The Certainty of Literature

The Certainty of Literature
Essays in polemic

George Watson
Fellow in English,
St John's College, Cambridge

St. Martin's Press
New York

First published in the United States of America in 1989

Printed in Great Britain

ISBN 0–312–04043–1

Library of Congress Cataloging-in-Publication Data

Watson, George, 1927–
   The certainty of literature: essays in polemic/ George Watson,
      p.   cm.
   Includes bibliographical references.
   ISBN 0–312–04043–1
   1. Criticism.   2. Literature—History and criticism—Theory, etc.
3. Critical theory.   I. Title.
PN81W299   1989
801'.95—dc20   89–24123
                                                                      CIP

for Robert Newell

The Apollo Belvedere is not beautiful because it pleases: . . . it pleases us because it is beautiful.

– Coleridge

CONTENTS

PREFACE

This book was prompted by an extravagantly publicised crisis in Cambridge English, where I teach – the celebrated 'Structuralism' crisis of 1980 – when an academic school of literature divided noisily over the certainty of literary judgements.

The media are not much to be blamed, then or ever, for neglecting the wider issues in favour of personalities. They often deal with party politics, after all, in much the same way. More so, perhaps, for obstinately misnaming the issue. It is late in the day to say so, but by 1980 not a single one of the Cambridge disputants was a structuralist. Misnaming the issue, unfortunately, has meant that the real bone of contention – the status of literary judgement as knowledge – has been largely lost sight of. It would be a pity, however, if the matter were left there: when a question goes unanswered, there is a natural disposition to think it unanswerable, and this one can be answered. Structuralism with its successor-dogmas was no more than a brief flirtation with scepticism about the arts in Anglo-America in the 1950s and after: the objective status of literary argument, by contrast, is of abiding importance.

The reason is severely practical, though not only that. Study is about learning and knowing, and literature could not long survive as a formal study if knowledge were not seen as there to be had; nor can those who believe it is there put their case with any effect to a doubting world unless armed with arguments to fight the sceptics off and talk them down. They need combat-training. Doubting Castle, in Bunyan, was kept by Giant Despair, and this book proposes arguments against doubts about literature that easily lead to despair. It is opposed to radical scepticism; it holds that we can, after all, know what the value of a work is, on occasion, and not merely imagine that we know; that many of the propositions of Renaissance humanism – not least its master-idea of a humanity that is ultimately one above all differences of race, class or creed – may well be true as well as interesting; that anxieties about ideology and the alleged distortions of the vantage-point are misplaced or, at best, wildly overdrawn; and that literary knowledge can be as certain as any that there is – as certain, for example, as mathematics or the natural sciences. The dogmatism that dogmatically denies all that betrays itself, in its very vehemence, as a self-contradiction, or what in my fourth chapter I call argument-against-itself. How can it claim such certainty, if all certainty is unjustified? And it is a practical issue whether literary studies can outlive a contradiction so evident to the outsider that he must sometimes wonder whether insiders know what they are about. Sceptical theory bowdlerises literature, what is more: it turns it into a polite gentleman's-library entertainment where it needs teeth to bite.

In these sixteen chapters, then – the first eight on modern critical theory laced with illustrations ancient and modern, the rest on instructive instances of the objectivist view since Shakespeare – I have tried to show why radical scepticism is unpersuasive and why humanism is true. That is to look forward by looking back. The millennia-long past of critical theory is still regrettably neglected in our times, except as an historical curiosity; though humanism, or the conviction that the arts are about the human world, past and present, and offer indispensable knowledge of that world, is a doctrine of flesh and bone, and its solidity is surely something to admire. It sees literature as one of the necessary arts of mankind, rather like architecture or plumbing, and it is no wonder the world of letters wants it back. It makes literature signify; it is death to fribble and contemptuous of the desperate view that criticism could never be more than a tired exercise of translating one set of terms into another and more fashionable set. Theory does not need to be a bored game for those who, to their sorrow, have outlived a taste for literature and for living. It can change lives; it can matter. Erasmus and Shakespeare knew that in their own century. The makers of the Enlightenment understood it two centuries later, and so did the pioneers of fictional realism from Henry Fielding to Henry James. They repay study still, and not just as curiosities; and I take up their cause here in admiring advocacy.

It is to that trinity, then – Humanism, Enlightenment, Realism –, that this book is offered as humble tribute and in contentious obedience. Theirs is a doctrine of hope, in the end, and it leads out of Doubting Castle; and of radical hope, since to know the world is to change it, or at least to see how it might purposefully be changed, and for the better. Contentious obedience is perhaps a paradox, but one readily understood by the great humanists and their successors, and it means that no submission to dogma is creditable if wholly untested by evidence, that any critical test – whether of humanism or of anything else – needs to take the two-thousand-year-long tradition of European theorising full-bloodedly into account, with due attention to its wealth of detail. This question was not born yesterday, and what is at issue here is nothing like the thin diagram offered by Heidegger years ago when he asked and dismissed the famous question 'How can we restore sense to the word?'[1] My concern is with a mature and complex view of the arts of mankind, and to see it as naïve and simplistic would be to belittle what it has to teach and to dismiss claims never seriously made by ancient or modern man in defence of the knowledge that literature has to give.

One or two of these papers now look a trifle battle-scarred, having profited (as I am vividly conscious) from exposure to Cambridge lecture-platforms since 1980 and various universities in Europe and America and their journals, as well as from the dissent they provoked there. I have now extensively reshaped them; others (about half the book) I lay before the public for the first time. All are offered as polemical essays designed to provoke further debate – to open questions, not to close them – and they concern issues that profit indispensably from the interplay of minds. To persuade, and only that, would be to fail. So, too, to incite opposition and nothing else. To excite reasoned opposition is to succeed.

The issues are in their nature contentious but not, soberly considered, alarming. Since the 1960s critical theory has sometimes been seen as a fatal infection in academia, and I have visited institutions where the question 'Do you have critical theory?' has sounded as fearful as an enquiry about Aids. My own view, which is developed at length here, is that theory is not a disease at all, still less a fatal one, but a natural and traditional aspect of literary enquiry at least as old as Plato and Aristotle. The real answer to bad literary theory, as Aristotle presumably understood when he answered Plato in the *Poetics*, is good critical theory; and it is a pity that radical sceptics like Neo-Marxists or Deconstructionists, in their heyday, were challenged as little and as timidly as they were.

Theory is not a distinctively modern activity – far from it. In England it is at least as old as Sir Philip Sidney, in modern Europe as old as the Italian and Spanish humanists he quarried as sources. Sidney, Fielding, Samuel Johnson and Henry James were, among other things, theorists of literature. It is not literary historians, on the long view, that are traditionalists – their craft is scarcely more than two centuries old – and the treatises of Roland Barthes, Jacques Derrida and their Anglo-American disciples would have looked more familiar to Aristotle or Sidney in their broader concerns than the writings of George Saintsbury or the sturdy blue volumes of the *Oxford History of English Literature*, which are genuinely involved, for better or worse, in something distinctively recent: in seeing a given literary tradition, like the Whig constitution itself, as an evolving activity over decades and centuries. That literary historians should lately have lacked the will to proclaim the novelty of what they do – that they should tacitly have accepted the tedious title of traditionalists, and as a badge of shame – marks a surprising and, I believe, still unexplained chapter in the records of intellectual self-abasement. Historians have no business to be so complaisant. They are needed. In recent years, regrettably, sceptics have largely had it all their own way, by default, and recent handbooks of critical theory have commonly supposed that the sceptical tradition was almost the only one there is.[2] Now that the current of philosophical opinion is turning the other way, however, and towards certainty, it is time literature too took account of the rooted incoherence of the sceptical case.

Acknowledgements

The first of these chapters, 'On being certain', was delivered in an earlier form in the oldest of all English departments, it is said, in the University of Edinburgh – aptly enough in its David Hume

Tower – and I am grateful for the warm hospitality to be enjoyed on an academic visit to Scotland: the more so because, in a long debate, its anti-sceptical thesis met with lively opposition there, as if the spirit of Hume still lived. 'The doubting of scepticism' was delivered at the University of Virginia in Charlottesville, where it encountered only the politest of doubt, and it appeared there in *Virginia Quarterly Review*. 'The stacked deck of language' I delivered at Walter Jackson Bate's invitation at Harvard; and my hosts urging it into print, it appeared in its original form in the *Sewanee Review*. Soon after, the University of Georgia was generous enough to appoint me as a stranger to its Helen Lanier chair of English, and my sixth and seventh chapters first saw the light there in the *Georgia Review*. 'The lost prophets of realism', also in *Sewanee*, was exposed to debate in Renford Bambrough's class on Wittgenstein and Critical Judgement at St John's College, Cambridge, a humanistic institution since its foundation in 1511. I confess myself shamelessly indebted throughout this book to that highly creative seminar of Michaelmas 1986, where literature and philosophy solemnly and creatively joined hands, and dedicate it to another of its participants, a philosopher generous to me with long evenings of post-Wittgensteinian advice. I hope both of them will agree that philosophy is far too important to be left to philosophers. 'The classic Marx' and 'The Whig interpretation of history' first appeared in *Encounter*; 'The phantom ghost of Modernism' in *American Scholar*; 'Orwell's Nazi renegade' in *Sewanee*. Seven other chapters are wholly unpublished. I am grateful to my college for its support and to Mrs Cecilia Green for her typing; and to the editors of these journals for permission to reprint even if, in the light of later reflection and the interests of a marshalled and not over-repetitious argument in favour of the certainty of literary judgements, I have nowhere felt obliged to stick to my original drafts or thoughts.

G.W.
St John's College, Cambridge

The Certainty of Literature

Notes

1. Martin Heidegger, *Über den Humanismus* (Berne, 1947), p. 7.
2. See, for example, *Modern Criticism and Theory*, ed. David Lodge (London, 1988), an anthology which sees the twentieth-century theoretical tradition as Saussurian and sceptical, apart from a mild retort to Hillis Miller by M. H. Abrams.

PART I

1

ON BEING CERTAIN

No one playing football is allowed to move the goalposts. They are essential to the game: no posts, no game.

In critical debates about morality and the arts, by contrast, that principle is not at all easily accepted, and it is often felt one might usefully question the premiss on which a dispute was based – refuse, so to say, to accept a rule and play the game. There is no right place to start an argument, it is said. Thomas Hardy once remarked in his diary, for example, on reading the Newman–Kingsley controversy, that though the style of Newman's *Apologia* was charming and its logic 'really human':

> only – and here comes the fatal catastrophe – there is no first link to his excellent chain of reasoning, and down you come headlong. (2 July 1865)

To which the Catholic Newman – or for that matter the Protestant Kingsley – might have replied that every argument has to start somewhere, that the argument between the churches starts with God, and that the agnostic Hardy is merely trying to move the posts while play is on, or starting the argument too far back.

I do not suppose that reply would would satisfy Hardy – still less all who have heard it since. A consensus, it is widely felt, is not as such to be respected, and we rejoice to doubt that there are certainties. Some years ago a young Cambridge philosopher, F. P. Ramsey, raised the point into a principle, remarking that the truth can sometimes lie 'in some third possibility which has not yet been thought of – which we can only discover by rejecting something assumed as obvious by both the disputants'. That celebrated remark from *The Foundations of Mathematics* (1931) makes goal-shifting sound like a duty as well as a pleasure, and it prompts questions that vitally affect the arts and sciences alike. I want to ask here if critics or moralists are entitled to move the posts, or even to try to do so; whether there are critical goalposts that justly survive any attempts to move them; and above all whether any literary judgement could in the end ever be called certain and immovable. And the course of debate here will find itself continuously indebted to Wittgenstein's late book *On Certainty* (1969), which he composed as notes in Cambridge just before his death in 1951; and to Samuel Johnson, who (not by chance) was one of his favourite authors.

Words in their ordinary use are not to be shifted, and by and large there is no reason even to wish to shift them. True, there have been numerous attempts down the centuries to suggest that all terms and language-systems are cripplingly confined – Fredric Jameson's *Prison-House of Language* (1972) is a recent and flagrant instance – but they are always, in the end, unpersuasive and self-refuting. Arguments are no more distorted by the confined sense of words than a game is distorted by its rules; in fact we need their confinement to make sense even of scepticism. 'Doubt itself', as Wittgenstein put it in *On Certainty*, 'rests only on what is beyond doubt' (§519); and Hardy could not have disputed the Christian notion of God had he not understood that, and much besides, in the same way as Newman and Kingsley. In fact it is only because he agreed with them about what God means that he could disagree about whether He exists.

It is with argumentative assumptions, then, and not with the meanings of words, that the issue lies; and here, it must be admitted, behaviour that would cause a footballer to be sent off can prove the mark of a critical genius. When Sir Philip Sidney, paraphrasing Aristotle, remarks in *An Apology for Poetry* (1595) that the poet creates through fiction 'another nature, in making things . . . better than nature bringeth forth', he is denying a perilous assumption common to realist and escapist alike: that reality is never more than what lies about us. But what if there should be a higher reality? 'The truest poetry is the most feigning', as Shakespeare put it shortly afterwards in *As You Like It*, echoing the point, and it seems churlish not to raise a cheer.

The opposite to moving the goalposts, in that fashion, is simply playing the game; and over the centuries most critics and moralists, it is likely, have done that and nothing but that. They have raised few cheers in recent times. But it is possible that their motives are something worthier than a servile reluctance to be sent off, and I want for the moment to allow consensus-arguing all the credit it can reasonably be found to deserve – the more so because it gets precious little, nowadays, from theorists of any persuasion whatever, whether conservative or radical. Believing something because it is widely or universally believed, that is to say, is not commonly seen as a dignified or interesting line of conduct. We esteem dissent. 'A very fine thing,' Flaubert once remarked of the Crystal Palace, on visiting London, 'in spite of being admired by everybody.' But that version of anti-humanism is wildly overdrawn. There is nothing plausible in the suggestion that anything whatever that looks like a consensus ought on that ground alone to be rejected or despised. Questioned, perhaps; but there are neglected grounds for suggesting that the outright rejection of a consensus, in the field of literary judgement, may be a greater nonsense than anti-humanists, ancient or modern, have encouraged us to see.[1]

A notorious instance of argument-from-consensus can be found in Samuel Johnson's 1765 preface to Shakespeare, where he argued that Shakespeare must be a great dramatist, and on the ground that all intervening generations of Englishmen had thought him so. He had enjoyed a 'continuance of esteem', like Homer and Virgil before him, and acquired over time something like the dignity of an Ancient.

Vulnerable as it is, baldly stated, Johnson's consensual argument is carefully protected. His concern is with competent opinion, in the first place, not any opinion; and it excludes mere whims and whimsies even among the competent, since some learned critics have been known to 'hope for eminence from the heresies of paradox', as he puts it – no mere trendies, then, however widely read or intelligent, need apply. But the chief weight of his argument lies in its distinguishing the 'gradual and comparative' judgements to which the arts give rise, on the one hand, from the 'absolute and definite' results of mathematical and scientific enquiry on the other:

> What mankind have long possessed, they have often examined and compared; and if they persist to value the possession, it is because frequent comparisons have confirmed opinion in its favour. As among the works of nature no man can properly call a river deep, or

a mountain high, without the knowledge of many mountains and many rivers; so in the productions of genius, nothing can be styled excellent till it has been compared with other works of the same kind.

That is why works 'tentative and experimental', like works of art, need to be 'estimated by their proportion to the general and collective ability of man'. Whereas the Pythagorean scale of numbers was instantly seen to be perfect, Johnson argues, Homer's poems can only with any security be judged great through the lapse of time, 'by remarking that nation after nation, and century after century, has been able to do little more than transpose his incidents, new-name his characters, and paraphrase his sentiments'.

Johnson's initial proposition here about continuance of esteem has a lapidary dignity of utterance but, to most recent theorists, not much other merit. I am not aware of any critical account in our times that has even remotely considered the hypothesis that the principle might be true as well as interesting: or, for that matter, Matthew Arnold's more analytical version of a similar view, in 'The study of poetry' (1880), concerning what ultimately constitutes poetic greatness. Passages from Homer, among others, represent what Arnold daringly called 'an infallible touchstone' of quality. Such claims are nowadays seen as of no more than anthropological interest. The myth of a theoretical bedrock or 'first link', as Hardy called it, is by now so potent that one American critic has confidently dismissed Arnold's notion of poetic greatness as nothing more than evidence of his 'weakness in reasoning on a high level of abstraction', with his touchstones serving him 'as a sort of mental crutch'.[2] But the demand for an abstract norm or formula does not persuade. It is about as convincing, in fact, as an official bar of metal – an alloy of platinum – exactly one metre in length and maintained at Sèvres, near Paris, at a controlled temperature, which was long held to be the standard against which all French measures in case of dispute were to be compared. A moment's reflection would show that if a million private measures in France were to read one length for a metre, and the official bar of platinum another, no one even of the most modest intelligence would conclude anything other, in the first instance, than that the bar itself had been tampered with or somehow allowed to deteriorate. There *is* no first link, no theoretical basis, no bedrock; and the charge against the human-istic mind, whether Johnson's or Arnold's, that it cannot under challenge produce a sufficient account of the standards by which its values may be measured is, on sober reflection, no charge at all. It is the interdependence of cases, be they tape-measures or poems, that offers certain knowledge here, not a single standard like a metre bar or a verbal formula. Those who complain that Johnson's argument from consensus is uncritical and authorita-rian are in a very weak position if their own preference is for a verbal definition to which one is summarily invited to submit. I would rather submit, as a free citizen, to the judgement of the ages about Homer or Shakespeare than to the formulations of a critic responsible to no one but himself.

It is sometimes suggested, for all that, that to accept the consensual judgement of the past is a blind and unthinking act. But Johnson and Arnold are not inviting blind acceptance, though they do invite acceptance. They are asking that proposi-tions like the greatness of the *Iliad* should be considered in the light of what mankind has long thought about them. That is not a refusal to think but an enticement to think. Nor is it blind, in its very nature, to accept what one is told. Much, and in all prob-ability most, of what we know, at least in an articulable sense, we know because we have been told; and much of it, like the multiplication table, is probably as old as Homer and certainly as old as any surviving critical praise of Homer. 'My life', as Wittgenstein remarks in *On Certainty*, 'consists in my being content to accept many things' (§344). If it is wrong to accept propositions on ancient authority, then every schoolchild is wrong when he learns arithmetic. I do not suppose that anyone seriously believes that – which is why a far-reaching contempt for consensus-thinking may justly be called insincere as well as mis-guided.

What would one think – to test Johnson's point further about continuance of esteem – of someone who denied that Shakes-peare was a great playwright?

Many a schoolchild bored with a prescribed play might be instanced here; so might Strindberg, who as an adult openly proclaimed contempt. If continuance of esteem had no weight whatever in our minds, we should be forced to regard such dismissals seriously; but surely no one in fact behaves in that way. If a child doesn't think much of *Hamlet*, we think, and perhaps say – even if we have not read Shakespeare, or read him lately – that he may feel differently when he is older; when Strindberg says something similar, we conclude that he was cranky or did not know much English. (Both, as it happens, were true.) But what is never said, on that sort of evidence, is that the whole critical question must now be reopened. And yet if Johnson's consensual principle counted for nothing in our minds, that is just what one would say.

The point can readily be made more immediate. I can easily bear listening to Haydn's music, but have never quite understood why musicians should think him as great a composer as Handel or Mozart. It bespeaks no exceptional modesty to add that it has never occurred to me to doubt where the fault is. I am missing something. And in accepting that, as almost anybody would, I am accepting a principle of authority: others know more about eighteenth-century music. But the case is not hopeless: its solution, presumably, or part of it, would be to play contemporary and comparable works inferior to Haydn's, like Boccherini's, drawing attention to ways in which they are inferior. That would amply illustrate Johnson's point about the arts as 'gradual and comparative' rather than 'absolute and definite'. It is also a commonplace method of critical instruction – so that one may say that education is even now pervasively humanistic in its assumptions.

The striking fact about humanism, indeed, is that it is commonly accepted in practice even by those who deride it in principle. That is a highly arresting paradox of critical antihumanism in the present age – that it is so seldom applied even by its warmest enthusiasts. Sceptical theories like Deconstruction tend to be proclaimed rather than used, and I do not suppose that any Deconstructionist would welcome an attempt by others to deconstruct anything he had himself written. It is even a question whether such theories *can* be used: they are rather like new shoes one is too proud to wear in the rain. They may look very fine – but will they keep the water out? Humanism, as the application of Johnsonian principle to the classroom shows, really does stand up to a bit of rain. Whether it stands up to all the rain there could ever be is the next question.

What would it take to make one abandon a consensus-judgement like the greatness of Homer or Shakespeare?

Such questions richly illustrate Wittgenstein's famous challenge in *On Certainty*: 'What would get judged by what here?' (§125). True, there is nothing impossible (to speak generally) about the view that a consensus might be wrong. Galileo, when he showed that the earth moved, proved that. Oddly enough, Johnson does not appear to see how much his own scientific contrast strengthens his case for the arts here, and his phrase 'definite and absolute' may contain one or two false implications. Like many men of letters then and since, he may have believed that the history of the sciences has been an accumulation of immovable certainties. But of course it is nothing of the kind – as the embarrassing case of Galileo's predecessors, or the scientific consensus in favour of phlogiston in Johnson's own age, the principle of inflammability in combustible matter, amply illustrates. There *is* no such thing as phlogiston, as we now know: the scientific consensus was wrong. It was none the less scientific, and historians of science rightly record it. Or again, the eighteenth-century scientific consensus in favour of Newton was shown by Einstein to have been (at least in a few details) fallacious. So if terms like 'definite' and 'absolute' imply something like irrefutable, then they imply something that is false. Science is refutable: it has been refuted.

A scientific consensus, then, can be wrong. Can a critical consensus like the Homeric or the Shakespearian equally be so?

With all due sense of temerity, I want to suggest that the answer is no, and that it would remain no even if some one were to write a better epic than Homer's or better plays than Shakespeare's. It may be objected that to answer like that is to foreclose the question – that no one has the right to reject an argument with material evidence unheard. But the difficulty about replying yes to the possibility of an Einstein in the arts is quite different from that, and different in kind. It is not just that one has not heard the argument: it is rather that one cannot even imagine the form such an argument would have to take in order to persuade.

The difficulties of imagining that are different in kind, what is more, from those that arise from many factual questions, whether in science or history. One can commonly discern in factual matters what a refutation would look like. In one daring sally, for example, in *Philosophische Bemerkungen* (1964), Wittgenstein surmised that it might even be possible to imagine new evidence proving that Julius Caesar never existed: a document might be discovered, he hazarded, 'from which it emerges that no such man ever lived, and his existence was made up for particular ends' (IV.56), such as justifying the principate of his grand-nephew Augustus. That provocative hypothesis has usefully proved a bone of contention; and Wittgenstein's English translator, in a paper called 'Hume and Julius Caesar' (1973), has briskly called it one of his 'rare pieces of stupidity', since the knowledge one would have to give up in order to believe the existence of Julius Caesar a conspiratorial invention would easily outweigh any authenticity reasonably to be attributed to a newly discovered document from the ancient world.[3] I presume Wittgenstein's disciple is right in this matter, and he wrong: 'Not everything can be put up for checking' in historical questions. Or, as Wittgenstein put it in *On Certainty*, 'we are forced to rest content with assumption – if I want the door to turn, the hinges must stay put' (§343).

The historical existence of Caesar may be left timidly on the borderline here: something probably, if not certainly, a limiting case. I want to suggest that the greatness of Homer and Shakespeare are not on the border of anything. They are not limiting cases to certainty, they are like hinges that stay put, and they cannot usefully be put up for checking. And that is because one cannot even conceive of the argument that would cause serious doubt or certain denial. It is one thing to keep an open mind in a critical issue, but surely no mind should be open enough to give serious credence to the hypothesis that the *Iliad* and *King Lear* are not great works. At least that is true in any sense that matters. No doubt there is a 'thin' or remotely hypothetical sense in which one might claim that *King Lear* could be shown to be a poor play: all that would have been demonstrated, one might say, if *Lear* could be shown to be incoherent, lacking in credible characterisation, ill-written and the like. But to thicken that thin sort of proof, one would have to show those charges true of that play. It is easy enough to imagine the first move, impossible to imagine the second.

Even if someone were to write a better poem or a better play, what is more, it is still doubtful if there is any form of argument that could cause one to doubt the *Iliad* or *Lear* to be eminent in their kind. 'If you don't like Titian, you don't like painting', an art historian once said – meaning that in the Western tradition of easel-painting since the Middle Ages, at least, it is something far harder than just difficult to dissociate what Titian did from what great works are: it is squarely impossible. Nor should one fall victim to the assumption that no hypothesis is to be reasonably believed until it has been fully tested. How do we know we are mortal? Or again: 'Can you play the violin?' 'I don't know: I've never tried.' The reason why anyone can see that exchange to be funny is that everyone knows there are certainties which, like mortality itself, do not need to be tested in order to be unhesitatingly believed. Wittgenstein's instance in *On Certainty* is the blind man's question 'Have you two hands?' Looking, as he says, would not help. 'If I had any doubt about it, then I don't know why I should trust my eyes. For why shouldn't I test my eyes by looking to find out whether I see my two hands?' (§125).

To argue like that for the certainty of critical judgement – I mean of some critical judgements – is to take Johnson's shoes out in the rain. It may be that he should have tried them further than he did. Continuance of esteem, as the instance of Titian suggests, might after all be more than the merely provisional principle that Johnson supposed it to be. Perhaps that is to underrate a little his argument in the 1765 preface to Shakespeare; combine his notion of continued esteem with what he calls 'gradual and comparative' judgements in the arts, and the radical beginnings of a certainty-principle in literary criticism begin to emerge which he might not have rejected. But it is equally likely that Johnson's remark about the 'absolute and definite' conclusions of mathematics and the sciences is over-concessive here. As Einstein illustrated when he refined and corrected Newton, seemingly absolute and definite conclusions in the physical sciences can be assailed, and successfully. If 'definite' means certain or not up for checking, then the details of Newton's law of gravity were plainly something less than that.

If that is so, then Johnsonian humanism, which many in these times have found too strong, may be thought somewhat too weak. It fails, that is, to give full credit to the sense in which one might be said to know, and certainly know, what some of the incontrovertible instances of artistic greatness are. It fails –

though it only just fails – to moot a possibility that looks at once dizzyingly difficult and yet hard to refute: that some literary reputations like Homer's and Shakespeare's may, on reflection, prove to be more certain than some findings of mathematics or the physical sciences.

Even that, perhaps, underrates the certainty of some literary judgements. For there is far more that would follow from concluding Shakespeare to have been a poor dramatist than a view of Shakespeare. We know and understand as much as we do – we are what we are – because of literature. To unthink oneself is harder than hard. It is highly implausible to suppose that, as an educated being, one could reimagine what a mind would be like without books. 'They are that which we know', as T. S. Eliot once said of the great authors in 'Tradition and the individual talent' (1919). The remark, which deserves to be the most famous he ever made in prose, was fittingly if unconsciously echoed years later by his admirer William Empson, who replied to an invitation to write in his praise that he would find the task impossibly difficult because he was 'not certain how much of his own mind Eliot had invented'.[4] That is admirably candid. In a similar way, the business of proving Shakespeare a bad poet is not just impossible but in a serious sense beyond imagining. 'Can you play the violin?' You would have to conceive of yourself as another being in order to conceive that.

That helps to explain, perhaps, why F. R. Leavis's notorious remark about the 'dislodgement' of Milton's poetic reputation is ultimately, and even initially, incredible. It was 'effected with remarkably little fuss', as he put it.[5] But if Milton's dislodgement was effected at all, it could not have been done without an enormous fuss, and the fuss would not have been confined to a sense of Milton. The world would have been forced to rethink its sense of works composed in the shadow of *Paradise Lost*, like Wordsworth's *Prelude*; and of works composed in reaction to it, like Dryden's *Absalom and Achitophel*. Not to mention ourselves . . . To say there was no fuss about the dislodgement of Milton, then, or not much, is close to saying that it did not happen. And of course it did not happen.

One unspoken but potent fear of modern critical theory, in that case, may have to be reconsidered: that literary studies have recorded no serious progress in certain knowledge beyond the severely factual, standing in consequence at a grave and permanent disadvantage to the achievements of the sciences. In the modern Battle of the Books between laboratories and libraries, in terms of reliable conclusions, the labs are often felt to have triumphed so completely that the contest is hardly worth debating. But surely it is worth debating. 'It has no meaning', as Wittgenstein put it in *On Certainty*, 'to say that a game has always been played wrong' (§496). That goes for literary criticism too. It has no meaning, he might have agreed, to say that Homer and Shakespeare have always been over-prized and falsely esteemed. 'What would get judged by what here?' as his famous challenge runs. The answer, in literary terms, is that the less esteemed gets judged by the more. Terence Rattigan gets judged by Shakespeare, not Shakespeare by Rattigan. And to be uncertain about that is to espouse an argument for which the defence cannot even be imagined.

Notes

1. For an exception to that neglect see Anthony Savile, *The Test of Time: an essay in philosophical aesthetics* (Oxford, 1982).
2. J. S. Eells, *The Touchstones of Matthew Arnold* (New York, 1955), p. 22.
3. G. E. M. Anscombe, *Collected Philosophical Papers* (Oxford, 1981), I. 89f.
4. Christopher Ricks, 'William Empson 1909–1984', *Proceedings of the British Academy*, 71 (1985), p. 554.
5. F. R. Leavis, *Revaluation* (London, 1936), p. 42.

2

HOW RADICAL IS THEORY?

The question may look surprising. But since the 1960s literary theory, against all probability, has attracted minds passionately dedicated to radicalism, even subversion: so much so that historians of literature have sometimes wonderingly heard themselves dismissed as traditionalists. Mephistopheles's famous advice in Goethe's *Faust* has been roundly ignored: 'All theory is grey...', and we have been asked, by contrast, to see it as exciting, even revolutionary. Those who are of the Devil's party and know it may need some further persuasion here. Theory might help, no doubt: but how could it ever excite or subvert? I want to ask whether any grand theory of literature – or, for that matter, any far-flung generalisation like a total theory of language or of tragedy – could ever be radical in its effects. Radicals seek transformation, and nothing less. Could a theory ever transform a sense of literature – or, for that matter, literary creation itself?

Philosophy, Wittgenstein once remarked, leaves everything as it is. I presume he was implicitly countering Marx's challenge, still carved on his giant tombstone in north London, that philosophers should not only interpret the world but change it. That head-on clash of views has now been dramatically re-enacted in critical debate. To interchange 'theory' and 'philosophy' should give little trouble here, since recent literary theory has amounted to an attempt to philosophise literary criticism, the critic bravely risking the charge of amateurism as he takes on himself the unaccustomed duties of a philosopher. Or so the twentieth century, left to itself, naturally sees the matter. On a longer view, no doubt, it is the other way about. European criticism began in theory, at least so far as its surviving documents suggest, with Plato's *Republic* Book IV and Aristotle's *Poetics*; and such ancient sources of European theory have been seriously undervalued in modern debate, as I hope to show. The English tradition began in theory too, if that beginning is to be dated to Sidney's *Apology for Poetry* and the Elizabethan rhetoricians. The neglect of such centuries-old theory may have been partly wilful. A recent critic has deflatingly remarked how familiar Jacques Derrida's scepticism would look to anyone who had ever studied ancient philosophy, comparing him to Pyrrho who (around 300 BC) held that 'custom and convention govern human action, for no single thing is in itself any more than that'.[1] We only imagine, then, that we know. And if Derrida was a Pyrrhonist, then the novelty of *la nouvelle critique* is indeed gravely in question.

The analysis, treatise-long, of literary works from the past is by contrast new – little more than two centuries old, so far as modern vernacular literatures go; and literary history in the annalistic sense, like George Saintsbury or the *Oxford History of English Literature*, newer still. Odd, then, that the literary historian since the 1960s should have accepted the dismissive charge of traditionalism so tamely. It is not the modern theorist who has pioneered anything much in criticism, he might reasonably counter: he has rather returned it, secret traditionalist that he is, to its ancient philosophical sources. Derrida is a closet Pyrrhonist . . . And he might have added – though out of a characteristic modesty he seldom did – that history, and not least literary history, can after all be highly radical in its effects, as George Orwell's remark about 'he who controls the past controls the future' implies. That, after all, is why revisionist historians trouble to write, and they have their proven successes. And it has yet to be shown that a literary theory could ever change anything, except to weaken certainty and create despair.

That last challenge is the nub. Could a theory of literature ever be radical in its effect?

To answer yes, in modest mood, it might be enough to show that a theory of literature had transformed an existing and educated sense of literature itself. Educated, since it is not in doubt that an ignorant view is easily – all too easily – transformed. Such a theory, if it could be found, might easily be radical in senses far beyond the literary, the ways educated minds live being connected with their understanding of novels, poems, plays and films in all sorts of visible and invisible ways. In that sense, a radical theory of narrative, say, or of language might ultimately have all sorts of devastating effects on how one worshipped, voted, or lived a daily life; in which case, it might be said, Wittgenstein would have been proved wrong. Philosophy, or theory, does not always leave everything as it is.

Plain and unequivocal instances, however, are hard to find. The fragment known as Aristotle's *Poetics* is a report on existing Greek tragedy, not a recipe-book for writing more, and there is no reason to think it changed the course of ancient literature or that Aristotle meant it to do so. No Elizabethan poet or dramatist, so far as we certainly know, wrote as he did (allusions apart) because he had read a theory of fiction called Sidney's *Apology*, though an early training in rhetoric may have influenced Renaissance style in ways not now easy to attach to the writings of any single rhetorician. The dramatic unities, it has been said, had a powerful influence on drama in the seventeenth century and after; but again, the theory may have arisen out of theatrical convenience rather than the other way around, and there is no convincing evidence that Samuel Johnson's refutation of the unities in his 1765 Shakespeare preface set a new fashion in dramaturgy. In the Paris of the 1950s and after, the *nouveau roman* was said to owe a lot to *la nouvelle critique*: a practice of literature to a theory. But the priority of events, as usual, is hard to establish here – Nathalie Sarraute and Samuel Beckett were publishing fiction before the Second World War, after all – and it is more than possible that the fiction inspired the criticism. Again, I can easily believe that the fictive devices with which John Fowles decorated his finest novel, *The French Lieutenant's Woman* (1969), were affected by an awareness of Parisian theories of the time. But the novel is fundamentally in a realistic tradition, for all that, with no more than a parodic garnishing from other sources.

The question 'How radical is literary theory?', then, remains largely hypothetical or, at most, marginal to the historical instances. That absence of clear instances of radical theory – radical in effect, that is, and not just in intent – might not deter some theorists of our times, or deter them much. Their claim over the past quarter-century has been to total innovation, after all, and a new start. The new theorist in that style was an inveterate avant-gardiste; and it is an essential part of the claims of an avant-garde to be doing something for the first time. Hence the excitement. The theory that the Arbitrariness of the Sign had destroyed any claim of language to imitate the real, for example, was seen as an axe laid to the root of any descriptive pretensions that literature in general, or criticism in particular, might ever make: whether fictional realism, or Aristotelian mimesis, or the analysis of literary works, or moral knowledge in general, or the entire humanistic claim that the arts can teach mankind how to live. Humanism had been laid on the block, in that view, and beheaded with a swift and single blow from the cutting edge of radical theory. Nothing like it had ever happened before to western man, in the estimation of Roland Barthes, Jacques Derrida or their Anglo-American disciples. That was why theory no longer looked grey but suddenly exciting. It had swept away the lumber of the ages.

All that sounds impressively radical, to be sure, and there can be no question here about radicalism of intent. If Aristotle, Coleridge and Matthew Arnold were no more than false starts, if criticism had not yet reached even its starting-point or settled its scope or its terms of debate, then the total sense of what literature is and does would indeed have to be reshaped. The mood was often compounded with a barely secret elation. 'It will be obvious', remarked David Lodge in *The Modes of Modern Writing* (1977), in a passage to which I shall later return, speaking of the Arbitrariness of the Sign, 'how this view militates against any mimetic theory of literature', not least fictional realism. Off with the king's head. One senses the hug of glee – the sudden, eager glow of vandalistic pride.

All that concerns intent. How radical is theory in its effects; how radical, for that matter, could any theory ever be?

One tempting answer to that question, in the most general terms, would be to say that no theory could ever be that unless it were at once credited and wrong. There is an embarrassing abundance of such theories: that all history is a history of class struggle; that all Jews are evil; that agreed criteria are needed to call critical judgements objective. A wrong theory that is none the less believed can indeed change the world, and enormously. If, on the other hand, a theory is not credited, then it presumably changes nothing, whether right or wrong, and the question of effect hardly arises.

If it is credited and right, then it is plausible, in a perilous sort of way, to suggest that it still changes nothing, since some would say that a right theory can only tell what is already known. It needs to fit. Plato famously argued that to define a concept is to recall what one has always known: one can only see it to be so if, in some buried sense, one knows it already. I presume that conclusion to underlie Wittgenstein's point in *Philosophical Investigations* (1953) about philosophy leaving everything as it is (§124). To be right, in that view, could only be to elicit something already, if unconsciously, understood. To apply the point to literature: if *Hamlet* defied some proposed theory of tragedy, it is not the play we should reject as an instance but the theory as a theory. We know that *Hamlet* is a tragedy, and *Twelfth Night* not, before seeking any general account of tragedy or comedy at all; and judge such general accounts by the instances, not the instances by the accounts.

That last point, which with some understatement I have called perilous, needs to be explored. Is it convincing to argue that critical theories, if credited and right, can have no radical force – can only tell us what is already known, only leave everything as it is?

In the *Meno* of Plato, which is one of his early dialogues, Socrates elicits Pythagoras' theorem about right-angled triangles by questioning an illiterate slave and convincing him that he knows it and has always known it. 'These opinions were already somewhere in him, were they not?' Socrates triumphantly asks, and Meno agrees that they were. So even the ignorant man, Socrates concludes, 'has within himself true opinions without having knowledge of them' (85b). The case is classic – and classically puzzling. Right theories, like Johnson's demonstration that a play can be excellent without observing the unities, tell what we already know even when they contradict what we may elsewhere over-confidently assert. We already know a playwright can defy the unities because Shakespeare has done so, and in plays known to be excellent. That amply illustrates Wittgenstein's point in the *Investigations* (§129) that the most important aspects of things may be 'hidden because of their simplicity and familiarity', that one might be unable to notice something because it is constantly before one's eyes. Like Socrates with the theorem, Johnson arranges knowledge already possessed rather than offering anything new; and in that sense, at least, we are all Meno's slave. Theory cannot tell us anything that is true, in that view, since we already know what it has to tell. And if it cannot tell anything, it will be said, then it cannot be radical in its effects.

The radical theorist, for all that, still has a card to play here, and he should be allowed and encouraged to play it. It is a good card.

Surely Meno's slave, he might answer, has been changed by being made to realise that he understands Pythagoras' theorem; and that change is more than a new-found ability to answer questions about right-angled triangles. It is not just that he can now give an account of the square on the hypotenuse, and for the first time. There is also a plain sense, however much he or Meno might deny it, in which it might reasonably be said that he knows it for the first time. Plato's own answer was that the slave recalls such knowledge from a previous existence. But that answer, whatever it is worth, is to the question how he could so easily have been brought to expound the matter under Socratic inter-rogation, and it does not help to answer the question whether there is any significant sense in which he now knows something he did not know an hour or a day before. The radical theorist will insist that such knowledge is indeed genuinely new: that theories like the Arbitrariness of the Sign, for example, or a theory of literary genre, if true and accepted, change a view of literature and of everything that pertains to it. Even Socrates admits that the slave is in some obscure sense a new man. 'At present these opinions, being newly aroused, have the quality of a dream' (85c), he remarks – meaning, perhaps, that they seem as strange to him as dreams do to the dreamer, even though they have emerged out of his own consciousness. A lot of critical theory is exciting because dream-like, in that sense: unaccustomed, insecure, fresh. And hence, at least potentially, radical.

That reply needs to be pondered. In what sense could an understanding of literature ever be changed by a theory that was at once new and true?

The Arbitrariness of the Sign will hardly do as an instance, since its novelty is controversial, and I shall defer an account of that controversy to another chapter. The familiar theory of genre, however, can be put to some useful illustrative work here. Imagine, then, a theatre-goer who has scarcely heard the words

'tragedy' and 'comedy' and who cheerfully watches Shakespeare, and much besides, in ignorance of any critical attempt to
define such terms. He might, after all, be an experienced, even a
percipient play-watcher. Suppose you now explain to him – or,
Socrates-like, encourage him to see for himself – that *Hamlet* is a
tragedy and *Twelfth Night* a comedy, and why; and, in addition,
that *Hamlet* belongs to a group that includes *King Lear* and
Macbeth, whereas *Twelfth Night* belongs to another group that
includes *As You Like It* and *Much Ado*. Or, more ambitiously, you
might give him Alastair Fowler's *Kinds of Literature* (1982) to read.
The playgoer is now, so to speak, Meno's slave. He may even say
that he always knew *Hamlet* to be more like *Macbeth* than *Twelfth
Night*. One might even accept that claim.

In what sense does the playgoer, newly armed with a theory of
genre (or, as Socrates would put it, 'aroused') know more?

It is tempting to answer that he can now, and for the first time,
explain why he always knew *Hamlet* to be more like *Macbeth* than
Twelfth Night. But that answer, however tempting, is wrong.
Shakespeare's tragedies, though not all tragedies, end with a
death; his comedies, though not all comedies, with a marriage;
and the imaginary playgoer could have noticed all that without
knowing any theory of genre and without possessing any terminology like Tragedy or Comedy. He could also have noticed significant contrasts in texture, as between the solemn and the comic.
And he could have done all that, and quite likely has done all
that, before his Socratic lesson. In fact it is only because he can do
it without a terminology that he can do it with one. He can only
see that the terms fit, that is to say, because he already knows
what it is they are meant to fit.

There is still something implausible, however, in the claim that
the playgoer newly aroused by theory knows no more than he
did.

If he knows more, one way of expressing what it is he now
knows would be to say that a theory has given him the skills to
work faster as he recognises things by their names and exchanges
views about them with others. A terminology can have all sorts of
effects, fortunate and unfortunate; and one fortunate effect might
easily be to speed things up. A gardener who knows some botany
may work no faster as a gardener, but he is altogether likely to be
able to explain the similarities and dissimilarities of plants faster

than a gardener who knows none. It is observable that people who know about plants know the names of plants, on the whole: those who do not, do not. Similarly with birds. All that is highly unlikely to be coincidental, however much one might insist that kinships and identities can be noticed without one's knowing the technical names for species and subspecies. In an article on 'Metre' (1960), for example, C. S. Lewis once defended the use of classical terms in English metrics, misleading as they arguably are, on the fiercely practical ground that one needs some agreed terminology to discuss the matter at all: 'Everyone knows what you mean', he remarked, even if English verse is accentual and Latin is not; and he added bluntly: 'Have you ever had a pupil not brought up on this scheme who was aware of metre at all?'[2] In other words, even a mildly misleading terminology can be better than none, since one can readily isolate the sense in which Latin metrical terms for quantity fail to fit an accentual language like English. Armed with terms like 'iambic' and 'trochaic', at least you can start; and it is a question whether, in a matter as technical as botany or metre or bird-watching, you could start at all except by learning a terminology.

This, then, may be the safe claim to make. Theory puts you in the fast lane; it does not just enable you to explain faster, what is more, since without it you might have grave difficulty in explaining at all. And the fast lane, in any advanced enquiry, is where everyone wants to be. Such accelerations can be dangerous, as accelerations often are in heavy traffic. But the radical theorist is entitled to claim that this still represents a difference. Whether that difference is big enough to justify the grand title of radicalism might be doubted, however, and reasonably. Whatever the tempo, it will be said, it is still the same road, and the destination is the same.

The larger claim that the radical theorist needs to make here is to say that a theory enables you to see something for the first time, and something that is there. A true theory, in that event, might be newly credited and still radical in its effects.

That claim, which is vaster by far than its predecessor, does not altogether run counter to ordinary experience. Lewis's point about using the traditional terms for metre was that you only begin to notice metre at all by using metrical terms, that learning what things are means learning what they are called. The botanist would doubtless wish to argue something similar about plants. So might the architect. St Paul's Cathedral in London, for example, is fronted with six pairs of Corinthian pillars, and there may be something in the view that I only know that because I know about the three classical forms – Doric, Ionic and Corinthian – having learnt them from a work of architectual theory. That claim far exceeds the modest claim that I can only explain the matter because I know the terminology. The more modest claim, in any case, is in a strict sense untrue. One *could* describe a Corinthian pillar without knowing the term. Knowing the term merely speeds things up.

But any ordinary experience of art surely suggests something more: that, as a matter of practice, it is only because one knows the name of the phenomenon that one notices it to be there at all. Consider a handful of instances: that baroque paintings tend to be based on the compositional device of a diagonal; that European music of a certain era is polyphonic; that foregrounds tend to advance in depth in Dutch landscapes in the course of the seventeenth century; that Shakespeare uses enjambment more daringly in his late verse than in his early; and that in right-angled triangles the square on the hypotenuse . . . If true theory is indeed radical, it is surely radical in these terms: that it offers a fresh, an almost indispensable compulsion of attention-giving. As Socrates would say, it arouses. It is all very well to say that, if it is right, it can only tell what we already know. Without Socrates, would Meno's slave have attended to right-angled triangles at all?

It is hardly to be imagined that such an answer will satisfy the radical theorist; but then he may, in all conscience, be happy as he is. If, on the other hand, he wants to persuade that all history is a history of class war, or that all objective judgements demand agreed criteria, then he plainly has a tough battle on his hands. Such propositions may indeed be radical; if one believed them, that is, they would utterly transform the ways in which history and critical judgement were seen. But the difficulty now is quite unlike learning metrical or architectural terms. We are not recalling, in Platonic style, what we have always known from the instances if we say such things. Who, after all, ever chose a meal, or a husband or wife – all instances, after all, of exercising critical judgement – by first establishing agreed criteria? Where in modern industrial history are the cases of class war? Such theories do not *recall* experience at all; we are dogmatising, not remembering, if we utter them. And the future of literary theory, if it has one, may rest on achieving a sturdier scepticism of dogma – including sceptical dogma – and a firmer awareness of how in life we truly learn and teach. There are theories that help us to look and theories that forbid us to look, and the business of the theorist is to tell the difference.

Notes

1. A. D. Nuttall, *The New Mimesis* (London, 1983), p. 36.
2. C. S. Lewis, 'Metre', *Review of English Literature*, 1 (1960); reprinted in his *Selected Literary Essays* (Cambridge, 1969), p. 284.

3

THE DOUBTING OF SCEPTICISM

In the summer of 1985 the Peking government, gravely concerned at the rise of juvenile crime in the Chinese People's Republic,
announced new and compulsory courses for all schoolchildren
'to teach them the difference between right and wrong.'

That moral confidence is impressive: not the difference between the legal and the illegal, but between right and wrong.
Laws, or at least good laws, embody moral principles; and such
principles are not merely to be observed. They must be seen to be
true.

Any western intellectual reaction to such moral confidence in a
Marxist state is likely to be embarrassed and confused. The non-
Communist world is by now accustomed to be told, even by its
clergy, that law is not the same as morality, which may be; and in
literary studies it is so used to the assumption that critical values
are a matter of personal judgement that many find it hard to
imagine any other view could be seriously held. When I presumed, some years ago, to entitle a chapter in *The Discipline of
English* (1978) 'Why literary judgements are objective', the
suggestion was considered so laughable that, on visits to schools
and colleges, discussion commonly began with a mocking look
and a remark like 'You are the one who believes that literary
judgements are objective.'

Well, yes; and no apology is needed here for confusing, so
early in the debate, literary and moral judgements – what Peking
thinks about right and wrong, and the greatness of Shakespeare
or Dickens – since it is rare, and in common experience simply
unknown, for anyone to be an objectivist in the one and not the
other. I do not certainly know what the Peking government
thinks about literary judgements, but would wager a large sum

that, since it is objectivist in moral matters and believes children should be taught the difference between right and wrong, it holds similar views on the arts as well.

That confidence contrasts sharply with the prevailing orthodoxy of the West. Here critics more commonly strive to distinguish factual and evaluative issues, and often imagine that it is always possible – even easy – to tell one from the other. Teaching in a Midwestern university in the 1950s, for example, I was told by the chairman of an English department to set students an 'objective test' during a Shakespeare course, to see if the prescribed plays had been duly studied; and it was to consist, as he explained, of questions to which there was only one right answer, such as 'What was the name of Richard II's queen?' It took little enquiry to ascertain that the entire department, and perhaps the entire university, believed that an objective question is one to which the answer is certainly known and unanimously agreed, as the very nature of the test implied; and that, since literary and moral questions are not reliably like that, they fall outside the range of objective enquiry. And the confidence with which these assumptions were held was Pekingese in its certitude, though directed towards an opposite conclusion.

For all that, western subjectivism was muddled as a consensus, and it seldom noticed how muddled it was. A friend in another university reported soon after that a student expelled for a sexual misdemeanour had provoked a noisy demonstration in his own support, the banner reading 'Morality is a matter of personal choice.' The expelled student was later discovered to have attempted blackmail. Nobody doubts that blackmail is a moral issue; nobody, equally, whether on that campus or any other, thinks it a matter of personal choice. The slogan so earnestly stitched on banners, and so passionately upheld by scores of eager demonstrators, suddenly looked tattered and in ruins: so much so, that the local philosophy department, which took its responsibilities seriously, spent several weeks conscientiously debating the matter.

It seems clear, then, that the whole question of moral and literary scepticism will have to be reopened. Among philosphers it has already been reopened; and the 1980s saw a battery of books about (and commonly against) scepticism as a philosophical idea, or the radical notion familiar to Ancients as well as

Moderns that all knowledge is illusory.[1] No need to conclude that, because philosophy is forever turning back on itself and reopening old questions, it is failing to achieve anything. That would be as pointless as to tell a housewife that, because her home will be dirty again tomorrow, she need not clean it today. Such matters need to be reopened, all the time; and there are forms of intellectual progress other than a simple trajectory or an unending accumulation of evidence.

The internal contradictions of radical scepticism have by now escaped few philosophers: that if we cannot certainly know any-thing, then we cannot certainly know even that; that if all dogmas are ideologically conditioned, and to their discredit, then so is that dogma; and that the critic who wishes to look knowing had better know something or stop looking knowing. Not all literary theorists, however, have so far noticed these self-contradictions. In A Map of Misreading (1975), for example, Harold Bloom has restated the familiar dogma of the undetermined text in as radical fashion as he dared: all reading is strictly speaking impossible, he argues in his introduction – or rather, it is 'a belated and all-but-impossible act', and 'if strong is always a misreading'. But a mis-reading can only be that if a right reading is possible; and if a right reading is possible, then it can only be arrived at by reading. So Harold Bloom must believe some reading habits (perhaps his own) to be an exception to his own principle. The instance illustrates the sheer inattention-to-itself that characterises so much critical theory – its refusal to look at the consequences of what it is saying. When Pontius Pilate asked 'What is truth?' he was jesting, according to Bacon, and did not stay for an answer. Perhaps he should have stayed. Nobody, after all, whether in moral or aesthetic matters, behaves as if values were merely something we choose to impute as individuals to any given behaviour or any work of art. Auschwitz was a given set of behaviour, and nobody (to my knowledge) believes that it can be made right or wrong simply by thinking it so. Scepticism can be credulous: as credulous as belief. Constrained by popularised versions of nineteenth-century anthropology, we are by now entirely accustomed to being urged to withhold moral condem-nation from other civilisations and ethical systems: but hardly anyone – perhaps no one – now thinks that principle should extend as far as the ethical system of Hitler's Third Reich. A muddle, then, as our anti-sceptical philosophers have rightly noted, is what we are in.

The history of philosophy is less like housework, perhaps, than a game of ping-pong where arguments are forever turned back on their originators; and even if the prevailing mood in morality and literary studies is still far less certain than that of the Peking government, at least the argumentative ball is nowadays being returned, and ever more briskly, into the sceptical court. It is less easy to be a radical sceptic now than it was in the heady days of post-structuralism and dogmas of ideological conditioning; though some ageing survivors of Deconstruction and radical feminism still struggle to keep their dilapidated scepticisms afloat. But the arguments of a tradition of critical theory that once emanated from Paris in the 1950s and 1960s, it is now clear, were seldom as good as they needed to be; and the stale fug of old-fashioned French *marxisant* criticism is now being dispelled by the fresh wind of humanistic debate. Our radical sceptics, in the long run, though sceptical enough to impress themselves and even one another, were nothing like sceptical enough.

In literary terms, the debate about the objectivity of judgement is little more than a century old, and it forms no essential part of Renaissance or eighteenth-century critical theory. In literary parlance, the terms 'objective' and 'subjective' entered English as late as the early nineteenth century, with Coleridge's *Biographia Literaria* (1817), inviting as terms some candid mockery from Thomas Carlyle. In his tenth chapter, Coleridge announced that he had decided to import those words out of philosophy into literary theory:

> The very words *objective* and *subjective*, of such constant recurrence in the schools of yore, I have ventured to reintroduce, because I could not so briefly or conveniently, by any more familiar terms, distinguish the *percipere* from the *percipi*,

the act of perceiving from what is perceived; and nearly forty years later De Quincey, in a note of 1856 to his *Confessions*, remarked of 'objective' that the word had been 'so nearly unintelligible in 1821', when his own book first appeared a mere four years after Coleridge's, 'so entirely scholastic' and 'so apparently pedantic', that it had taken a generation or two to render it 'too common to need any apology'. In literary theory, then, the debate in these familiar terms can be dated to the early nineteenth century, which makes it little more than a century and a half old. Time to get it right, one might say; and yet we seem hardly nearer than in Coleridge's day, or De Quincey's, to getting it right, if nearer at all.

Some of the capacity of late twentieth-century literary theorists to get it wrong looks little better than obdurate. There can be no serious excuse, for example, for confusing the claim to objectivity, whether in morality or in the arts, with a general claim to certain knowledge. Nobody working in the physical sciences, unless corrupted by bad philosophy, imagines that an enquiry becomes objective only when the answer has been found and agreed. A scientist performing an observation, or an experiment in a laboratory, can hardly fail to be aware that his enquiry is objective even though he does not know the answer to it. (If he already knew the answer, why would he bother to conduct the experiment?) To take an observational instance from astronomy: when John Couch Adams, in 1845–6, noticed irregular movements in the planet Uranus and decided that there must be some hitherto unnoticed planet there to account for them – calling it Neptune – his early observations were based on the twin assumptions that something was possibly there and that he did not yet know what it was; and, at a later stage, that something was probably there and that he did not yet certainly know what it was. There is nothing exceptional or paradoxical, then, about the suggestion that an enquiry is objective and unanswered: that moral and aesthetic values are objective and that, in some given case, we do not know what they are. Henry James's fiction often deals with moral truths that exist but are not yet known. Richard Rorty has called objectivity 'a matter of ability to achieve agreement on whether a particular set of desiderata have or have not been satisfied'[2] – which, if seriously pondered, might rule out much or most of the physical properties even of this cosmos, let alone others; and yet it seems extravagant to deny that physics and chemistry are objective enquiries. Objectivity is far wider than that. Humanism depends on the claim that the study of the arts, as of the principles of human conduct, is an objective enquiry. But the claim to literary objectivism is in no way a claim to universal knowledge, still less to universal certainty. It is a comment on the logical status of the question. Like any experimental scientist, a critic might sensibly argue that his literary enquiry was objective without claiming that he knew the answer to it, and even (perhaps) without claiming that the answer would ever certainly be known. That is why it remains so absurd to imagine that to call literary judgements objective is to claim in all cases to know, and to know for certain, what they are.

Another aspect of critical obduracy has been to confuse knowledge with an ability to give a sufficient account of what one knows. That demand, at its crudest, expresses itself in an insistence on definitions and statable criteria. But a definition is not the first stage in an argument, and not even clearly the last. G. K. Chesterton once remarked that 'the man next door is not definable because he is too actual to be defined':[3] a perceptive remark, especially when one reflects that nobody would think it a ground for denying that one knew the man next door. Knowing literature is often like that. You do not recognise a play to be a tragedy by measuring it against an agreed form of words that defines Tragedy in general: *Oedipus* and *Lear* are known to be instances before any critical debate about tragedy has even begun; and any account of what constitutes Tragedy has to conform to those plays. Definition is not where to start, then, though it may occasionally be where to choose to stop. A recent commission on pornography decided at its first meeting, which was chaired by a philosopher, not to begin its deliberations by trying to define pornography, and it did not even end by doing so. One might perfectly well know what literature is, in the same way, or some species of literature like Tragedy, without possessing a definition that satisfies anyone; and as for an *agreed* definition, that is an even remoter prospect, and one even less essential, than a definition satisfying to a single mind.

The simple truth is that no agreement is needed, whether in morality, in the arts or elsewhere, in order to be certain. No one would think it an objection to being sure that the earth is round rather than flat to be told that not everyone agrees that it is so. Tolstoy thought Shakespeare a poor dramatist: but no one hesitates for long between the two most evident explanations for this – that he was right, or that he did not know much about Shakespeare. Some murderers have continued to believe and proclaim, even after conviction, that they behaved well: Franz Stangl, for example, when serving a prison sentence after the war as a Nazi camp commandant, remained fully convinced that since he had acted efficiently as an exterminator and under orders not of his making, his sentence was plainly unjust;[4] but it would seem more than strange to suppose that his agreement to the proposition that mass murder is wrong would have to be gained before it could certainly be known that it is. Nor is my agreement required before the conclusions reached in a chemical laboratory are accepted, since I know little or nothing about experimental chemistry. There is no substance at all, then, in the claim that a critical proposition needs to be agreed in order to be certain.

The demand for a verbal definition, whether agreed or not, is in any case misconceived. We perfectly well know what certain familiar fruits taste like, such as apples and pears – so much so as to distinguish them blindfold when laid on the tongue – and yet without being able to give any sufficient account of how to perform that easy and familiar process of distinction. It seems plain, then, that one can know something without being able to give an account of it; so that the complaint that there is no agreed definition of literature looks like a very odd ground for denying that we know what literature is. A Hollywood director once said: 'If it's all in the script, why make the film?'; and a Russian ballerina, when asked what she meant by a dance, once replied: 'If I could say it in words, do you think I should take the trouble to dance it?' If we could say everything that Tragedy is, in any reasonable number of words, who would take the trouble to act, read or watch *Oedipus* or *Lear*? It is because, in an absolute sense, we cannot say everything they are that we want them.

Another theoretical fallacy is to confuse precision with accuracy. An account is precise when it is in no sense vague or blurred: a map of Britain in the form of a perfect triangle, for example, would be precise. So is a newspaper caricature; so is the ethical injunction 'It is wrong to tell lies'. But all such accounts, though precise, are inaccurate. The triangular map fails to describe the ins-and-outs of the British coastline; the caricature of President Bush or Mrs Thatcher leaves most of the facial details out and exaggerates those that are left; and the rule against lying, as any thoughtful moralist or casuist could show, is subject to exceptions. In complex cases like these, the more precise an account is, the less accurate it is likely to be. A map of the Gobi desert could not fail to be more inaccurate if its limits were made to look precise: since desert merges into surrounding non-desert, anything with the precision of a line is sure to be misleading. Some phenomena are by their nature blurred at the edges: the Gobi is not bordered in the sense that France is bordered by Germany. The demand for definition takes no account of the difference between precision and accuracy: it rashly assumes, that is, that any account is likely to be more accurate for being more precise.

That distinction may be called Wittgenstein's chief contribution to philosophy; and it is a pity it has been so little noticed by literary critics, and more especially by literary theorists. It was summed up years ago in an article by John Wisdom in *Mind* (1952) with the question 'Can you play chess without the queen?'[5] That is a vivid instance of Wittgenstein's own famous proposition: 'If I tell someone "Stand about here", may not that explanation work perfectly?'[6] Both remarks illustrate the distinction between precision and accuracy in memorable ways. In photographing a building, the best place to stand is 'about here'; it would not matter to move a step or two, but it would matter a great deal to move twenty yards. If, before beginning a game of chess, the players remove the two queens and then play according to all the usual rules, are they playing chess or some other game? All such cases represent the scrubland, so to speak, that fuzzily divides desert from farmland. And to ask whether Samuel Beckett's *Waiting for Godot* counts as a tragedy, or as a comedy, or as neither, or whether the metre of Milton's 'Lycidas' is a canzone – or whether it is always wrong to tell a lie – is to be back in scrubland. It is not that one is failing to find right or accurate answers to such questions in declining to give a single and precise answer. Precision is not there to be found.

The point, Wittgensteinian as it is, is to be found in the writings of Samuel Johnson. In the twenty-eighth chapter of *Rasselas* (1759) the hero hotly debates with his sister the rival claims of marriage and celibacy, and Rasselas tries to convict Nekayah of a logical fallacy: 'Both conditions may be bad, but they cannot both be worst.' His sister rounds on him in Wittgensteinian style:

> 'I did not expect', answered the princess, 'to hear that imputed to falsehood which is the consequence only of frailty. To the mind, as to the eye, it is difficult to compare with exactness objects vast in their extent, and various in their parts. Where we see or conceive the whole at once, we readily note the discriminations and decide the preference: but of two systems of which neither can be surveyed by

any human being in its full compass of magnitude and multiplicity of complication, where is to wonder that, judging of the whole by parts, I am alternately affected by one and the other as either presses on my memory or fancy? We differ from ourselves just as we differ from each other when we see only part of the question, as in the multifarious relations of politics and morality; but when we perceive the whole at once, as in numerical computations, all agree in one judgement, and none ever varies his opinion.'

To the multifarious relations of politics and morality, Nekayah might have added those of the arts. Many critical disagreements, like many moral disagreements, spring from the complexity and lack of precise borders to the questions at stake. To persuade Tolstoy of the highly multifarious question of Shakespeare's greatness in *King Lear* 'in its full compass of magnitude and multiplicity of complication', as Johnson grandly put it, one would have to disentangle at length the causes of Tolstoy's mistake, as I do not hesitate to call it: a lack of English, a bad translation, a false expectation about the nature of drama or a crippling ignorance about Jacobean theatrical conditions. Of course his agreement might still in the event be hard to have. But it would be profoundly misleading to suggest that there nowhere exists the critical argument by which, in principle, it could be had.

Beyond and above all that, the most potent enemy of humanism in our times has been the doctrine of conditioning.

In the twentieth century, reductive attacks on humanistic discourse have most commonly been either racial or class-based. 'You only believe that because you are Jewish', for example, or 'You only believe that because you are bourgeois'. Even Sidney and Beatrice Webb, warmly pro-Soviet though they were when they wrote *Soviet Communism* (1935), were mildly disturbed to discover an academic slogan in Stalin's Russia that ran 'We stand for Party in Mathematics', as if Bolshevism affected numbers; and the Nazis, similarly, had a mathematical journal full of 'Party in mathematics'.[7] More recently a third, sex-based ground has been offered: 'You only believe that because you are a man.' In the 1970s, for example, when a woman scientist was elected for the first time head of a French *polytechnique* – one of the great academic institutes of the French Republic – the event, though welcomed by some, was publicly rejected by radical feminist opinion on the grounds that she would be teaching 'male-dominated science'.

I am less concerned, for the moment, with the elements that distinguish these three forms of anti-humanism – racialism, class war and radical feminism – than with what they have in common. What they have in common is the assumption that it is enough to identify the cause of a belief, or claim to identify it, to dismiss it. 'You only believe that because you are Jewish/bourgeois/male . . .' That assumption is a blunderbuss. Since it is commonly possible to identify the principal cause of a belief, and always possible to claim to have done so, any certainty can be briskly and conveniently discredited by arguments in that form.

But to all such simple reductions, whether Fascist, Marxist or feminist, there is a brisk and convenient answer. And that answer is that to know anything at all, at least in an articulate sense, is a mental state that is caused – most commonly by observation or by teaching – and that to identify such causes has very little to do with endorsing or discrediting knowledge. To take a simple example: being more literate than numerate, and scarcely scientific at all, I know that water consists of two parts of hydrogen to one of oxygen only because I was taught it. That may be a highly inadequate ground for believing it; but it is nothing like an adequate ground for doubting it. Any grounds for believing that water is H_2O are simply independent of my personal inability, as a non-scientist, to grasp or justify that formula. To call science male-dominated, in a similar way, or Mendelssohn's music Jewish, or Victorian fiction bourgeois, might help to identify some features of that science, music or fiction, and might help in ascertaining, in part, how they came to be what they are. But such judgements could not, of themselves, prove the achievements of artists and scientists to be anything less than they are; and those who accept the Fascist, Marxist or feminist view of conditioning have never shown that they do. The value of a belief is not to be confused with the causes, inadequate as they often are, that have led to its acceptance; a certainty may be ill-based and yet justified.

Nor have such sceptics ever shown how their own arguments are to be rendered exempt from themselves. For if all beliefs are conditioned, then racialism, Marxism and feminism, being beliefs, are conditioned too. Miss Glenda Jackson is a feminist, it may be presumed, because she has been conditioned into it: she has heard people talk feminism, that is, and believed them. But that does not show whether or not her convictions are true: merely that the apostles of easy reduction are the victims of a self-contradiction. For if all beliefs are conditioned, then the belief that all beliefs are conditioned is itself conditioned. And if it is an objection to a doctrine to say that it is that, then it is an objection to the doctrine of conditioning too.

All such reductions, it seems clear, are subject to silent and convenient self-exemptions. There has probably never been a Marxist, for example, who believed that Karl Marx believed as he did because he had been conditioned into believing it. One is still entitled, none the less, to ask on what ground exemption is made in his case. If Marx is allowed to be exempt, might not others claim exemption too? When a feminist calls science male-dominated, she is plainly implying that she, and exceptionally she, can discern those features that male scientists have put there specifically because they are *men*. But if it is possible for her to discern them, then it cannot be true to say that science is altogether male-dominated. For if that domination were total, everyone would be subject to it; and the feminist has plainly implied that she, for one, is not.

Samuel Johnson, again, has shown the way out of the difficulty here. In a conversation reported by Boswell from the Isle of Skye, in September 1773,[8] he unashamedly insisted that all good manners are acquired – and all critical judgement too, he might have said – and that it is no objection to say that they are so:

> Common language speaks the truth as to this: we say a person is *well bred*.

When Lady M'Leod asked if no man were naturally good, Johnson replied categorically: 'No, madam, no more than a wolf.' 'Nor no woman, sir?' asked Boswell mischievously. 'No, sir', said Johnson. To which Lady M'Leod is reported to have remarked shudderingly, and under her breath, 'This is worse than Swift.'

But if worse-than-Swift means misanthropic, then one may reasonably doubt that it is. Johnson's point is common to the Enlightenment of his own century, after all, and to the long humanistic tradition stretching behind it; and it is not of itself pessimistic. Man knows what he knows about science, morality and the arts because he has learned it: he has watched and listened and tested. He has acquired his mother-tongue, in the first instance, by such means; and other languages too, if at all, by such means. Of ourselves we know little or nothing: we know because we learn. To object against cognitive process, whether in literature or elsewhere, on the ground that it derives from sources beyond ourselves is to say nothing of consequence. It *needs* to derive from elsewhere. 'He that was only taught by himself', as Ben Jonson remarks in *Timber*, 'had a fool to his master.'

My own helplessness before the multiplication-table, or the chemical composition of water, was saved by teachers working through an accumulation of principles built up since the ancient Babylonians, and it is no objection whatever to what I know to say that I could not have thought of it for myself – still less that I did not in fact think of it for myself. Just as well... Any mathematical or chemical principle conceived of in isolation from that tradition, by now thousands of years old, is highly unlikely to be of any value whatever. In a similar way, what I know through criticism about literature is none the worse for being derived from others, and may easily be all the better for it. Criticism, like life, is a teacher.

The case for radical scepticism, then, contradicts itself. But it is an instance of a wider habit of self-contradiction that it will require another chapter to delineate.

Notes

1. See, for example, *The Skeptical Tradition*, ed. Miles Burnyeat (Berkeley, 1983), on the Ancients; A. C. Grayling, *The Refutation of Scepticism* (London, 1985); and Peter Strawson, *Skepticism and Naturalism* (London, 1985).
2. Richard Rorty, 'Texts and lumps', *New Literary History*, 17 (1985), p. 13.
3. G. K. Chesterton, *Charles Dickens* (London, 1906), p. 1.
4. See Gitta Sereny, *Into That Darkness* (London, 1974).
5. See Renford Bambrough, 'Discipline and discipleship', in *Philosophy and Life: essays on John Wisdom*, ed. Ilham Dilman (The Hague, 1984), pp. 208f.
6. Ludwig Wittgenstein, *Philosophical Investigations* (Oxford, 1953), §88.
7. F. A. Hayek, *The Road to Serfdom* (London, 1944), p. 120.
8. James Boswell, *The Tour to the Hebrides*, edited by G. B. Hill, revised by L. F. Powell, in *Boswell's Life of Johnson*, vol. 5 (Oxford, 1950), p. 211.

4

ARGUMENT-AGAINST-ITSELF

There is a story about an Oxford philosophy seminar – presumably a fiction – where the speaker announced: 'Ghosts have never existed, and so all assertions about them are meaningless'; to which a voice from the back replied: 'Including that one?'

The story neatly illustrates self-refutation: argument by suicide, so to speak, or argument-against-itself. A critical argument, not least, can easily prove suicidal in that way: if it is true, then it is false. In fact it has just demonstrated, unknowingly, why it is false.

The present age cannot claim to have invented arguments in that style – Socrates, after all, in his lust for definition in others but seldom in himself, has plausibly been accused of an overfondness for them. But they have been used with an exceptional and characteristic confidence in the present century – with the sort of confidence, first to last, that asks not to be questioned. One imagines the Oxford ghost-sceptic as aggrieved by his heckler as if he had been bitten by his own guard-dog. Radical sceptics, above all, confidently expect their own arguments to be used against anyone but themselves. In fact it is the hallmark of the sceptic to assume that his own assertions are somehow miraculously exempt from their own fire-power – rather as if he were standing inviolate on some Archimedean point far outside the range of argument. That is perhaps to risk some unfairness to the memory of Archimedes: if he ever said anything like 'Give me a place to stand, and I will move the earth', he was knowingly offering a significant hypothesis about weight and mass. The self-refuter of our own times, by contrast, is not knowingly uttering a hypothesis. He imagines he really has found somewhere to stand, argumentatively speaking: an Archimedean base outside the scope of all debate from which, unchallenged, he can direct sceptical fire-power against any assertion but his own.

He has exempted himself. It would be easy, and partly persuasive, to suggest that the twentieth-century vogue for argumentative self-exemption has its famous nineteenth-century sources, notably in Marx and Freud; and certainly, whatever those two great originals may have meant and said, their disciples have often claimed self-exemption by invoking the Master's name. Refutation, being self-inflicted, then takes a familiar course. If all beliefs are socially conditioned, then Marxism is so too, since it is a belief; if all theories are mere rationalisations, then Freudianism too is that, since it is a theory. Such easy reductions as social conditioning and rationalisation, considered as total explanations, are by now rightly seen as demolishable, and these are crude and summary accounts of how their demolition is familiarly performed. Nor will the demolition-ist be impressed to be told that what Marx or Freud once wrote or said was a good deal less crude or better protected than those summaries imply. For one thing, it is not always so: Marx did write like a crude Marxist, on occasion; Freud could be crudely Freudian – among other things. In any case, such reductions are by now characteristic of whole schools. They exist and flourish; and it is beside the point to object that their dead masters, if strictly or subtly interpreted, believed in something less vulner-able. Argument-against-itself, for whatever reason, is the fashion we are in; and it matters little how we got into it, though a good deal how to get out. That is why I am less concerned here with historical issues, except as illustrative cases, than with the fashion and its cure.

Any self-exempting argument is self-refuting. If an argument is good, then it has no counter-instances – least of all itself; and as the Oxford ghost-sceptic's discomfiture illustrates, over-bold ver-sions of scepticism can instantaneously self-destruct. That is not to disparage generalisations in any general sense. The better sort – 'women are often unpunctual', for example – can conscientiously offer themselves in some well-protected guise, and a single case like a relentlessly punctual woman would do them little if any damage. Self-exemption cannot claim that. It excludes cautious qualifiers like 'often' and 'commonly'; it is characteristically sweeping. A scattering of instances, old and new, may help to document the spread of cases here.

1. 'Nothing is certain.' The radical sceptic, who is commonly a disappointed foundationist, is fond of claiming that, since there are no certain and agreed foundations to knowledge, there is no certain knowledge – least of all in morality or the arts. But if nothing is certain, then that is not. And if all truths need certain and agreed foundation, as he believes, what is the certain and agreed foundation to the proposition that all truths need certain and agreed foundations?

2. 'Ideology'. Everything that passes for knowledge, it is sometimes said, is merely perspectival, arising (for example) out of class, race or gender, and marked by some ideology characteristic of its origins. To reread I. A. Richards's *Practical Criticism* (1929), for example, Terry Eagleton has suggested,[1] is to be

> struck by the habits of perception and interpretation which they [the undergraduate critics and their teacher] spontaneously share. . . . None of this is really surprising: for all the participants in this experiment were, presumably, young, white, upper- or upper-middle-class, privately educated English people of the 1920s. . . . Their critical responses were deeply entwined with their broader prejudices and beliefs,

and he adds, in a sudden spasm of generosity that does not entirely escape the charge of condescension:

> This is not a matter of *blame*: there is no critical response which is not so entwined, and thus no such thing as a 'pure' literary critical judgement or intepretation. If anyone is to be blamed it is I. A. Richards himself, who as a young, white, upper-middle-class male Cambridge don was unable to objectify a context of interests which he himself largely shared.

But if *all* critical responses are distorted by matters of origin, how is Richards at fault for failing to 'objectify' his ? Any attempt he made at objectification, in that case, would itself be open to the same complaint. And if all responses are distorted by social and racial origin ('white, upper-middle-class') and even by sex ('male'), how can one accept that Eagleton's are not? It is hard to doubt that he had a social and racial origin, or that he has a sex.

3. 'Morality is merely personal'. Many historians have lately

invited us to detach ourselves from moral judgements in history. 'The historian', wrote David Knowles, 'is not a judge, still less a hanging judge.' E. H. Carr, quoting the passage approvingly, remarks: 'What profit does anyone find today in denouncing the sins of Charlemagne or of Napoleon?'[2] Neither Knowles nor Carr seems conscious of making any moral judgement in such pronouncements; and yet Knowles is entirely aware that there *are* hanging-judge historians, as he calls them, like Acton: in fact he quotes from them. So when he writes that 'the historian is not a judge', he plainly means that he ought not to be one. And Carr's declared objection to condemning the sins of Charlemagne and Napoleon is that it would be unprofitable. These are judgements – just or unjust. If judgement lies outside the historian's business, then so do these.

4. 'Interpretation is merely personal.' It is often denied that works of literature, even works in general, can ever have an existence independent of their interpreter. In *The Politics of Interpretation* (1983), for example, Ronald Dworkin and Stanley Fish scarcely doubt the assumption. But that does not inhibit them from disputing whether the one has properly understood the other. 'There is no trace in my essay', Dworkin writes indignantly,

> of any claim that the identity or characterization or interpretation of a work of art is a 'brute fact' . . . or that the nature of a work of art is 'independent' of the interpreter, or that the constraints of interpretation are 'self-executing'. . . . Fish has read my essay through lenses of quite amazing power. They enable him to see, in what I said, claims I never embrace and firmly reject.[3]

But if the sense of a text is *in no way* independent of its interpreter, how can any reader ever be said to have misunderstood it? Dworkin does not even have the defence that his claim refers to works of literature rather than to treatises like his own, since his total argument plainly relates to essays and documents as well as to poems, plays and novels. Neither of the combatants, in fact, has noticed that if his theory were true, he would have lost the right to complain that he himself had ever been misinterpreted about anything.

5. 'The Arbitrariness of the Sign.' Since any given language is

arbitrary, it has been said, in the sense that its words could be other than they are, none imitates the real. But in that case the assertion must itself fail to imitate the realities of the question. After all, it is itself in words.

6. As an extended example: a critic once claimed that George Orwell's reports of the Depression and the Spanish Civil War had been radically misdescribed by critics, since they reflect nothing that happened in Lancashire or Spain in the 1930s. When evidence for their accuracy was produced, he replied that since reality exists simultaneously and language only sequentially, no text can ever accurately describe any state of affairs, whether past or present. But in that case his own account of Orwell cannot have been accurate, since it is itself a text; in which case Orwell may indeed have been reporting things as they were.

7. 'The Death of the Author.' Announcing it as a critical principle in 'What is an author?' (1969), Michel Foucault called for a new style of criticism based on 'texts as texts' rather than on authorial intention. 'What difference does it make who is speaking?' But if it makes *no* difference, then it makes no difference that the author of 'What is an author?' was Foucault. The consequences of concluding that would be far-reaching, and not just for such immediate and practical concerns as sending him (or someone else) a royalty cheque. They would include refusing to make any connection on assumptions of common authorship between that essay and other writings by Foucault: an inhibition that the editor of *A Foucault Reader* (1987), where it is reprinted with other papers by the same author and because they are by the same author, has understandably felt himself entitled to ignore.

8. 'Reality is unintelligible.' In *Reading Myself and Others* (1975), Philip Roth retells a notorious newspaper-story about a brutal murder of two Chicago sisters, whose grief-stricken mother was consoled by well-wishers with gifts of a new kitchen and a pair of parakeets; and he indignantly concludes:

> The American writer in the middle of the twentieth century has his hands full in trying to understand, describe and then *make credible* much of American reality. It stupefies, it sickens, it infuriates. . . .

Roth may be indulging in rhetorical hyperbole here. But if he really finds it hard or impossible to understand his Chicago crime-story, how can he be stupefied, sickened or infuriated by it? It is altogether plain, one suspects, that he can and does understand it – that he readily and confidently understands it, in fact – and that he knows that he does, and wants others to share his indignant understanding. It is a story which (in his view) exemplifies the extravagant effects of the tabloid press on popular behaviour. And it is only those who claim to understand those effects who can plausibly protest against them.

9. 'Literary judgements are personal.' A scholar editing a medieval poet once remarked on the absurd critical state of his subject. 'People think he can't have written some poems just because they aren't good enough,' he said, roaring with laughter. Some weeks before, he had roared still louder when someone picked up a freshman essay in his college room and asked 'Did you write this?' Clearly he thought himself exempt from his own rule that, in terms of value, anybody can write anything; in fact his scholarly reputation, as he rightly saw, altogether depended on that self-exemption. One thing to insist theoretically on the subjectivity of critical judgements: another to accept it in one's own case. When it really matters – when one knows it really matters – almost everybody believes in the objectivity of judgement: as in trusting an engineer to design a bridge that will not fall, or a surgeon with his knife.

10. Laws of history. Historians often claim there are no general conclusions or 'laws' to be drawn from the study of history, or none that matter – such laws being either false or trite. Karl Popper, for example, has declared that 'the host of trivial laws' that historians take for granted have no serious interest or ordering function equivalent to those of the natural sciences. A law of history, he argued, could only be true at the cost of being trivial: where two armies are equally well led, for example, big ones tend to defeat small ones.[4] But the notion that laws of history are always trite or false is itself a law of history, if it constitutes a law to make a sweeping claim about the past in general terms. It can hardly be trite, since Popper is aware that he is arguing against a host of intelligent adversaries; and he is plainly unready to acknowledge it might be false. So it refutes itself.

These instances suggest that a silent claim to self-exemption is by now a highly fashionable style of argumentative effrontery among the learned. As fallacies go, it is more or less the flavour-of-the-century: not utterly unique to our times, that is, but unique in its force and audacity. It infects philosophy as well as criticism. In fact a modern historian of ancient scepticism has recently remarked that 'inoculation', as he aptly calls it, is nowadays commonplace among professional philosophers in a way an Ancient might have felt innocently puzzled by; and he instances a philosopher applying for a research grant to study the question 'Is time real?': neither the applicant nor his committee troubling to consider that, if the question were in any way in doubt, they could hardly vote funds for a specific period like an academic year.[5] Theorists readily assume themselves to stand outside their own speculations; like moralists and critics, philosophers too can sound efficiently inoculated against their own arguments, and especially against their own doubts. They behave as if matters were as certain as they publicly and lengthily doubt them to be.

Self-exemption in that style is likely to be late Victorian in origin, though in the last years of the century it was the property of a few advanced spirits rather than a wide intellectual class. More continental than English, it was more central European, I suspect, than anything else. Victorian England could be highly impatient of pretension, by contrast, in the sense of gaps between what is said and done, and noisily anti-hypocritical in a no-nonsense way. Dickens is a loud, hectoring instance of that view, George Eliot a trenchant one, Matthew Arnold a suavely refined one; and so fervent is their insistence that pretence and practice must match, so lusty their horror of prating, that hypocrisy-hunting might be called the chief Victorian sport after fox-hunting. 'We live and learn', says Martin Chuzzlewit grimly, after his adventure on the American frontier. 'Sometimes we nearly die and learn.' Dickens's Mr Pecksniff is not a lonely caricature in the fiction of the age, or his Mrs Jellyby either: living up to your own claims, and offering yourself as a first instance of them, is firmly at the heart of the Victorian conscience. Ordinarily a temperate author, George Eliot borders on stridency when she attacks silly novelists for being 'oracular', or continental sociologists for the aching gap between what they claim to know about the human world and what they truly know. In her own fiction, implacably, no such gap is countenanced. To know, morally speaking, is to have lived; and mankind accumulates moral knowledge by something far more intimate than mere observation. We learn by doing and by failing to do, and books are no more than a crutch. Marx's note-taking in the Reading Room of the British Museum, had she known about it – and she may easily have known about it, and even met Marx, who was only eighteen months older than herself – or Freud's notes scribbled unseen at the head of a patient's couch, would have excited her liveliest derision. You know life less by looking at it or hearing about it than by living it. And until you have lived, you cultivate the humility of silent, earnest attention or risk the censure of experience.

That high Victorian assumption of humility before experience is notably absent from the writings of Nietzsche, Durkheim and Freud. Such writers claim, or effortlessly assume, an Archimedean point; they insist that superior understanding belongs to an observer armed with rules and techniques newly designed for the purpose. By the early twentieth century the claim had become the trade mark of entire intellectual professions – most notably anthropology, sociology and psychology. Like Margaret Mead among the Samoans, such professions readily assume a personal inoculation against the phenomena they describe. They are openly impatient of experience; they attribute to observation the total function of truth-gathering and interpretation; and they regard self-exemption as a natural right of the observer, even a proven duty. The enquirer is nowhere a part of his own data. That sudden swerve into self-exemption has its philosophical or quasi-philosophical sources. Nietzsche, cheerfully deriding human pretensions to knowledge in *Götzendämmerung* (1888), suddenly abandoned his insistence that all belief is merely perspectival to praise the literature of the Ancients for what it had abundantly taught him – 'What I have to thank the Ancients for', as he called it – and we are suddenly plunged again into that new, self-contradictory world. For if all knowledge is damagingly perspectival, then it is hard to see how one can learn from ancient literature, or indeed from anything; and yet the argument plainly implies Nietzsche has learnt something that is the case, not merely a set of convenient fictions. Or when Durkheim in *Les règles de la méthode sociologique* (1895) remarks that the aim of sociology is to enable the modern mind to acquire a knowledge of social structures that science alone can provide, we are there again, since the claim that only science knows reality is a claim exempt from itself, being itself unscientifically based. 'Consider social facts as things', Durkheim proposes:

> Instead of a science concerned with realities, we have so far produced no more than ideological analysis – proceeding from ideas to things, not from things to ideas. This method cannot give objective results. (ch. 2)

Society is not to be seriously understood, he continues, until a new terminology has been devised on the analogy of the physical sciences; what once passed for social knowledge in such authors as Dickens and George Eliot, in that view, being no more than gossip and old wives' tales – 'ideas', not 'things' – unfounded because without scientific foundations. But the claim that there are foundations to social knowledge, or that they are needed, is itself scientifically unfounded; and it is notable that no attempt is ever instituted by Durkheim or his followers to reveal or devise scientific foundations for that claim. It is exempt from itself.

We are now silently enjoined to step off the whirligig of life, in fact, and look at it; and not allowed to ask whether it is so much as possible to step off, or where to stand if we did. Archimedes' point has ceased to be ironical or hypothetical. It is literal and urgent. Mankind will not understand itself, it is now suggested, until the analyst has moved to a place from which entire societies can be studied and compared from outside themselves. And it is only a short step from such Archimedean fantasies to the science fiction of H. G. Wells in *The Time Machine* (1895), to Aldous Huxley's *Brave New World* (1932), and to the totalitarian systems anatomised by George Orwell in *Nineteen Eighty-Four* (1949). If man can stand outside mankind, then he can remake it. 'Caesarism and science together', as Sir Oswald Mosley boldly put it in his memoir *My Life* (1968), announcing his programme, 'could evolve Faustian man.' There is no saying what one might not do, in fact, and license oneself in duty to do, if only one could claim to stand outside the human condition and judge it with the lofty vision of those who have ceased to see themselves as human or humane.

There is no longer any need to ask whether such arguments

convince, since they plainly bear within themselves the evidences why they do not. There is some need, however, to ask why they once did. It is not just isolated thinkers of the last century like Durkheim and Nietzsche, or inchoate armies of intellectuals in our own times, but real armies too that have marched to that drum. Self-exemption was not commonly seen as self-refuting by the Modernist mind of the early years of the twentieth century, though it was often seen, and rightly, as precarious and difficult. From his youthful dissertation on F. H. Bradley, *Knowledge and Experience* (1964), submitted to Harvard in 1916, down to *Four Quartets* (1943), T. S. Eliot agonised for a lifetime over the rooted incompetence of inherited human speech – unaware, apparently, for all his awareness, that his own eloquence had proved English at least to be a good deal more than barely competent as a language. Samuel Beckett's *Waiting for Godot* (1954) is an amusing play about the sheer impossibility, in this vale of tears, of ever being amused, so that it gracefully and self-consciously refutes itself; and Picasso's Cubist paintings deny classic representations like traditional portraiture in favour of conceptual forms which yet recognisably represent their sitters. Modernists have knowingly as well as unknowingly luxuriated in the contradictions of self-exemption, so that there can be no question of catching them out by drawing attention to such contradictions. They insist, at times, on being caught. In a similar way, any anthology of Anglo-American poems from our mid-century is certain to abound in poems about how difficult or impossible it is to write a poem. And yet they are *poems*, in the judgement of poet and anthologist alike: how else should they be there? Modernism is about the impossible-that-is.

Why should the western mind, in the past hundred years, have taken such evident delight in denying the very thing it did? Part of the answer may lie in the sudden charms of a new generation-struggle – new, that is, in its argumentative form. To deny the value of experience in favour of some formal logic yet to be devised can act as a conveniently instant refutation of the claims of parent, magistrate or critic to know better. 'What are your criteria?': that recurrent challenge, well known to be unanswerable and meant to be so, can feel exhilaratingly like putting the rook on the back line in a game of chess – and in a game, like many another, played out between young and old.

Another part of the answer can lie in the fact that, for radical intelligences, the gap between private conduct and the fervour of moral principle is all too patent and habitual. The teacher who proclaims a belief in the equality of educational provision and yet deliberately gives good classes undeniably has a problem of consistency, unless he silently self-exempts, since good classes are likely to create even more educational inequality; and if inequality is wrong, then that is wrong. The rich socialist who condemns private wealth and yet wants to remain rich (and even get richer) undeniably has a problem too, rather like Mr Pecksniff, and it is a pity Dickens did not live long enough to dissect a specimen. The provisional answer of the egalitarian here, bold rather than persuasive, can be to count oneself out of the argument altogether, perhaps out of all arguments – much as diplomats and journalists count themselves out of arguments about whether it is right to visit apartheid-ridden lands or totalitarian regimes. (They are only observing and reporting, after all.) The trouble is that the notion of moral immunity, so easily conceded to diplomats and journalists, does not work at all clearly for the egalitarian, as he shamefacedly knows. It does not work if only because his immunity is conferred not by some accredited authority, as it needs to be in order to count at all, but by himself.

A further motive lies in self-assertion. Many self-exempting critical stances involve what logicians have lately come to call the Higher Redefinition: this language is not what *I* call descriptive, though you may . . . this poem is not what *I* call a poem . . . this amusement is not what *I* find amusing. . . . The 'I' in all these assertions, claiming as it does to stand outside language, poetry, or amusement, is easily imagined as standing above them too: superior, deprecating, and above all 'knowing', in the sense that a friend or relative might wear a knowing expression when he claims an intuition he will not reveal. In his own pretension, at any rate, the self-exempting critic is something of a Superman. He would like to convince others, and himself, that his long-standing dissatisfaction with familiar truths is a mark of superior virtue and taste. 'This is not a matter of *blame*. . . .' His claims mask a secret elation. He will not play the game, so to speak, because he would have the world believe that he, and he almost alone on earth, knows of a better one.

But to all that there is a reasonable challenge, and it has not been answered. Show your game; explain why it is better; and see if you can do either without using language as it is commonly used or abandoning a radical scepticism about values. But beware: if it is indeed better, then you have made a value-judgement; and if all such judgements are merely personal, then that is. Until that string of challenges is met, the cult of argument-against-itself will look like mere posturing and the febrile fashion of one brief age of Western man: a teasing play with no winners, no prizes and no game.

Notes

1. T. Eagleton, *Literary Theory* (Oxford, 1983), p. 15.
2. David Knowles, *The Historian and Character* (Cambridge, 1955), p. 19; E. H. Carr, *What Is History?* (London, 1961), p. 72.
3. *The Politics of Interpretation*, ed. by W. J. T. Mitchell (Chicago, 1983), pp. 288–9.
4. Karl Popper, *The Open Society and its Enemies* (London, 1945), II.251. See p. 139, below.
5. M. F. Burnyeat, 'The sceptic in his place and time', in *Philosophy and History*, ed. by Richard Rorty, J. B. Schneewind and Quentin Skinner (Cambridge, 1984), p. 225.

5

THE STACKED DECK
OF LANGUAGE

Literary theory since the 1960s has revealed two characteristic weaknesses.

First, it was often philosophically and linguistically out of date, being based on a tradition of thought – mainly German and French – that flourished in continental Europe between the 1840s and the First World War: above all early Marx, Durkheim's writings in the 1880s and 1890s and Saussure's Geneva lectures of 1906–11. Its sense of Modernism was severely arrested: even its literary awareness could only with difficulty be stretched beyond the 1930s, when its cult novelist James Joyce ceased to write. 'Modern critical theory', or *la nouvelle critique*, was an intellectually antiquated doctrine even in its heyday. Some old doctrines, it will be said, are valuable and just, and deserve to be maintained or revived; and so they are, and do. But in that case literary theorists should have presented their case as a revival, and it was disquieting to hear them talk as if what they believed were the latest thing.

The other weakness is more specific. Post-structuralist theory was based on a plain and yet apparently unnoticed contradiction; and as with all contradictions, at least one of its propositions must be false. Consider *Modern Literary Theory* (1982), a collection of essays edited by Ann Jefferson and David Robey of Oxford. In its introduction, the editors complained that literary scholarship has always lacked agreement about 'a truly adequate definition of its subject-matter', implying it was high time it had one; and in the second chapter Robey proclaimed modern linguistics had demonstrated 'the essential disjunction between language and reality', any language being a closed system 'wholly independent of the

material world'. In other words, criticism can reliably proceed
only by agreed verbal definitions; but any such definition is
necessarily and always false, being itself couched in a language
disjoined from reality. So you are damned if you do and damned
if you don't.

The contradiction is patent. Language, it was said, being based
on a system of arbitrary signs, cannot imitate reality. In that case
why do critical theorists use it so much – or indeed at all? The last
time I heard Jacques Derrida lecture, he talked for two and three-
quarter hours, causing me to miss dinner; and yet his argument
was that the truth cannot be told and that language is only seemingly and delusively referential. In that case I would rather have
had dinner.

A black mood of self-contradiction has settled over the theory of
language, though far less among professional linguists than
among literary critics. And it arises from a fear that the whole of
human speech might, in the end, prove nothing more than an
instrument radically disabling to thought: loaded dice, a distorting looking-glass, a stacked deck of cards.

The mood is not entirely new. In 1786, for example, the English
linguist Horne Tooke remarked in the introduction to his *The
Diversions of Purley* on the dominance of words over thoughts,
nervously measuring the prospect that even man's proudest and
profoundest cogitations might prove utterly helpless before them:
'If . . . Philosophy herself has been misled by language, how shall
she teach us to detect his tricks?' Language might be less an aid
than an 'imposition', in that case, mankind less its master than its
slave.

The mood revived briefly in American linguistics between the
wars. In the late 1920s Benjamin Lee Whorf and Edward Sapir
concluded from a study of Amerindian languages that 'ideology
follows phoneticism'; Whorf even spoke of 'inexorable laws of
pattern' that unconsciously control the thoughts of every one of
us. 'Men do not live in the objective world alone,' wrote Sapir in
1929, 'but are very much at the mercy of the particular language
of their society.'[1]

All that, by now, sounds amiably tentative and engagingly
mild. In the 1950s and 1960s a far extremer view was to be heard,
mainly from Paris: that one cannot even hope to describe reality

in words, all language being arbitrarily imposed and ideologically conditioned; that men are always and forever the victims rather than the beneficiaries of speech, and all the more so when they do not know it. It is later than you think . . . Variously garnished – for even pessimism can be beguiling, not least in Paris – that is among the master-ideas of Lacan's *Ecrits* (1966) and of Roland Barthes's treatises since 1957. It lay at the root, too, of Derrida's dogma of *différance* – of that infinite postponement of knowledge allegedly imposed by an inescapable and crippling dependence on words.

Early in the century, Ferdinand de Saussure had spoken of language as a conjuror's forced card; since then, his metaphor has been indefinitely extended by those who judge themselves his disciples. Being arbitrary, language gives us no choice. It may console with an illusion of liberty; but having tasted of modern critical theory, we are consoled no more. We are the prisoners of words, and liberty is not for us. Mankind may shake its manacles gratefully hereafter, even gleefully, but will not shake them off.

Several arguments, it seems clear, have gone off the rails here – leading, as derailments do, to a pile-up of accidents.

First, a historical point about language as an arbitrary system. Like the French word *arbitraire*, *arbitrary* is riskily ambiguous. In strictly neutral terms, it can mean 'depending on passing chance'; more darkly, it can mean 'ill-intentioned, damaging, despotic'. It is itself, then, something like an illustrative example of the forced card. When modern literary theorists attribute to Saussure the discovery that language is arbitrary, as they habitually do, they commonly imply both senses.

Saussure did not discover that language is largely arbitrary or conventional, however, or claim that he did. His *Cours de linguistique générale* appeared in 1916, three years after his death, edited from his lecture-notes; and if that text is to be trusted, he was explicit that the Principle of the Arbitrary had long been commonplace: 'No one disputes the principle of the arbitrary nature of the sign' (I.i). It is only the full significance of that commonplace view, he held, that had been overlooked: '*Le principe de l'arbitraire du signe n'est contesté par personne; mais il est souvent plus aisé de découvrir une vérité que de lui assigner la place qui lui revient*'; and he goes on to except onomatopoeia and interjections: exceptions too deeply involved in the sound-system of a language to do much more, in any case, than dent the principle itself. Linguists have usually been aware Saussure was uttering a commonplace here – the more so because, like the honest Swiss he was, he bluntly said so. Literary theorists have been more inclined to follow what other theorists have said, and to attribute to Saussure a theoretical originality he neither possessed nor claimed.

The Principle of the Arbitrary is ancient, medieval and modern. Plato's view largely depends on whether one takes Socrates' exciting nonsense about etymology in the *Cratylus* to be serious or spoofing – a moot point among experts; but in the *Organon* Aristole saw words as arbitrary, and his view was accepted by schoolmen such as Aquinas and by many humanists after them. Rabelais put the principle into the mouth of Pantagruel: '*Les voix ne signifient naturellement, mais à plaisir.*'[2] The point was restated by Bacon, Hobbes, and Locke in the next century; and it was to be memorably reiterated by Samuel Johnson in the preface to his *Dictionary* (1755): 'Words are the daughters of the earth, and things are the sons of heaven.' Locke admittedly had opponents who had proposed a 'scriptural' theory of Adamic language, where the relation between the Signifier and the Signified was God-given rather than arbitrary and a better guide, accordingly, than man's fallen reason. But in the *Essay* of 1690 Locke insists that words are man-made, and he turns the Genesis story of Adam naming the animals into a common charter for all mankind as it discovers and invents: 'The same liberty . . . that Adam had of affixing any new name to any idea, the same has anyone still' (III.vi). An inventor, then, would have the linguistic rights and privileges of first man.

The sinister sense of *arbitrary* may be judged by replacing it with a more innocent term like *conventional*. Signs are conventional or, if you will, 'merely conventional'. In *The Hunting of the Snark* (1876), Lewis Carroll wittily imagines a crew presented with a map that is an absolute blank:

> 'What's the good of Mercator's North Poles and Equators,
> Tropics, Zones, and Meridian Lines?'
> So the Bellman would cry: and the crew would reply
> 'They are merely conventional signs!'

That obedient crew sounds very much like the *nouveaux critiques* of the 1960s; and if not everybody can see what is the matter with all that, at least everybody can see that something is. A description, whether a map or a critical account, need be no less helpful or accurate for being based on conventions that amount to merely provisional and arbitrary agreements between mapmaker and sailor, author and reader. Plain as it is, that is something *la nouvelle critique* could not, or would not, understand. And yet a seaman who refused to read maps on the Bellman's principle would end up on the beach or in the sea.

Consider, however, the sceptical gloss confidently put on the Principle of the Arbitrary by certain literary theorists in more recent years. In Jean-Marie Benoist's *La révolution structurale* (1975), for example, a French critic exultantly hammered nails into the coffin of humanism, as he imagined, by suggesting that Nietzsche's death of God had now been followed by the death of man – men being obliged to efface themselves, as he argued, 'before the differential structural and semiotic relationship which articulates the signs that are produced among them'. So humanity must forever renounce the illusion of rationality, even of individual consciousness, every individual creature being 'no less spoken than speaking'. All that sounds like a late echo of Roland Barthes, who had claimed as early as *Mythologies* (1957) that the study of signs showed a sense of the real world to be a mere function of language. Barthes is rumoured to have read Saussure as late as 1955 or 1956; whether he read him at all carefully, however, remains unclear. Was he reinterpreting Saussure, we may ask, when he so confidently repudiated any certain knowledge of the real, or boldly inventing a scepticism all his own?

Literary scepticism in that mode, it seems likely, was entirely mid-century Parisian. Saussure makes a highly improbable sceptic in the Barthesian sense; and when he spoke of cards being forced, it seems clear he meant no more than individual words. In any given language, as he argued, the signifier is fixed and not free. 'The man in the street has no voice in the matter, and the signifier chosen by language could be replaced by no other' (*Cours* I.ii). We are not socially permitted to call cats dogs, in fact, or dogs cats, and would achieve a reputation for myopia, or eccentricity, or worse if we did. On that level the native speaker simply has nothing to think about: 'Reflection does not enter into the use of an idiom', as Saussure remarks; and he ingeniously adds that language is harder to modify than morality – is more conservative – precisely because it is arbitrary, change failing to happen not because it is impossible but because it is pointless. It is quite different in that sense from moral issues, he argues, such as the rival claims of monogamy and polygamy. No wonder language evolves more slowly, then, than social custom. What would be the *point*, after all, in calling a cat a dog? 'Of all social institutions, language is the least amenable to initiative', as Saussure puts it: 'Because the sign is arbitrary, it follows no law but tradition; and because it is based on tradition, it is arbitrary' (I.i.1).[3]

The passage may be nothing like a political declaration, in intention, though it can all too easily be mistaken for one. So too might that notorious passage, later in the *Cours*, where Saussure speaks of language as being 'without positive terms' ('*sans termes positifs*', II.iv.4) – a passage easily misinterpreted as suggesting that language does not (and cannot) describe the real, and even that there is no knowable reality to describe.

The truth is, however, that no exceptional political or philosophical views can be attributed to Saussure. He lived the uneventful life of a Swiss professor; and when he called language 'the prime conservative force' of human society, he may have been making nothing more than a severely anthropological point. It is highly unlikely, in any case, that he saw the familiar Principle of the Arbitrary as in any way radical, whether in linguistics or in politics. It was the conventional wisdom of linguists since the Renaissance, and even earlier; Saussure knew that it was, and said so; and nobody in the years after 1916, when the *Cours* first appeared, seems to have thought it had radical implications, whether for linguistics or anything else. Leonard Bloomfield reviewed it unenthusiastically in the *Modern Language Journal* in 1923, finding it unremarkable; C. K. Ogden and I. A. Richards dismissed it scathingly in the same year in *The Meaning of Meaning*. Its reputation for radical originality belongs to the 1950s and after, and it arose among those largely untrained in the history of linguistics. Anyone who imagines that Saussure founded modern linguistics must be remarkably ignorant of that history, and content to remain so.

It was in the 1950s that Saussure was suddenly turned into 'the father of modern linguistics' and the man who made possible 'the achievement of twentieth-century linguistics'[4] – a sort of

Latin-Quarter literary theorist before his time. Hard now to be sure whether that misunderstanding, in its origins, was innocent or deliberate. Few literary critics have read the *Cours* through, in all probability; fewer still bothered to study the tradition of nineteenth-century linguistics out of which it once grew. Geoffrey Strickland, for example, has suggested that Saussure believed in semiology because he 'regarded all forms of human communication as systems of what are, at first, arbitrarily adopted signs'. That is true enough: but then what linguist of his time – he was born in 1857 – did not think that? David Lodge, in *The Modes of Modern Writing* (1977), commits himself to the still rasher notion that the Principle of the Arbitrary was Saussure's own idea, and 'an idea of the greatest importance'. Thus it is that myths are born. The truth is that the idea had been a learned commonplace for centuries, even millennia.

It matters less, in the end, what Saussure might be supposed to have said, or said for the first time, than what the Principle of the Arbitrary can reasonably be thought to entail for literature. For David Lodge, and not only for him, the arbitrariness of the sign has an instant and damaging implication for literature, and above all for the realistic novel: 'It will be obvious how this view of language militates against any mimetic theory of literature' – and he adds, perhaps with a touch of glee, that the whole notion is bound to be 'disconcerting' to Anglo-American critics, who are cast here in the usual Latin-Quarter stereotype of men cosily gullible in their inherited faith in mimesis and realism, and hopelessly conservative in consequence.

Practically everything is wrong with that. There is nothing obvious, to begin with, or even plausible, in the thesis that the Principle of the Arbitrary militates against any mimetic use of language. *Dog* is no less an accurate name for a well-known kind of quadruped because, like *chien* in French and *Hund* in German, it could just as well have been something else. As Lewis Carroll's Bellman and crew so signally and so disastrously failed to understand, signs can be arbitrary and at the same time accurate, helpful, and even indispensable. Road signs, which are arbitrarily fixed by international committees to save lives, are an obvious instance. Ignore them if you dare: they portray the real.

The great realistic novelists of the nineteenth century, in any case, lived in an age when the arbitrary principle of language was simply uncontroversial. If the principle is anti-realistic, which I doubt, the sense in which it is so can hardly be called obvious. It was not obvious to Balzac, or Dickens, or George Eliot; and we may continue undisconcertedly to ask what in the world is inimical to realism about it. George Eliot derided the idea that to make free of an abstract terminology in morality or sociology was to understand human affairs, and one of her essays is called 'How we come to give ourselves false testimonials and believe in them'. On the opening page of *Great Expectations* (1861), Dickens calls it unreasonable that the infant Pip should imagine the shape of his unseen parents to resemble the letters on their tombstones. It would be pleasant to offer a cash prize for a single scrap of evidence that any of the great realistic novelists ever doubted the Arbitrariness of the Sign. I know of no such evidence.

Lodge puzzles needlessly over the thought that continental structuralism 'took so long to make itself felt in the Atlantic cultural hemisphere'. He is apparently unaware that C. S. Peirce, a pioneer of semiology, was an American who died before the First World War, so that the doctrine was Atlantic before it was French at all.[6] That fact was cleverly concealed by the French New Critics of the 1960s, perhaps on the celebrated principle that originality is the suppression of sources. (Saussure, who died at much the same time as Peirce, was not a Frenchman, though he wrote and taught in French.) Lodge declares himself surprised that the doctrine made no impact in Anglo-America before the 1960s. But it did: Richards and Bloomfield were writing about it on opposite sides of the Atlantic in the 1920s. In *The Meaning of Meaning* (1923) Ogden and Richards dismissed Saussure's argument, as they understood it, as 'neglecting entirely the things for which signs stand', and being hence 'cut off from any contact with scientific methods of investigation'. By the 1960s, when the chief writings of Barthes, Lacan, Foucault and Derrida were becoming available, Saussure's views already looked old-hat to English-speaking linguists of an older generation, who by then had moved to Chomsky and beyond.

In 1951, for example, in 'General linguistics and descriptive grammar', J. R. Firth called Saussure's doctrine of the sign 'overvalued', years before *la nouvelle critique* was launched in Paris; and he demonstrated how familiar much of it might have been even to the Victorian mind by quoting from an 1877 lecture by Henry Sweet entitled 'On English philology and phonology'. Sweet had announced there that 'language is essentially based on the dualism of form and meaning, and all attempts to reduce language to strict logical and psychological categories by ignoring its formal side have failed ignominiously'. That is the ancient and medieval Principle of the Arbitrary, couched anew in Victorian terms. Sweet had urged his audience to pay less attention to fashionable German historical philology, and more to 'the phenomena of living languages', concentrating their energies in an imperial age on what he called 'living philology' around the globe, or languages as they actually are. British linguistics were encouraging '*la synchronie*', then, long before Saussure, though seldom that highly exclusive version of the synchronic advocated in Geneva in 1906. Saussure was a highly traditional linguist, in many ways, and it is a pity that literary critics are sometimes so easily inclined to assume that what is new to them is new absolutely.

There is something profoundly puzzling, in any case, about the claim that mimesis in general or realism in particular is politically conservative. In his *Essais critiques* (1964) Roland Barthes, as a radical, called all literature fundamentally unrealistic – '*la littérature est toujours irréaliste*' – and on the curious ground that the verb 'to write' is intransitive, which it is not. If he were correct, however, it is hard to see how anyone could ever change the world with the help of literature, whether realistic or unrealistic. For a radical, Barthes is extraordinarily eager to draw a conservative conclusion, and extraordinarily unaware that he has done so.

How could one change the world, after all, in any purposive sense, *without* using language as a descriptive instrument? Radical change, whether legislative or violent, commonly implies a shared sense of injustice. The French revolutionaries of 1789, like the British parliamentary reformers of 1832, believed they could alter their worlds for the better – by extending the suffrage, for example. That involved a claim to know injustice and to be able to describe it. The French Declaration of the Rights of Man was composed in language; so was the British Reform Act of 1832. If we are not allowed to believe that language imitates the real, then it is hard to see how we can convey a radical case to others, or even understand it ourselves. It is notable, what is more, that it is never suggested that the objective claims of science require scientists to be conservatives.

That is the important sense, in the end, in which David Lodge's use of 'disconcerting' is itself just that. The great realists are offered as stuffy old Establishment types ruffled or alarmed by a whiff of new and radical doctrine from Paris. But any stuffy old Establishment type could swallow the Lodge view with equanimity, even quiet rejoicing. Since the onus of proof always lies with the advocates of change, anything that militates against a mimetic view of language is likely to be good news for conservatives. As Lassalle once remarked, the most revolutionary act is, and always remains, to say out loud what is. That is the crucial, and highly neglected, sense in which *la nouvelle critique*, whatever its intentions, was always conservative in its effects, and always likely to be so.

A puzzle here, and one more French than Anglo-American, lies in the appeal of the Principle of the Arbitrary not just to radicals but to revolutionaries. The post-Saussurians of the 1960s were often post-Marxians, and Barthes's famous remark about smashing the Naturality of the Sign had a smack of true revolutionary fervour: *'battre en brèche la naturalité du signe'*. But one is never told who in his day believed in that naturality, and it is highly incredible to suppose that Barthes himself can have been taught at school or college to think of language as other than arbitrary. How ignorant would you have to be? There is a story about the Mitford girls, whose nanny is said to have resented the gravely misleading French habit of putting the letter C on hot-water taps; and if you are ignorant enough, no doubt, the sheer fact that other languages are different from your own can seem wilful and even perverse. But only then. Barthes's revolutionary claim here, it may be, is little more than a revolutionary pose. The French literary intellectual sometimes loves to imitate the Flaubert of *Bouvard et Pécuchet* (1881), where the bourgeois is held up to ridicule as capable of the silliest idea you can think of. The satirical image is archetypal, and one is not supposed to object that no bourgeois can be found who readily conforms to the type. And so with the great realistic novelists: in spite of repeated claims that they were ignorant of the Principle of the Arbitrary, not one among them can be produced whose ignorance is probable or remotely demonstrable.

In the fanciful Barthesian view, however, language is chock-a-block with conservative assumptions that the *marxisant* intellectual would love to smash to smithereens. That is a political argument; and to convince, it would need political instances. What are the linguistic signs in French or English, then, that allegedly weight those languages in a conservative interest? Only contrary cases come easily to mind. 'Socialism' can be easily used as a synonym for social reform, though there is abundant evidence from both sides of the Iron Curtain that it favours the rich and the powerful: a perfect doctrine for a ruling class like the governing parties of the eastern bloc. The workers of West Germany are easily better fed and housed than those of the East, with more generous provision of state welfare. And we have just lived through an era in which state monopoly or nationalisation was offered as a solution by the Left, with competition advanced by groups and parties that called themselves conservative. Those who believe that monopoly favours the rich, and competition the poor, can only be puzzled by all this, and you would expect anyone whose dearest wish was to smash the Naturality of the Sign might attack the socialist claim to favour the poor, and the familiar terminology of Right and Left.

And yet nothing like that, in the event, happened, and it seems never to have occurred to Barthes or his followers to doubt that socialism was radical. That is the second large sense in which *la nouvelle critique* was conservative: it could not even begin to see that much of our political language, including the conventional spectrum of Left and Right, has from the start been despotically arbitrary and gravely misleading. It missed the best instances of its own case.

Another difficulty is more general and less political. If it were true that the Principle of the Arbitrary destroyed any claims of language to describe the real, that destruction might be expected to extend to all the uses of language that there are. The writings of Barthes and Derrida, then, being themselves instances of language, would have to be seen as non-descriptive: in which case they must fail to describe how language works, or fails to work. The argument is neatly antagonistic. Hamlet switched letters of execution on Rosencrantz and Guildenstern as they slept, dispatching them to a death planned for himself, and it would take far less ingenuity than Hamlet's to hoist the French New Criticism with its own petard and blow it to the moon. Every dogmatist who claims that all uses of language are ideologically conditioned should be asked whether that stricture applies to the remark he has just made.

Another consideration may look familiar to philosophers, but less so to literary critics. I mean that the 'impositions' of language might be positively helpful – even essential – to the tasks of intellection and radical thought.

That is an Enlightenment view, and it is one worth reviving. More than two centuries ago a learned French *philosophe* undertook the education of an Italian prince. The *Cours d'études* of Condillac is too wordy to make lively reading, but at least the book breathes an invigorating air of confidence in the power of an advanced language like French to lick a thought into shape – '*dégrossir la pensée*', as he puts it. Condillac encouraged the young Prince of Parma to perform an exercise which he called '*décomposition*' – glimpsing the contents of a room, or a view from a window, in a flash, and then naming the constituent parts one by one, the essential linearity of speech thereby forcing upon his pupil the salutary task of describing item by item something he had glimpsed simultaneously. Readers of Kipling will recognise the exercise as Kim's Game; in America it is called 'Concentration'.

'*Décomposition*' implies a polar opposite to the Barthes–Derrida view of language as a prison-house, but it aptly describes much of what the critic does. Consider the following, written by an architectural critic: 'The building is of reinforced concrete, faced with Portland stone, and has bronze windows. It is four storeys high and has in addition a number of penthouses. One approaches it in studied meanness through the middle of New Court. The surprise is supreme . . .'[7] Unlike Kim, or the Italian prince, the critic can go back and look again. But that apart, he is playing much the same game as they are, if more deliberately.

There is, what is more, a larger sense in which criticism is always likely to be something more than Kim's Game. The game necessarily assumes that the sheer identity of objects is obvious; but in aesthetic criticism that is not always, or even usually, true. It is not clear at a glance, after all, that a building faced with Portland is invisibly based on reinforced concrete; not even obvious to everyone that Portland, visible as it is, is that. We need to be told things by critics, being more ignorant than they, and language is essential here in a sense far beyond its linearity. To describe is to know. 'When I think in language,' as Wittgenstein remarks in *Philosophical Investigations*, 'there aren't "meanings" going through my mind in addition to the verbal expressions: the language is itself the vehicle of thought' (§329). An indispensable vehicle, that is. 'You learned the concept "pain" when you learned language' (§384).

Learning what words mean is often the same as learning what things are. As Meno's slave discovered, a new vocabulary can mean new attention-giving. The post-Saussurian critic does not just misunderstand Saussure. He misunderstands the larger issue. Language does not get in the way of thought: it is the way of thought. To ask of language 'Where would we be without it?' is to ask a question not even to be posed, let alone answered, except through language itself. And when Condillac speaks of licking a thought into shape, he is almost guilty of understatement. Without words, what thought would there be to lick?

Language is nothing like the prison-house once imagined by the post-structuralist critic. It is more like a luxury hotel: marvellously plumbed, richly fed and wined, and with a gymnasium and a sauna in the basement. And nobody has slept in all the beds that there are. Far from being constrained by language, one is offered more chances than one could ever take. No one, not even the greatest poet, can persuasively claim to have used all the linguistic resources that lie to hand.

Since the British have somehow acquired a bad reputation for failing to keep up to date in this matter, two British critics – Coleridge and I. A. Richards – may be usefully offered here as exemplars, in their day, of advanced thought.

In September 1800, in the last weeks of the eighteenth century, Coleridge sent a letter to William Godwin inviting him to write a book. It was to be 'on the power of words, and the processes by which human feelings form affinities with them'.

> In short, I wish you to *philosophise* Horne Tooke's system, and to solve the great questions: . . . Is *thinking* impossible without arbitrary signs? and how far is the word 'arbitrary' a misnomer? Are not words etc. parts and germinations of the plant? And what is the law of their growth? . . . I would endeavour to destroy the old antithesis

of *words and things*, elevating, as it were, words into things, and living things too.[8]

That is a good deal to ask; and it is no wonder if Coleridge wanted someone else to write the book for him, or if Godwin failed to oblige him.

But there is a sense in which countless theorists have been writing that book since 1800. The letter is seminal. Over fifty years ago I. A. Richards hailed it in *Coleridge on Imagination* (1934) as a total summary of the theory of signs: 'I can think of no piece of writing in which so many problems of what is now known as semasiology are so brought together.' That is a remark to astonish those who imagine that British critics took no interest in semasiology or semiotics before the 1960s, when they borrowed it shamefacedly from Paris. But then the theory of signs was already old when Coleridge spoke of it as a young man to Godwin, and both of them knew that it was. Not being Lewis Carroll's Bellman, however, they knew that the arbitrary is nothing like a licence for irrationality. Language is more salutary, as they knew, than disabling: a master-guide, though never an infallible one, and not a stacked deck. Language is indeed potent; but its power, by and large, is beneficent. Coleridge himself did not doubt it. In the fourth chapter of the *Biographia Literaria* he was to remark in a revealing footnote that language, like a mathematician's slide-rule, can 'as it were *think* for us', and proudly called that gift the 'reversionary wealth in our mother-tongue'. That is an Enlightenment point, and it pays due tribute to words. Needing language as we do, we are no more its victims than a sighted man is the victim of his eyes. It is a gift beyond price: a path of knowledge, indispensably, and the way by which we see.

Notes

1. Benjamin Lee Whorf, *Language, Thought and Reality* (New York, 1956), p. 252; Edward Sapir, 'The status of linguistics as a science', *Language*, 5 (1929). On the origins of the Whorf–Sapir hypothesis see Julia M. Penn, *Linguistic Relativity versus Innate Ideas* (The Hague, 1972).
2. 'Utterances are meaningful not by their nature, but by choice.' See M. A. Screech, *Rabelais* (London, 1979), pp. 379 f. for a full account of Rabelais's view of language and its sources; and more generally, Hans Aarsleff, *From Locke to Saussure* (London, 1982) for eighteenth- and nineteenth-century views.

3. The point was anticipated by George Eliot by more than thirty years. 'I never called everything by the same name that all the people about me did', remarks Dorothea in *Middlemarch* (Edinburgh, 1872), to which Mrs Cadwallader replies in Saussurian style: 'But I suppose you have found out your mistake, my dear '. . . and that is a proof of sanity' (ch. 54).
4. Jonathan Culler, *Saussure* (London, 1976), p. 7.
5. Geoffrey Strickland, *Structuralism or Criticism?* (London, 1981), p. 13.
6. Umberto Eco, in *A Theory of Semiotics* (Bloomington, 1976), is broad-minded enough to call Peirce and Saussure the twin pioneers of semiotics, 'two scholars who foretold the official birth and scientific organization of the discipline' (0.5.1). He nowhere mentions Coleridge but eventually allows a place to William of Ockham and John Locke (3.3.4).
7. Nikolaus Pevsner, *Cambridgeshire* (London, 1970, 2nd edition), p. 156, describing the Cripps building of St John's College.
8. S. T. Coleridge, *Collected Letters*, ed. by E. L. Griggs (Oxford, 1956), vol. i, pp. 625–6, from a letter of 22 September 1800.

6

A WORD FOR THE UNSPEAKABLE

Though language is indispensable, sense is often conveyed without it. What does it mean to do so?

A literary example may help. In Henry James's *The Ambassadors* (1903) there is a conversation between the hero's mistress and his friend which, delicate as the occasion is, proves surprisingly successful – the novelist remarking that 'it ended in fact by being quite beautiful between them, the number of things they had a manifest consciousness of not saying' (ix.i). Of not needing to say, James evidently means here, indicating a truth entirely familiar in friendship, where words count for less than the total sentiment that informs them. James may even have meant that his characters could not have expressed all there was between them in words. Language is irremediably less subtle, after all, than the congenialities of life itself.

Significant silences like these – silences beyond language – are commonplace in ordinary experience, and often remarked on by the great poets and novelists. But they are damagingly neglected, even denied, by many theorists of literature: to a point, sometimes, where their theories risk losing touch with reality and literature alike. I want to say a word for silence and the unspeakable.

It is manifest (to use James's own portentous word) that one often communicates without language, and that one sometimes has to do so. To take the simplest case: there is a story about Rudyard Kipling in old age, driving across Czechoslovakia and getting out of his car to converse with a farmer working his own land, to return full of information about local agricultural conditions –

even though he and the farmer, as his companions noted with amusement, had no language in common. I have enjoyed a broadly similar experience, as it happens, in Indonesia, and imagine it to be widely familiar. When people exchange knowledge without a common language, it would usually be untrue to say that they do not speak at all: they first gesture, especially by pointing, and then give names and repeat them, as if beginning to learn the language of the other. Just how matters as complicated as the rotation of crops can be conveyed in that way is a harder thing to explain – so hard, that it is impossible to explain it even to oneself after it has happened: a combination of names-with-objects, gestures, and the advantages of a knowledge already shared, no doubt – a sort of interpreted silence. And it is unlikely to be accidental that in all such instances – the Czech and Kipling, the Indonesian and I – it was something visible that was discussed, namely the farm beneath our feet. Wittgenstein once remarked how ridiculous it would be to suppose one could replace any sentence whatever by a gesture.[1] It is plainly unlikely that Kipling could have discussed any question other than farming with his Czech, at least for long; and certain that he could not have discussed any theoretical question at all.

Silent or nearly silent communion, aptly supported by gestures of eye or hand – all that is strikingly absent even as a possibility from much contemporary thought, and notably from theorising about the arts. In its place, it is now common for critics to present a figment I shall call *Articulate Man*, and a fashion I shall call the *Cult of the Explicit*. By Articulate Man I mean a fictive creature imagined as dependent, for all he knows or can ever know, on the power of speech; by the Cult of the Explicit a dogmatic assumption that knowledge and speech are coextensive. If you cannot tell, in that view, then you do not know; if you cannot name your criteria, then you cannot judge. . . . All that sounds as if modelled on a classroom or exam-room: in any literary or historical subject, that is, a pupil who cannot answer a question is always and inescapably assumed not to know the answer; and such, no doubt, are the necessary conventions of ny educational system. There could be no marks for replying: 'I *do* know the answer to this question, as it happens, though I cannot say what it is.'

'Necessary' here is a small but essential concession to the Myth of the Articulate, since it is plain that no educational system could be conducted otherwise. But it is by now vitally important to insist that intellection, in the wider sense, is strikingly unlike formal education; and that formal education, in that respect, offers a highly misleading picture of what a life of mind is altogether like.

That encourages, even demands, a pre-empted conclusion: that those who believe in the Myth of the Articulate do so, in all likelihood, because they suppose that all thinking life is (or ought to be) like a classroom or exam-room. It is natural, then, that the Cult of the Explicit should flourish in colleges and universities, and that much of the business of growing up, after college, can consist in a process of unlearning that assumption: by allowing essentials to go unsaid, on occasion; by ceasing always to demand answers, whether of oneself or of others; and by giving manifest consciousness in general a chance to breathe. If that process of useful unlearning is sometimes slow and hard, it is because the formal aspects of education are in themselves of enormous prestige in the present age – the first in all human history, after all, to attempt mass higher education – so that the demand for answers is prodigious. 'Be still and know that I am God', as the Lord of the Psalmist put it – that is very far indeed from the guiding motto of the late twentieth century, where silent knowledge can even be made to sound like a contradiction in terms. In fact silence is more commonly taken to signify argumentative defeat. We have lately created an entire class of the educationally self-conscious – an enlarged clerisy suddenly wide enough to argue within itself as if its own world of assumptions about language were the only world there is.

Here are some examples – in most of which, significantly enough, the hypothesis of Articulate Man is assumed rather than asserted. To assert it, after all, might risk making it look silly; to claim that what we know is necessarily and always coextensive with what we can precisely express is a view so implausible, baldly stated, that nobody is likely to want to argue it in just that form, so that the argument offered is in practice usually about something else. For Jacques Derrida, for example, man lives out his thinking life trapped within a labyrinth of language not of his own making and yet inescapable: that assumption, if largely unstated, is powerfully omnipresent in a work as highly pessimistic about the prospects for human reason as *Glas* (1974). It does not appear to have occurred to him that much of what we know – and even, as in the conversation in James's novel, much of what we convey to others, one way or another, such as friendship, love, or the taste of a glass of wine – does not demand any use of language at all, unless incidentally. 'Don't talk of love: show me', as the heroine sings in *My Fair Lady*. I am not, of course, doubting that friends, lovers, and wine-tasters converse: just that they can converse about matters other than friendship, love or wine, and still know (and even convey sense) about such things. They hardly need language at all.

In all this Derrida was echoing the assumptions of Jacques Lacan, for whom man was the victim of language and never, apparently, its master – man's nature being 'woven by effects in which is to be found the structure of language of which he becomes the material'; for which reason 'man cannot aim at being whole'.[2] Far more than by what they say, such arguments are astounding by virtue of what they simply take for granted, namely that language is the boundary and limit of all knowledge. The wider notion that one's thoughts are often shaped and guided by language is of course an unexceptionable truism, if mildly stated. But it is a truism which can easily be made to look sinister, and since the 1950s we have supped full of sinister accounts, notably doctrines about the ideological conditioning that all language allegedly imposes. Little enough has been heard of the contrary view – that an individual like a great poet might help to shape the language he uses, or that a language might shape and guide thoughts *for the better*. To those under the sway of the Articulate Myth, it is inconceivable that one might have a life of mind even partly independent of language: still less that the guidance it gives might be beneficial to thought or clear-sighted in itself.

Consider a more recent and more specifically literary instance. Reviewing P. D. Juhl's *Interpretation* (1981), Frank Kermode has reproached its author for appearing to imagine that a literary work could ever have one, and only one, correct interpretation.[3] I acquit the reviewer at once of the elementary fallacy of supposing that the One Correct Interpretation, in this instructive dispute, means the One Correct *and Universally Accepted* Interpretation. Many a correct interpretation remains unaccepted, after all, in and out of literature: the shape of the earth, for example, has only one correct interpretation, as I suppose, however many flat-earthers there may happen to be. But what is arresting here is his assumption, as an experienced examiner, that having One Correct Interpretation of a masterpiece like *Hamlet* could only be the same as being able to offer one: 'What we are waiting for now', he writes challengingly, 'is an instance of a literary work with one and only one correct interpretation.' Stand and deliver. I do not suppose it would meet that challenge, in his view, to reply: 'As a matter of fact, I do know what the One Correct Interpretation of *Hamlet* is, though I cannot tell you what it is.' No examiner is going to give marks for that. And yet it might, after all, in some exceptional being, be a broadly sensible thing to say. And one could judge how sensible by watching a course of behaviour that was directly related to it, such as a director coaching actors in a rehearsal of the play, telling them how to move and which words to emphasise. The sense in which some interpretations are better or worse than others – even right or wrong – would arise there sharply and inevitably, in decisions affecting many thousands of choices scattered over two or three hours of living theatre. And to speak of many thousands here is to render the rank absurdity of the articulate assumption instantly and shatteringly clear. In his review of Juhl, Kermode writes as if a sentence or two, a paragraph or two – perhaps at most a book or two – ought to embody the One Correct Interpretation he finds so damagingly wanting. But how could it? It would surely take a large library, and an infallible library at that. Ambiguity represents no exception here: if two meanings are of equal weight, then an ambiguous interpretation is correct. Translate the question into domestic terms: 'What is the One Correct Interpretation of King's College, Cambridge?' That is a question Kermode, as a member of that college, might understandably feel impatient with. Why, then, will he not allow that the same question, applied to a literary classic, is not one to ask in any mood that calls for a quick answer? I dare say *Hamlet* is as complex as King's.

And even more than an infallible library, an answer would surely require congenial understanding of a Jamesian sort – some sympathy for the unstatables of human consciousness where rich and complex issues concerning human relations are at stake. Even an infallible library would leave much unsaid, after all, simply because there is so much that cannot be said. Much of human reality is unsayable. The demand for an instance here sounds reasonable, moderate, and modest: give me a single instance in criticism of the One Correct Interpretation. It takes some reflection to see how unreasonable, immoderate, and immodest it is.

Learning humility in such matters may involve acquiring, or reacquiring, a proper respect for the unspeakable. The Old Owl Trick of putting the head on one side and pretending to know more is rightly suspect; but it remains true, for all that, that men know more than they can tell. Oppressed as we are by a Cult of the Explicit, the task now is painfully to regain a sense of language that answers to ordinary experience. T. S. Eliot in *East Coker* (1940) once aptly called writing, 'a raid on the inarticulate / With shabby equipment always deteriorating'; and a commando-raid on the unspeakable is all, surely, that many advanced assertions can reasonably hope to be. In some cases, what is worse – a point that Eliot, as an admirer of past time, might have found harder to swallow – the equipment has simply never been there, since any given language is after all finite. Sir Ernst Gombrich is fond of saying that there is no English equivalent for that common German expression of indignant astonishment: '*Man greift sich an den Kopf*'; adding generously that there is no exact German equivalent for 'I could kick myself'. For some yars I have been trying to discover a French equivalent for that common, knowing little English phrase 'What's the catch?', and wonder if there is one. Any experienced translator knows there is no presumption that a language should contain the means by which everything in another can be said – or at least by which it can be quickly and exactly said. Why, then, should a failure to answer be seen as infallible evidence of ignorance, ignominy or mulishness?

What is more, not all that is knowable and known, even when it can be expressed, is expressible briefly and at once, and it is perilously easy to confuse the demand for answers with a demand for answers that are brief and all-embracing. Napoleon, it is said, could only put up with brevity in his advisers, and there is a story how he once asked an official whether he should introduce sugar-beet into France; when the reply began: 'One would first have to consider . . .', Napoleon shouted: 'Bah! I'll ask Berthollet.' A lot of literary theory nowadays is Napoleonic, not least in its demand for the One Correct Interpretation. Deliver or be damned. One effect of that accelerated pace of argument is that the critic easily loses any Jamesian respect he may ever have had for sympathetic silences, phatic communions, and the empathy of like minds. Another is that, demanding only simple answers, he gets simplistic ones, as Napoleon must often have done, and arrives by quick stages at the easy habit of proffering them himself. The Napoleonic challenge quickly leads to a Napoleonic dogmatism, an insensitivity of one's own; the road to Waterloo is paved with glib intentions.

It is odd that the profession of literary studies, of all things, should ever have allowed itself to enter into this confusion. The arguments just paraded ought to be truisms. Most literary scholars have a knowledge of other languages, after all; and it is a commonplace fact of the relations between language that not everything is translatable. Not all cerebral activity, in any case, is verbal. The French have a proverb, 'The great griefs are dumb'; and a great mathematician notorious for his taciturnity, when asked why he spoke so little, replied after a thoughtful silence: 'Because so many of the things I want to think about cannot be expressed in words.' It is a truth often proclaimed by poets themselves that the profoundest experiences are beyond description: when Milton in 'Lycidas' calls the angelic singing of heaven inexpressible, or rather 'unexpressive'

> And hears the unexpressive nuptial song
> In the blest kingdoms meek of joy and love

he is using the classic rhetorical figure of *occupatio*, or a refusal to describe, describing after some inadequate fashion even as he does so: '. . . when he saith something, in saying he cannot say it', as Henry Peacham characterises the figure in his *Garden of Eloquence* (1593). One would expect a man of letters, of all people, working daily with the highly limited instruments of language, to know about this, just as one would expect him to have studied rhetoric and to have read Milton. Why, then, is the Napoleonic challenge that offers only a crude choice between assertion and ignominy so widely accepted by the very caste that should respect it least? Why have men of letters forgotten the unspeakable?

It might be admitted in reply, lame as it is, that language is an instrument of enormous potency, and that professional critics who confuse that potency with omnicompetence are committing what (in tolerant mood) might be seen as a natural mistake. Natural for them, that is: they are men of letters because they once felt that power in youth, and long before they ever became authors or critical theorists. Those who argue as if knowledge were totally bounded by language are genuflecting before an undeniable god. If we do not depend on language for everything that we know, it is as certainly true that without it we should all know enormously less: so much less, that it is hard to be clear whether the verb 'to know' could apply at all intelligibly to a word-less state. The notion of Marxist theorists like Antonio Gramsci, as mediated through his latter-day disciples, that the weaponry of a given language is of necessity ideologically confining and its grammar class-bound is an odd, even self-contradictory way of paying tribute to that power: it is a dogma which, if absolutely true, would be certainty unstatable and probably unknowable; and such theorists claim to state it and to know it. If it is impossible to stand outside language, as Lacan and Derrida often imply, then it is hard to see how they – or anyone else – can be certain that language is inadequate, distorting or confining; and when told, as we often are, that every utterance is ideologically constrained, it is useful to recall that the charge, whatever it amounts to, must apply to that utterance too.

This is the supreme paradox of such arguments about conditioning. They imply a moment in which the Marxist or post-Marxist theorist of language ceases to be that in order to perceive that his certainties about the ideological or social conditioning of language are there at all. A kind of moment of grace, perhaps, in the fallen life of a sinner? Many religions and quasi-religions call upon man to be more than a man, if only for a moment, in order to see what man truly is. The demand is puzzling. To be pure in heart, even for an instant, or conscious even for a moment of a utopia of classlessness, one would need a moment, at least, in which sin or class-consciousness was less than dominant in the mind. To step out of a system, after all, is to deny its force, and a law of nature that can be defied by an individual act of will is not much of a law; just as it is not much of a prison that keeps an open door. Such theories are classic cases of self-regarding paradox, or what I have called argument-against-itself. If they were true, that is, they would be false. They represent refutations of themselves.

Genuflection to language in the present age, superstitious as it ultimately is, may have another more strictly literary aspect. Great literature, it might be said, does not give much attention to significant silence, by and large, or to expressive gesture or unspeaking communion; and anyone who spends a lifetime studying it might be forgiven for thinking words can do anything. I have already offered two reasons for thinking that view, at best, an exaggerated one. The great poets have often used the figure of *occupatio* and openly avowed that words cannot sufficiently describe: 'I cannot paint / What then I was . . .', as Wordsworth puts it in 'Tintern Abbey', declaring the sheer impossibility of depicting his boyhood; and the great realists of European fiction, like Henry James in *The Ambassadors*, have often illustrated the paradox that in conversation and in silence we subtly and powerfully imply far more than could ever be said. If any critic thinks that literature has said it all, then he cannot even have paid proper attention to literature, let alone to life. The great poets and novelists have proclaimed, and often, that no language is omnicompetent.

The trouble is that failure, for all that, is not what strikes one first or last about a great poet. In Shakespeare, for example, speech is all but coextensive with character. There is barely a handful of ordained silences in all his drama. There is a highly exceptional moment, it is true in an early play, *1 Henry VI*, when Joan of Arc as a sorceress vainly summons up fiends to succour the defeated French. According to a stage direction, the fiends 'walk and speak not', though they hang their heads as a gesture of refusal (v.iii). Coriolanus' wife Virgilia, likewise, is so touched by his safe return from the wars that she cannot speak at all, and he addresses her in mocking tenderness as 'my gracious silence' (ii.i). But when Timon of Athens has no more to say, it is simply the end of him: 'Lips, let four words go by and language end' (v.i), and he exits to die. Silence is so fundamentally alien to Shakespearean theatre, beyond a few isolated instances, that any actor who allows it to invade his delivery, or who uses gesture to replace rather than support it, is plainly running counter to the genius of a style.

For all that, limits to Shakespeare's language have been courageously sought, and one notable Shakespearian has suggested that Lear uses language 'not as an adequate register of his experience, but as evidence that his experience is beyond language's scope.'[4] The notion is perhaps more engaging than persuasive. What Lear does say surely drowns out any failure to say more; his remark on waking in fresh clothes, tended by Cordelia – 'I know not what to say' (IV.vii) – looks more like classical *occupatio* than any serious failure in articulacy; and when Edgar, at the bitter end, offers to 'speak what we feel, not what we ought to say', contrasting the demands of honesty and decorum, he sounds confident of being able to manage either of them. One could still come near to forgiving the critic who, nourished on such an author, allowed himself to feel that words alone are certain good, even sufficient good. The trouble is that they are not.

The literary critic may not find it easy to climb down from his Napoleonic perch of claiming and demanding total, brief and instant articulacy. That would be a climb-down indeed. To claim to be able to say and define everything, or to need to do so, is a literary version of the sin of pride; and once a critical tradition eats of that apple, it is unclear how it can recover its innocence except as a ritual humiliation. No profession has an interest, on the whole, in diminishing its own role. The danger now is that for so long as the assumption of Articulate Man is widely accepted inside the fraternity of letters, demanding and forever demanding definitions and criteria, and for so long as the Cult of the Explicit dominates its affairs, the attack may all too easily come from without; and it could be as merciless and unselective in its destructive power as napalm, and as damaging to what is good in literary studies as to what is extravagant or false. There are tactical advantages, after all, in allowing a profession to put its own house in order. Yet by claiming too much for itself over the years, critical theory may now find it hard to put itself to rights without abandoning some traditionally inflated notions of what words and only words can do.

It could begin, at least, by learning respect for what words cannot do. Hard as it is for a man of letters to counsel the value of silence, it might on occasion be the most significant advice he could give.

Notes

1. Ludwig Wittgenstein, *Philosophische Grammatik* (Oxford, 1969), I.iv; see also Renford Bambrough and R. F. Holland, 'Thought, word and deed', *Proceedings of the Aristotelian Society*, supplementary volume 54 (1980).
2. Jacques Lacan, *Écrits* (Paris, 1966), pp. 688–9, 692. Cf. Martin Heidegger, *Über den Humanismus* (Berne, 1947): 'Language is the abode of being . . .' (p. 5).
3. *London Review of Books*, 7–20 May 1981; with reply, 6–19 August 1981; reprinted in Frank Kermode, *Essays on Fiction 1971–82* (London, 1983) p. 209.
4. Winifred Nowottny, 'Some aspects of the style of *King Lear*', *Shakespeare Survey*, 13 (1960). See also Anne Barton, 'Shakespeare and the limits of language', *Shakespeare Survey*, 24 (1971).

7

HOW TO BE AN IDEOLOGUE

In literary debates, at least, 'ideology' is a word that loses none of its vogue.

But its vogue over the years has become ever more puzzling; and ever more difficult, by now, to relate to anything in the verbal contests over morality or politics from which the term was once drawn. The specifically literary sense of the word, however, demands to be understood; and it needs to be asked whether its older political meanings cast any useful light on how critics commonly use it today.

To start with a characteristic instance from recent literary theory:

> Some traditional critics would appear to hold that other people subscribe to theories, while they prefer to read literature 'straight-forwardly'. No theoretical or ideological predilections, in other words, mediate between themselves and the text. . . . It is therefore difficult to engage such critics in debate about ideological preconceptions, since the power of ideology over them is nowhere more marked than in their honest belief that their readings are 'innocent'.[1]

The passage is representative of a large body of critical discussion – most notably in its confident talk of theoretical or ideological preconceptions. With their quietly sinister implications of distortion, or at best incomprehension and mindless folly, such phrases are enough to give pause. Who are these gullible and uncomprehending traditionalists? And what is their unspoken tradition?

The answer can hardly be much of a secret, however secretive it is made to sound. No critic, it may be supposed, would deny having predilections and preconceptions, and one can hardly even imagine what it would be like to approach a novel, play, or poem – or a human situation either, for that matter – in that state of ignorance. And yet the passage succeeds in implying that a serious charge has been brought. And the final world, 'innocent', seems to be contrasted with something too dark even to be mentioned.

This is all very strange. Nobody is foolish, mistaken or guilty merely because he has predilections, whether in art or in life; and it is not obvious, in any case, that it is necessarily ideological to have them. Are there no non-ideological predilections in literature, like preferring claret to burgundy? It is true, no doubt, as in sexual matters, that guilt can attach to having predilections of a certain kind, such as pederasty; such tastes being usually enjoyed in secret and revealed (if at all) only in conduct. So perhaps that is the point that is being made – confused as it is. Certain traditional critics are secretive about revealing their preconceptions; and their critical preconceptions are by their very nature falsifying and shameful. The charge is double.

Again, that is more than strange. Everyone prefers some books to others, and some kinds of books to other kinds, and it is highly unclear what would be 'straightforward' about denying it. Critics exist to judge, and it is not in doubt that judgement occurs by way of considerations already present in the mind, whether expressible or not. A judge knows laws and precedents before he considers evidence and pronounces sentence, and all that is not usually thought of as discreditable. The charge of preference – even silent preference – strikes one as boneless.

There is a famous illustrative story. When Robert Graves was an undergraduate at Oxford just after the First World War, a don remarked to him at a college meeting after his first term: 'I understand, Mr Graves, that the essays that you write for your English tutor are, shall I say, a trifle temperamental. It appears, indeed, that you prefer some authors to others.' That celebrated anecdote from *Good-bye to All That* (1929) was once reproachfully quoted by F. R. Leavis as an epigraph to *The Common Pursuit* (1952), presumably under the apprehension that it illustrated a favourite theme of academic stupidity. Easier, perhaps, to see it as a shared irony between a clever don and an ex-army undergraduate older than most who had already earned some reputation in his college for strong and vehemently expressed opinions. That interpretation was once confirmed by Graves himself, in conversation:

'He was simply trying to be very sweet to me', I remember his saying of the don, with a smile. At all events, it ought to be clear that there is no serious opposing party to anyone who says that some books are better than others, or even some kinds of books. The contest only begins when it is asked what they are, and why.

Let us presume, then, that it is specifically ideological preconceptions that are under attack here, not just preconceptions in a general way – and above all ideologies that do not, and dare not, speak their name.

The charge of silence, in its turn, need not be very grave, since not everything that is known or believed can be said. A critic who denied subscribing to a theory might mean no more than that. What might be considered grave here is wilful or self-deluding secrecy, presumably, or a furtive refusal to produce grounds which, as a critic, you know that you have and know you could articulate. Furtive ideology in that style might be compared to a Swiss bank account: why would anyone keep his money abroad unless he were trying to conceal something discreditable? If that is the charge being made against what is called 'traditional' criticism, at least it is a charge to be met. It is not merely nebulous, that is, like some others that have been made. Ideology is guilty when for dubious motives it is known and yet undeclared.

This is the supreme puzzle of all. I happen to be an ideologue, and by admitting it may be presumed to have removed myself at least from the charge of furtive behaviour. Indeed I once wrote a book called *The English Ideology* (1973) about the Victorian tradition of parliament, and did not hesitate to suggest that much of that literature was not only interesting but true; and would not easily know what it meant to read literature 'straightforwardly', where the word is meant to exclude all possibility of principled and dedicated preference.

There is evidently something unusual in this avowal. In literary discussion nowadays ideology, like bad breath, is something one is aware of only in others, and the subject is by now as bedevilled with false shame as sex and alcoholism once were. Perhaps someone should start a society called 'Ideologues Anonymous'; its meetings could begin with members rising to their feet in a sympathetic atmosphere, intoning the words 'My name is X, and I am an ideologue . . .'.

Let me explain, then, what the term itself may be generally taken to mean. Ideology signifies a total view of the human world that is at once coherent and publicly available: total in its claim to explain everything, or at least everything in question; coherent in that its incompatibilities, if any, are either unnoticed or unaccepted as such by its adherents; and available, in that it looks to a body of published scripture. That is a use of the word by now traditional; and whether it ultimately derives from Napoleon or not, it was certainly thought in the last century to do so. Sir Walter Scott, in his *Life of Napoleon Bonaparte* (1827), called ideology the 'nickname' by which Napoleon had distinguished 'every species of theory which, resting in no respect upon the basis of self-interest, could, he thought, prevail with none save hot-brained boys and crazed enthusiasts' (VI. 251) – like the revolutionary sects he had supplanted in 1799. You would have to be young or mad – or both – in that view, to believe in any total theory of government: you rule by the seat of your pants. Napoleon's disdainful view of the word is the traditional view, and the only view current in English in the nineteenth century.

Totality, admittedly, is a lot to ask. But then that is a matter where elasticity may be allowed, and the requirement needs to be understood reasonably and in its context, which is normally political. Marxism and liberalism are total answers to politics, or can claim to be; one might prudently defer the question whether they are, or could even claim to be, total answers to everything of human concern, inside politics and out. Monetarism might just qualify, to the extent that there are those who believe that the defeat of inflation by that means is the chief or whole object of domestic policy; but it seems more natural to call the total system that informs it, or Neo-Conservatism, an ideology, with its broad moral emphasis on hard work and thrift. A borderline case like that demonstrates that there is after all a border, and that one is near it or on it.

It may be asked why ideology must be publicly available: are not some ideologies secret, even unconscious? But then one could only expose them by bringing them to the surface and relating them to some existing body of scripture. Some people are more or less positivists, for example, without admitting it and perhaps without even knowing it, and they may never have so much as heard of Auguste Comte or his followers. But the business of

showing them to be positivists is inescapably that of showing
how closely their views resemble some of Comte's.

Total, coherent, and available. A further limitation is perhaps
more precarious here, and not logically necessary, but still hard
to avoid. I mean that ideology is modern, in the sense of being
Enlightenment or post-Enlightenment; and for just that reason,
secular. The great religions are not ideologies. If the word itself
originated in the Paris of the 1790s, then the thing itself, in any
sense that matters now, is not much older. There is little to be
gained here, in general, by calling Christianity or Islam an ideology; and to speak of scripture here is to speak in metaphor. On
the other hand, the way modern ideologies like positivism,
liberalism and Marxism have imitated the great religions by
cherishing sacred texts, even priests and messiahs, is a formidable aspect of their appeal. The positivists in their day even
invented a chapel ritual, along with a canon of secular saints; and
for two hundred years or so it has been possible to hold ideological convictions, as Jefferson and Lenin did, with the intensity of
religious conviction. It does not follow that ideology *is* a religion,
still less that religion is an ideology.

The struggle to delimit the word is a large part of the struggle to
understand it. No doubt that delimitation could go too far: it would
be easy enough to identify a context where Christianity or Islam
might helpfully be called ideological, as in the Spain of Philip II or
the Iran of the ayatollahs. In such states, religion and politics are
inseparable. But in modern debates about literature, at least, the
great religions play remarkably little part, and the part they play is
not usually secretive. There are indeed Christian literary critics, like
C. S. Lewis or Helen Gardner, but they are in no way open to the
charge of being closet ideologues who claim to read literature without preconceptions. On the contrary, those preconceptions are the
most obvious fact about what they write. Nor do Marxist critics
usually fit the charge of furtive predilection, and for similar reasons.

The Marxist case is admittedly odd, and its influence is hard to
account for. Like Napoleon before him, Marx and his disciples
used 'ideology' or 'ideologue' as deprecatory terms. In Marx's
case the deprecation arose from alleged links with a social class
which, as he claimed, used ideas as mere economic self-interest,
rationalising a system of production from which its privileges
derived. But that notion of class, rapidly polarising into social

civil war, is no longer in working order. History has failed to deliver it; the wars between the classes in industrial states have simply failed to happen. That Marxist usage should still dominate so much of what passes for modern literary thought in this matter does little credit to its modernity or to its thoughtfulness. Its application to literature, in any case, was never clear.

But then the assumption that ideology is invariably falsifying is itself difficult, whether held by Napoleon, Marx or anybody else. Why should a world view that is total, coherent, and available never be true?

The last two properties at least – coherence and availability – present no difficulty at all. True accounts need to be coherent, in the sense of internally self-consistent. They also need to be available – if not to be true, at least to be tested. It would sound impossibly evasive to say that one adhered to a view of the world that had been irretrievably lost. All that is the plainest of plain sailing.

That leaves totality. And it must be admitted that there *is* something inherently plausible about the suggestion that any total view of the world, if contentious, is likely to be false. That is above all because it is always likely to be, at best, excessively simple. Reductions are always suspect, as in 'X is only Y'. Reality is 'not a given whole', as Iris Murdoch once memorably remarked in explaining her own departure from youthful Communism: 'It is here . . . that one is forever at odds with Marxism.'[2] In denying that reality is a given whole, it hardly matters whether the emphasis is laid on 'given' or 'whole', since both propositions convince. We have no certainty, and can have none, that human reality is a whole, in the sense of always subject to the same law or set of laws – if only because we can never certainly know it all. Anthropology has taught caution here. And for the same reason, reality is emphatically not wholly 'given', so much of it being unknown and even beyond the reach of language and of mind. Ideology is always open to the charge of intellectual vainglory; it characteristically underrates the extent to which any single human intelligence is weak, finite, and fallible. Its simplicity is suspicious.

All that is reason for finding the deprecatory emphasis conferred by Napoleon and others to be at least initially plausible. Ideology is a distorting mirror, it is often said, and by its very nature partial and simplistic. The trouble with that argumentative sword is that it is fiercely two-edged. Napoleon and Marx saw it sword is that it is fiercely two-edged. Napoleon and Marx saw it as a weapon against the Jacobins or the bourgeoisie; and modern Marxists are still fond of convicting their opponents of ideological distortion, overt or (more usually) implicit. But the charge notoriously applies to Marxists too, and in heaping measure, as Althusser discovered in his quarrels with fellow-Marxists in the France of the 1960s and after. How can one reasonably doubt that Marxism too is an ideology? The Marxist tactic of accusing others of ideological preconception always smacks strongly of the argumentative equivalent of the pre-emptive strike. 'I may have an ideology', the Marxist critic seems always on the point of saying in self-defence. 'But then so does everybody else. And so do you.'

It may now be possible to explain the hostility of modern literary theorists, and not least of Marxists among them, to the hidden hand of ideology in literary criticism.

Such hostility makes sense, though still confusing sense, if it is supposed that it is less the three primary attributes of ideology that are resented than certain secondary attributes the word has gathered to itself in recent years. The primary attributes are to be total, coherent, and available – and last two no objections to truth-claims at all, as anyone can see, and the first an objection that can hardly be plausibly offered by the victims of a dogma claiming to be as total as Marxism.

But the secondary attributes of ideology, I suggest, have lately tended to push the primary out of centre-court. Secondary here means modern, secular and furtive, and it would not be far out to sum up those secondary attributes under the title of 'liberal' in the larger sense – one larger, that is, than the name of any political party. It is not accidental if George Eliot, that supremely refined in-stance of liberal intelligence in English fiction, is the butt of a good deal of easy denigration here, and her admirers of still more. She is, after all, the Eternal Mother of the modern secular intelligence in our fiction. In her unflagging conviction of the duty of every individual to achieve righteousness outside the bonds of traditional faith, in her belief in the primacy of the particular over the general, and in her certainty that individual moral choice is even more significant than political reform, whether constitutional or violent, she is a sitting target for every Marxist literary theorist for whom 'ideology' represents a charge of unparalleled intellectual gravity.

In recent critical debate liberalism has become the very type of the modern, the secular, and the furtively unspoken. The only term that gives any difficulty here is the last. What in the world, it may reasonably be asked, is furtive or unspoken about liberalism? It is avowedly based on the great figures of the French, British, and American Enlightenment, and on a vast corpus of interpretation now two centuries old. Do not the great liberal authors, like George Eliot, explain their convictions as they go; and cannot their modern admirers point to the very passages where they do? Of course all that is true. But the mystery can usually be explained by the simple truth that the great liberal authors are nowadays seldom read even by academics. That can easily be demonstrated by the number who still believe that classical economists like Adam Smith believed in *laissez-faire*, or that John Stuart Mill believed in political democracy – or, for that matter, that George Eliot never explained or justified the ideological scope of her moral beliefs. All these views are mistaken; they all depend upon unexamined certainties. But then you do not bother to read in an enquiring spirit, or at all, if you believe you have the answers already, and the Marxist believes he has the answers already. The truth has already been spoken, by a nineteenth-century German; the task is less analysis, as he sees it, than dissemination. His ideological certainties are uncritical and unquestioning.

'Some traditional critics would appear to hold that other people subscribe to theories. . . . No theoretical or ideological predilections . . . mediate between themselves and the text.' Eagleton is as accurate as a parrot in his repetition of familiar charges against the liberal critical tradition. At its simplest, the charge is that liberal critics do not know what they are doing, theoretically speaking, when they read; that they refuse to reveal what their assumptions are; that they even deny any theoretical problem exists at all. And they reveal their secret ideology nowhere more clearly than in their 'honest' assertion that they have none.

The use of 'honest' here is nothing like as generous as it may wish to look; and since this account is an ignorant parody of the liberal case, it cannot be allowed to go unanswered. In post-Marxist criticism it is commonly buttressed by routine arguments about social conditioning. Honest as we are, or think ourselves, we believe what we do about the dignity of the individual, or the value of elected institutions, because such values are all we know; though they are ultimately the property of a social class intent on preserving its own privileges and power. All of which sounds like no more than the honesty of convenient self-persuasion. Such is the Marxist charge. And there are those who would rather be convicted of dishonesty than of honesty in that fashion.

The appeal to social conditioning, in any case, defies both observation and experience. Experience, because I do not in fact hold the ideology I was brought up in; and observation, because it is observable that a great many others do not. Neither did Karl Marx, since he was not brought up to be a Marxist. Nor did Marx's own views ever represent an attempt on his part to maintain the power and privileges of his own class; and, what is more, nobody has ever seriously claimed that they did. It is plain, in fact, that people do not reliably behave in the manner that theories of social conditioning confidently describe. And that is what makes the sociology of thought from Marx to Lukàcs and Mannheim, from the 1840s to the 1940s – however lively one may judge that century-long tradition of enquiry to have been – so profoundly disappointing in its substantive results.

A great Spanish liberal shortly before the Civil War, Salvador de Madariaga, once made an anti-clerical speech in the Cortès in Madrid in which he unexpectedly defended religious schools: 'If there were no church schools, where should we draw our anti-clericals from?' Counter-suggestibility is a phenomenon that Marxism is powerless to embrace or explain. The truth is that there are few if any clear, brief and reliable laws that govern human opinion beyond the merely truistic. It would hardly be an exaggeration to conclude that the sociology of thought has so far produced only one such sound general conclusion: that when you tell someone something, he sometimes believes you and sometimes does not.

There is still a substantial sense, for all that, in which liberal theories of the arts must always look radically deficient to their Marxist adversaries.

In one way or another, the great liberal thinkers have often managed to appear, at least to hostile witnesses, as anti-theoretical, even anti-ideological. One way is Emerson's. 'Where do we find ourselves?' he began his essay 'Experience' (1844), and answered himself:

> In a series of which we do not know the extremes, and believe that it
> has none. We wake and find ourselves on a stair; there are stairs
> below us, which we seem to have ascended; there are stairs above
> us, many a one, which go upward and out of sight.

There is no prospect in life, then, of anything like a total answer
that is also true – only of progressive and accumulative cognition,
acquiring more and more understanding as one goes. Emerson's
staircase is perhaps the most compelling single image left by his
century of what it is like to be a thinking being. But compelling as
it is, it is also inescapably tentative and inconclusive, and no one
would presume to call it an ultimate answer to the more searching
problems of cognition: it is far too richly agnostic, for that, about
how knowledge is lost and won, and resolutely thrusts the prospect of solving such larger problems into an ever-receding distance. If it is anti-ideological to be anti-total, Emerson is certainly
that. Living, as he sees it, is getting on with it; and he is emphatically liberal, too, in his sense of the immovable centrality of individual perception and individual will. No other philosophical
remark in its century, perhaps, sums up so completely the cognitive ethos of its greatest fiction, from Jane Austen to Henry
James.

To turn to the nineteenth-century novelists themselves is to
find the fullest and most various illustration one could ask for of
Emerson's Mind-on-a-Staircase. Scott's Waverley or Jane
Austen's Emma, like Dickens's Copperfield or Trollope's Palliser
after them, are never seen by the reader as blank sheets of
experience, since he meets them first as grown beings or (in
Copperfield's case) as children endowed with language and
ideas. They are already on the staircase, in fact, when the novel
begins, and already some way up it. They continue up it, as you
watch, occasionally falling back a step or two, and advancing
again as they perceive something they once failed to see; and of
course they never reach the top of the stairs. No such hero ends
by possessing, or imagining that he possesses, a total answer to
experience. In that highly special sense, the great realistic novels
are confessedly anti-ideological. One can always hope to understand more: one can never understand everything. There is no
key to total understanding, and you learn enough, if you try
hard, to get along. It is a pleasant symbol that the last words of
David Copperfield are 'pointing upwards'.

All that may help to explain how it is that the liberal idea, while still arguably meriting the name of ideology, is less plainly or candidly that than its Marxist critics could wish. It insists far too heavily on the primacy of the particular instance. That has sometimes been seen as a bit of cosy British provincialism, surviving blissfully in ignorance of what is called philosophy – which usually means late versions of nineteenth-century German idealism – and all too probably based on a cloistered national allegiance to a half-forgotten empiricism. If empiricism means the view that there are no innate ideas, all knowledge being derived from the senses, then one could comfortably accept that it is, historically speaking, a British view – one among others – if only because it derives above all from Locke, Berkeley and Hume. I do not know that one should be ready to accept simplistic accounts of what it involves, however, or to admit that it represents the limits of the theoretical interests of the great English novelists in the realistic tradition. For one thing, it has been amply shown by A. D. Nuttall in *A Common Sky* (1974) to lead as easily to solipsism and mysticism as to competitive capitalism or a sternly practical view of human relations. In literary terms, at least, the tradition of Locke is not a single highway but a road that forks, some of its forks running inconclusively into forests and waste-lands. If sense-perception is all that we have, how can we be certain that the real world exists at all? Wordsworth once described how, as a boy walking to school in the Lake District, he would desperately seize a stone wall to assure himself of a reality outside his own mind. The truth is that empiricism has no easy place in the literary argument; and the case for calling the great realistic novelists philosophically backward or Lockean is based on a series of mis-conceptions.

But then the primacy of the particular instance is not, or not only, an easy assumption in realistic fiction, but a conclusion that was hard-won. If *Tom Jones* stands as a sort of foundation-stone to that tradition, then the multiple critical apparatus that Fielding equipped it with in 1749, in a series of prefaces that contrive to adapt Aristotelian mimesis to a new and contemporary social context, demonstrates that the relation between fiction and life did not look to him and his readers either self-evident or unprob-lematical. Scott's jokes about fictionality in some of the Waverley novels shows that the issue was alive and kicking in his mind.

And the essays of George Eliot, surprisingly neglected as they nowadays are by critics and philosophers alike, offer conclusive evidence that in the mind of at least one great Victorian realist – and one without formal philosophical training – the deeper problems of cognition, and the relation of language and reality, were matters for conscious and painstaking deliberation. It is a misunderstanding to suppose that the great English novelists of the realistic tradition accepted empiricism, when they did, because they knew of nothing else. It does not follow that they were right. But at least it disposes of one objection against them that is commonly made and commonly believed. Ideologues they may have been, in some extended and secondary meaning of the term. But they were not furtive or unthinking ideologues, and that can be demonstrated from what they wrote.

In 1856, and before she had published any fiction, George Eliot wrote an article for the *Westminster Review* entitled 'The natural history of German life: Riehl'. Wilhelm Heinrich Riehl was a Munich professor of conservative convictions whose *Bürgerliche Gesellschaft* (1851) illustrates the deep affinity that can exist between the conservative and the Marxist mind, and his book abounds in naïve general terms supposedly descriptive of social classes, such as 'the bourgeoisie', 'the proletariat', and 'the peasantry'. George Eliot's refutation begins briskly with an attack upon the supposed primacy of the abstract, the 'images that are habitually associated with abstract or collective terms – what may be called the picture-writing of the mind, which it carries on concurrently with the more subtle symbolism of language'; and she illustratively suggests that the word 'railways' would mean little more than a printed railway-guide to someone who knew at best one track or station, whereas to anyone who had worked and travelled on them for years 'the range of images which would by turns present themselves to his mind at the mention of the *word* "railways" would include all the essential facts in the existence and relations of the *thing*.'

It is the ignorant man, then, who characteristically craves the total:

> He may talk of a vast network of railways stretching over the globe, of future 'lines' in Madagascar, and elegant refreshment-rooms in the Sandwich Islands, with none the less glibness because his distinct conceptions on the subject do not extend beyond his one station and his indefinite length of tram-road. But it is evident that if

we want a railway to be made, or its affairs to be managed, this man
of wide views and narrow observation will not serve our purpose.[3]

The application to glib social ideology is instant and obvious –
'proletariat' and 'peasantry' representing, to those who 'theorise
on those bodies with eloquence', as little knowledge as 'railway'
might have for someone who knew only one station or one line.
Among painters, George Eliot argues, and on similar grounds,
the great Dutch masters surpass the Pre-Raphaelites:

> Appeals founded on generalisations and statistics require a sym-
> pathy ready-made, a moral sentiment already in activity; but a
> picture of human life such as a great artist can give surprises even
> the trivial and the selfish into that attention to what is apart from
> themselves.

Such attention to detail she finely dubs 'the raw material of moral
sentiment'. General terms, by contrast, tend to falsify: they direct
our sympathy outwards 'towards a false object instead of the true
one'.[4]

Such arguments draw a line, hard and fast, between the literary
Marxist and the literary liberal in our times; and since the line
runs through politics as well as the arts, there can be no confusion
in mixing politics and letters here. It equally distinguishes the
severely philosophical interests of such critics, amateurish as
they often are. To the Marxist mind, still fundamentally revolutionary, change is ultimately an all-or-nothing affair, and
mankind has no business to think itself on Emerson's staircase at
all. Nothing important happens one step at a time; we are not
learning progressively about society, in that view, since the truth
has already been spoken by an early nineteenth-century German,
and some already know what it is. Progress is not a slow climb:
one should pull down the house that maintains that staircase,
and start afresh.

To the liberal or reforming mind, by contrast, progress is a
climb step by step; the house is to be lived in and improved, not
destroyed, and the slogan is not All-or-Nothing but Make-Do-
and-Mend. In critical terms that war of words is the noisiest there
is in the present age. In fiction it marks the difference between
realism, which can easily accommodate an Emersonian (or George
Eliot) view of knowledge, on one hand; and on the other a
demand for 'philosophical fiction', as it is misleadingly called,
like Kafka's stories or Thomas Mann's *Magic Mountain*, where

mighty abstractions are handled and juxtaposed. (It is a paradox here, and a significant one, that distinguished instances of specifically Marxist philosophical fiction do not easily spring to mind.)

Useless to ask whether Marxist theories of literature are what they are because revolutionary politics encourages a contempt for painstaking literary realism or because literary realism, with its caution, has by reaction created a demand for something politically more immediate, apocalyptic and absolute. Marxist contempt for mere reform, and Marxist critical disdain for fictional realism, are chicken-and-egg; and it is enough here to note their natural association, and to ask what it involves and whether it convinces. For it cannot be doubted that, on a long view, George Eliot's concept of cognition is right and Marx's wrong. (I call them that as a matter of convenience here: neither view is original to those authors, and neither ever supposed or claimed that it was.) I mean that a knowledge of the instances is, in the end, primary in a way that George Eliot's talk about railways suggests, and there is nothing that can take its place without falsification or loss.

Any Anglo-Saxon critic who argues in that manner has by now grown used to being called an empiricist, and I have already suggested why the word is unneeded and misleading in this context. In his only surviving literary essay, the fragment known as the *Poetics*, Aristotle discusses tragedy as if he were entirely satisfied that it is a particular group of plays like the *Oedipus* of Sophocles that demonstrates what tragedy is, and he plainly does not suppose that mankind has innate ideas of the great literary forms to which given instances are required to conform. It is notable that Aristotle can argue in that way without being an Englishman and without (altogether clearly) being an empiricist. In other words, when it comes to the primacy of the particular instance, empiricism is the flower and not the root: one possible effect of perceiving that primacy and not the only such effect. So little English criticism survives from the age before Locke's *Essay* of 1690 that it could only be a remote hypothesis to guess what a non-empiricist tradition of English criticism might have been like. But it is observable that Sir Philip Sidney in his *Apology for Poetry* is contentedly Aristotelian in his critical procedures; and though Dryden sometimes starts an argument from general rules, he does not think them immune to revision from particular instances. It is entirely possible, in fact, that the English critical and fictional tradition would have been little different if Locke, Berkeley, and Hume had never written. The grand fictional exception here is Sterne's *Tristram Shandy*, in part a parody of Locke's theories about the association of ideas; but his parody is so far from reverential that it will hardly stand as a positive instance of the influence of empiricism on the English novel.

It remains a question, for all that, why so many literary theorists have sensed a failure in what I here call liberalism or in what they call 'traditional' criticism: a failure, above all, to articulate ideologies and preconceptions or even to admit to them.

That complaint is not merely Marxist: René Wellek, a highly anti-Marxist critic, made it against F. R. Leavis half a century ago.[5] It is, or was, more strictly a continental versus an Anglo-Saxon view. There is no longer any safe national point to be made here, happily, since many British and American critics have been continentalised, in that sense, over the past twenty years: usually through contact with *la nouvelle critique*, where pre-1914 versions of German idealism were enlivened and turned to literary effect in their slow passage through mid-twentieth-century France. That debate or intellectual civil war exists by now in every literary culture in the western world. It is more likely to end in exhaustion than in victory; and there are already plentiful signs that *la nouvelle critique* is going or has already gone the way of the New Left. But before it does, there are arguments that need to be offered in favour of the liberal or realistic view of literature, if only for the record.

Literary theorists are trained in methods of exposition as well as in literature itself, and they do not always realise that an expository method is only that. The adolescent who is trained to write a literary essay – even the advanced student whose thesis needs to be shaped and marshalled to qualify for a doctorate – is often advised to state a general position at the outset and only later to adduce evidence in its support. It is significant that this pedagogic advice, common enough anywhere, is even commoner in France than in English-speaking countries. It would be easy to extend that procedural method into a thoughtless belief in ideological preconceptions or theoretical bases underlying all serious intellectual enquiry: an assumption all the easier to make because of the evident advantages to clarity in moving from the general to the particular. Mathematics offers a sparkling model here, rich and inviting in deductive achievement.

In literary argument, however, the mathematical model serves better as a mode of exposition than as a way of thought. The warning instance here is that of the student who misguidedly begins his essay: 'Before discussing whether *King Lear* is a tragedy, we must first define what tragedy is.' Northrop Frye's *Anatomy of Criticism* (1957) owed its brief, intense vogue to its inventive skill in offering definitions to initiate such essays; and it would not be hard to widen such definitions, where they cohere, into something that merited the name of a theory and even an ideology.

And yet, however definers may define or theorists theorise, the bottom rung of knowledge is not there. For tragedies are like trains, to revive George Eliot's illustrative point. You learn what they are, in a larger sense, by learning to know them: by studying them, by trying them out, by testing their strengths and their failings. The most favoured mode of literary exposition, by contrast – the movement from the general to the particular – represents a wholly and dangerously misleading inversion of how knowledge is in practice acquired and justified. Critics argue backwards, often enough, in literary essays – starting with something which is in fact a conclusion. In our end is our beginning. . . .

The misunderstanding that lies at the heart of phrases like 'ideological preconception' and 'theoretical basis', then, may in part be explained here. With admired examples of critical essays before his gaze, the student might easily suppose that the general precedes the particular, and even that such precedence has a rational as well as an expository aspect. No wonder he believes in criteria. The notion that critical theory necessarily underlies practice, that political ideology necessarily underlies opinions and policies, and the demand of some schools of historians for 'models' of social behaviour, may all take their rise here.

The mistake is in the end an academic mistake. But then the years since 1945 have been the first age of literary criticism in the history of the world to have been dominated by academe. No great critic of earlier times, from Dryden to T. S. Eliot, was an academic; though a few of them, like Arnold and Eliot himself, occasionally lectured in a university. The situation, being historically unique, is open to unique and unthought-of dangers. Theorists have allowed themselves to be misled, at times, by the sudden prestige of academic procedures, and have tended to forget that ideology, like any other kind of general assertion, needs to be earned before it is worth anything: to be tested by a knowledge of real instances before it can count as credible. That was the ringing message of Henry James's essay 'The lesson of Balzac' (1905), where he praised the great master of French realism for the clear certainty he offers in his fiction that 'his spirit has somehow *paid* for its knowledge'. Such knowledge is the latter end of a process of learning, seldom a beginning: a post-conception rather than a preconception.

All that is as plain in reading as in living: we generalise, if prudent, only upon instances. But in schools of literature the exposition of thought has sometimes come to be confused with thought itself, as if the ordering of an argument were the same as the act of discovery. That error stands as an enormous tribute to the potency of the written word; to the power of the pedagogue, above all; and to the sheer dignity of academic attainment in our times. No mistake could be more natural to the teacher of literature than to confuse composing an argument with having one. The worst folly is to imagine that Balzac or George Eliot may have shared the illusion, and to dig beneath the surfaces of their works like seekers after hidden gold, imputing ideologies where only tentative hypotheses are to be found.

No wonder if the seeker emerges empty-handed. What the great realists have to tell is seldom, at its best, a total view of life. They are as much on Emerson's staircase as anyone, if a little further up; they might teach patience, if nothing else. It is above all through an endless craving for generality, perverse and inverse as it is, that the theorist may easily forget – or strive to annul – the endless riches of earned experience they have to give.

Notes

1. Terry Eagleton, *Literary Theory: an Introduction* (Oxford, 1983), p. 198. See also his earlier work, *Criticism and Ideology: a Study in Marxist literary theory* (London, 1976). For a political account of the word, see John Plamenatz, *Ideology* (London, 1970).

2. Iris Murdoch, 'Against dryness,' *Encounter* (January 1961); reprinted in *The Novel Today*, ed. Malcolm Bradbury (London 1977), p. 30.
3. George Eliot, *Essays and Leaves from a Note-book* (Edinburgh, 1884), p. 229–30.
4. *Ibid.*, p. 235.
5. See René Wellek, 'A letter', *Scrutiny*, 6 (1937), on *Revaluation*, with Leavis's reply *ibid.*; both reprinted in *The Importance of Scrutiny*, ed. Eric Bentley (New York, 1948), pp. 23–40.

8

THE DREAM OF FICTION

'What's Hecuba to him?' Contemplating an actor whose tears were real, Hamlet pondered the enormous mystery of fiction, and called it a dream of passion, marvelling that any unreal event could move anyone to emotions that were themselves real

> But in a fiction, in a dream of passion,

and wondering how stories can move mankind, across centuries and continents:

> What's Hecuba to him or he to Hecuba,
> That he should weep for her? (II.ii)

That may be almost the most famous rhetorical question in Shakespeare. But it is only technically rhetorical, and it may still be worth trying to answer it, as Hamlet does. Why should one care about people who may never have existed, about speeches they may never have made, about incidents that may never have occurred?

These are questions, then and now, to nag the mind. The problem of fiction, though not fiction itself, is a discovery of Shakespeare's world. The Ancients had fiction but no sustained theory of the matter. Nobody is likely to have doubted that Plautus' plots were inventions, even if they were not invented by Plautus; and when Aristotle speaks of *poiisis* in the ninth chapter of the *Poetics* as more philosophical than history, which is merely about 'what Alcibiades did and suffered', he significantly implies that it is different. But the difference is not plainly one of veracity: his contrast between the particular and the universal is not certainly a truth-difference, since universals too are truths about the world. The historian relates what happened, he suggests, the poet what might – and if Herodotus were turned into verse, Aristotle penetratingly adds, it would still be a history and not a poem. That amounts to a defence of poetic invention; but it is still fairly remote from a theory of fiction. The poet is more truth-loving than the historian because universals belong to a higher order of truth than particulars.

That illustrates the cardinal difficulty, for ancient and medieval man, of achieving a fictional theory. The matter is unclear, but Aristotle does not seem to doubt that Hector and Oedipus were real men, even if he leaves himself free to doubt whether they behaved as Homer and Sophocles suggest. In that case he is offering a theory of literary story rather than of fiction. The poet shapes rather than creates, in that view; and what he shapes is already there, in a collective memory of the Greek past. Shaping, as Plato had objected, can easily be mendacious: one of Plautus' characters, in the *Pseudolus*, bluntly calls poets liars and complains that they can 'make a lie look like the truth' (404). But so long as the Ancients were content to echo Plato's strictures against poets as unreliable reporters, whether solemnly or whimsically, they were unlikely to hit on any sustained theory of fiction. So it looks as if the Ancients lacked such a theory, even though they had – and knew they had – fiction itself.

The flood of narrative make-believe is thought to have begun in Europe in the twelfth century, at least so far as written sources suggest, in a shift from epic to romance that arose in the new conditions of court and urban life.[1] The shift was silent, in critical terms. Medieval story was based on no stated theory of fiction, however fictional it may have known itself to be; and it needed none, since it continued to offer itself as history – 'as the old book saith' – and to be received as such, at least by the unsophisticated. Many must have doubted its historical claims, and in increasing measure; many must have been expected to doubt it. The richly ironic point of Chaucer's *Troilus and Criseyde*, for example, lies in the character of the narrator himself, an ageing antiquary in love with a heroine who, as all the world knows from common proverb, is bound to prove false – 'as false as Cressid'; so that his reluctance to accept the certainty of her fall from virtue is a joke shared, as the story unravels, between Chaucer and his audience. Given that the story, though set in the Trojan wars, is a medieval invention and not in Homer, the fictional intuitions of fourteenth-century England may be judged already advanced and subtle.

There is nothing surprising in the conclusion that fiction existed before, and well before, any sustained theory of itself. 'The owl of Minerva', as Hegel remarked, 'flies only by night': an art does not need to be described or accounted for until it is seen to exist – if then. No one needs a theory of fiction in order to write fiction. Theories like Sir Philip Sidney's *Apology for Poetry* (1595) are a response to something relatively new: a theory designed to explain a practice. Allegory must have sharpened the need, since it is openly fictional in its nature; the allegorical tradition that stretches from the *Roman de la rose* in the thirteenth century to Spenser's *Faerie Queene* and Bunyan's *Pilgrim's Progress* could only have been accepted by a literary culture prepared, in some self-conscious sense, to admit stories that laid no claim to be true. Sidney's talk of a poet creating a second nature, then, is fittingly daring, since fiction is no longer bounded by any visible world that ever was or is. It stands boldly outside history. The 'poetry' of Sidney's title means fiction in that radical sense; and the argument, for just that reason, is licensed to go beyond Aristotle's. There is no question of real events here, as in the Theban plays or the Trojan epics. The poet does not shape but create: he does not just see significant patterns in myth and history, as Aristotle seems to have implied, but starts anew. Such arguments plainly fit allegory like *The Faerie Queene* better than the plays of Marlowe and Shakespeare which – almost all – have claims to historicity in whole or part. (Tamburlaine existed, after all; so did Shakespeare's English kings, so did Othello and Lear.) Nobody, by contrast, was ever asked to believe Spenser's Red Cross Knight existed. He is a pattern of Christian virtue, and belongs to a world that Sidney calls golden.

That leaves Hamlet's famous challenge about Hecuba looking all the more exacting. As Priam's wife and queen of Troy she is not, in the estimation of the Ancients or of the Elizabethans, a fiction. It is entirely likely that Shakespeare and his audience believed she was an historical being and believed, with the Ancients, that the Trojan wars happened, and happened with the characters Homer names and describes. The Troy play that Hamlet recalls, then, and asks the First Player to recite from, is not strictly speaking golden, in Sidney's sense, or a pure fiction.

At least it is not golden all the way through. It is an alloy of gold and brass, presumably, of fiction and fact; it belongs as surely as Homer or Sophocles to a poetic past.

Hamlet speaks of the play he remembers as stylish and shapely – both of them merits Aristotle would have approved: 'well digested in the scenes', he says, and 'set down with as much modesty as cunning', with no phrases that 'might indict the author of affection' or affectation. All that strikingly lacks the conceptual radicalism of Sidney and Spenser, and I defer Shakespeare's more ambitious critical ideas, such as Theseus' 'forms of things unknown' and 'aery nothing', to a later chapter. But Hamlet's searching point about the actor's tears applies, after all, to stories of whatever claim to historicity, whether great, little or none. Hecuba, if she lived at all, is long since dead, and it does not much matter to his argument whether she is fact or fiction. What *is* strange, as he rightly sees, is that the actor should 'care for her': that he should care, what is more, as he recites his speech on the fall of Troy, more than Hamlet cares for his own urgent duty to revenge a murdered father:

> What would he do
> Had he the motive and the cue for passion
> That I have? He would drown the stage with tears ... (II.ii)

It is not always noticed that Hamlet answers his own question, by implication, though the implication is so remote as to leave it still formally rhetorical.

His reply is to contrast his own guilty indecision with some highly immediate situation that would test his courage:

> Who calls me villain, breaks my pate across,
> Plucks off my beard and blows it in my face,
> Tweaks me by the nose?

His indecision cannot be based on cowardice, then, since in any such situation he would react at once. And yet, in the face of his highest duty, he is 'dull and muddy-mettled', devoid of all urgency, and inactive –

> Like John-a-dreams, unpregnant of my cause ...

A John-a-dreams is a listless, dreamy fellow, so the contrast here is less between fiction and fact than between the immediate and the deferred. Like the sudden insult of a twisted nose, the ringing diction of the Player's speech is immediate: the ghost's charge, by contrast, can wait. We are moved by stories, then, not because we think them true but because, unlike much of the reality we live, they are *there*. An imagined grief like Hecuba's can usurp a real grief over a murdered father and a dishonoured mother.

But why, one may continue to ask, should it? To characterise the power of fiction in those terms is to redescribe the problem and not to solve it. Nobody *has* to attend to fiction, after all; and yet by choice we do. We seek out novels, plays and films. Hamlet asks the Player to perform his speech; children demand to be told tales. As Marghanita Laski used to say, mankind needs stories as it needs food and sex. Stories are not optional to life: they are necessary. Hamlet could have chosen to be utterly unconcerned about the fall of Troy, with so much else on his mind; but he eagerly asks for it. So his proffered solution – that we naturally concern ourselves more with instant problems like a twisted nose than with vaster and remoter issues – is not, as he can see himself, a reasonable one, any more than it is clearly reasonable to go to the cinema when there is work to perform. It is an excuse. With business to be done, and soon, there is a plain case for saying that no one should allow himself to be distracted by fiction at all.

There is no answering such a challenge, as I suppose, in the blunt sense of justifying those who behave as undutifully as Hamlet does, unless it is a justification to say that everyone does it. On the other hand, the Hecuba problem might be teased out, in some degree, if Hamlet's own hints towards a solution were closely observed. The play that he remembers and asks the actor to recite was excellent, he says, though unpopular ('caviare to the general'), and its excellence was artistic ('well digested in the scenes'), which implies a dramaturgical skill in selecting and shaping detail, along with an absence of affectation and 'modesty and cunning', or a sense of stylistic decorum. These arguments are fully within the world of the fictional, in that they are unconcerned with historical accuracy. It is not so much what Hecuba really said or did that is in question here as the shaping spirit of the playwright and his command of style. Fiction, in that view, is compelling because it is high art. To press the case further – further, perhaps, than it can go – it is not story that charms in stories, but the authorial skill that is brought to them. As people say of good anecdotists, 'It's the way he tells them.'

That tentative conclusion is only part convincing. It may be plausible to say that stories only sound good when they are well told: plainly implausible to say that no story is good in itself. To look at that argumentative dilemma from either end: in an attack on anthropological source-hunters among critics of the great romances, C. S. Lewis once stoutly defended the role of the poet: 'It is either in art, or nowhere,' he wrote in one of his last essays, 'that the dry bones are made to live again.'[2] That view is confirmed by source-hunters themselves. When the great medievalist Eugène Vinaver read all the surviving sources of Malory's *Morte Darthur* – perhaps the only scholar ever tireless enough to do so – he was emphatic in the introduction to his edition (1947) that Malory was hugely superior to the old Arthurian romances he had reworked. Art is made by art, such critics would say. It *is* how you tell it. As Hamlet put it, it has to be well digested, modest and cunning.

But does it? It is striking that Hamlet promptly produces his own counter-instance to that view: a play of his own devising called *The Mousetrap* about a villain who murders his sleeping brother and marries the widow. Hamlet is the author, and what he writes is not much of a play: the scene is ill digested and the style, at least by Shakespearean standards, is strikingly lacking in modesty and cunning. And yet it moves its principal audience, King Claudius, and for the simple reason that it is a diagram of his own crime. Idle to ask if it is a good story: it is, after all, the story of *Hamlet* itself. It is a good story, then, ill told; and yet it moves.

No doubt the counter-instance of Claudius comes too pat here, and it will be said that his horror is stirred not by a fiction but by an account that looks bent on turning into the story of his own life and scarcely fictive at all. But then no fiction is about nothing, in that sense. Any play or novel bears on life as it is known and lived, so that the case of Hamlet's *Mousetrap*, it might be countered, simply represents the force of that impact in a bold and highly simplified form. And there is a stronger reason than that for supposing some stories excellent in themselves and capable of surviving ill performances and poor versions. That reason is that there are stories that last; and on the Johnsonian principle of continuance of esteem, that must surely mean something: Faust, Don Juan, Quixote, Robinson Crusoe and Frankenstein, to name a handful. These are archetypes the world wants, seemingly, and goes on wanting: the salesman of his own soul, the great lover, the foolish knight with a shrewd attendant, the solitary on a desert island, the seeker after perfection who creates a monster. Though Faust, Juan and Crusoe have sources in historical person- ages, they plainly count here as fictional archetypes, since hardly anyone in centuries had doubted that the incidents attached to such names are imaginary. And they look built to last. Fielding imitated *Quixote* in *Joseph Andrews*, Dickens in *Pickwick*, and P. G. Wodehouse in the Jeeves stories; Thomas Mann reinterpreted Nazism in his *Doktor Faustus*; William Golding's *Lord of the Flies* is a late extension of the myth of Crusoe; and so on.

If there were no such thing as a good story – a story, that is to say, that is intrinsically good – how could that continuance be explained? It could not be explained, and there can be no doubt that there are good stories. Shakespeare, like his audience, must have known that there were; if challenged about Hecuba, he would surely have agreed that the fall of Troy is such a story, and that it is not just a matter of how you tell it – though telling it well, with modesty and cunning, can make it better. The story of King Arthur's Round Table – its rise and fall – which Malory inherited and improved, is likewise a good story, and it would still be that if he had never written. Permanence is not much regarded in recent theory. But it may represent a dislocation in critical debate to disdain the commonplace or assume that what is well known does not count as knowledge, and certain knowledge at that. No wonder, in that case, if the certainties of literary judgement are widely underrated; no wonder if the greatness of abiding stories like Faust or King Arthur is made perilously easy to underrate and overlook.

Johnson needed only a brief insistence, in his 1765 preface to Shakespeare, to establish the principle he called continuance of esteem. In the works of David Hume and his successor-sceptics, by contrast, that principle was rapidly inverted, and not only in respect of the authenticity of miracles; so that by the early nine- teenth century a cleric called Richard Whately, later Archbishop of Dublin, was moved to compose an anonymous pamphlet called *Historic Doubts Relative to Napoleon Buonaparte* (1819) to mock fashionable scepticism in that style. Whately's spoof claimed that Napoleon, by then a resident of St Helena, had never existed, on the ingenious ground that his reported career echoed epic events so strongly – total victories and total defeats on 'that grand scale so common in epic poetry, so rare in real life', and with 'that roundness and completeness which is characteristic of fiction' – that the whole thing can only have been made up by governments to induce people to pay their taxes. The point is acute as well as witty; but it has still to be taken, and historical reports can still be glibly dismissed as fictional merely because they resemble one another. A Bishop of Durham, for example, has recently doubted the Virgin Birth and Christ's walking on water on the ground that they are not unique to that case: 'There are stories about Tibetan holy men being able to do some quite remarkable things', he has remarked, 'so I have an open mind.' His mind may not be open enough. No argument against miracles needs to be as weak as that – just as the historical existence of Napoleon is unimpaired by resemblances between his career and the great epics; and the question whether Mary was or was not a virgin is independent of whether other messiahs, real or alleged, claimed to have been conceived in unusual ways.

The pendulum, then, has swung so far that even history can be readily doubted as a fiction, and perhaps it is time to swing it back. Before fiction was dreamed of, narrative was a report (or misreport) of real events, and stories concerned the past. To the sceptic, by contrast, as Whately's spoof suggests, the very resemblances that unite the human condition are sufficient grounds for suspecting history itself to be fiction too. That easy assumption is familiar to all readers of J. G. Frazer's *Golden Bough*. But both those extremes – anti-scepticism and scepticism – are exaggerations, and their exaggeration is best corrected by re-examining where the chief overlaps between history and fiction lie.

One extensive overlap concerns the might-have-been and the must-have-been – that freedom of hypothesis that historians, dramatists and novelists share, and necessarily share, as a traditional licence.

The classic instance is Thucydides. In a highly contested passage in his *History of the Peloponnesian War*, he remarks that where memory and report are lacking he has allowed himself to compose speeches for his historical characters 'roughly as I thought they would have spoken, keeping as close as possible to the general purport of what was actually said' (I.22). That licence to invent, for some eight centuries past the prerogative of the romance-writer and the novelist, was once the accepted licence of the historian too. No ancient historian, it seems clear, would have denied himself the liberty of inventing speeches; no Ancient would have doubted he had the right to do so.[3] The principle can run wider than speeches and as far as events: the Gospel of St Luke, for example, has been seen as an exercise in imagining what might or must have happened, given some earlier account, so that if Luke had been challenged – 'What is your evidence for that?' – he might have countered with: 'Can't you see it *must* have been like that?'[4] Modern historians no longer invent speeches, as Thucydides did, but they still speculate on what might or must have happened, and far beyond the evidence of documents or archaeology. To see how it must have been is to see how it was. When Clarendon as a royalist interprets the motives of his old enemy Oliver Cromwell in his *History of the Rebellion*, or when Macaulay as a Whig muses on why William of Orange invaded England and took the crown, they are indulging the ancient liberty of the Might and the Must.

That exercise in imagination can only be based on a widely accepted sense of the common nature of mankind. How could one know or guess that historical beings did or said what the surviving evidence does not declare them to have done or said, unless by attributing to them a nature that belongs to humanity itself – a nature the historian shares? That doctrine of a common nature is fundamental to humanism, and it is pre-eminently a doctrine of empathy. 'Each man bears the entire form of a man's estate', as Montaigne remarked. Shakespeare's Roman plays are classic instances of a sympathy daringly stretched across civilisations and centuries. John Donne enlarges the point in his verse letter 'To Sir Edward Herbert at Julyers' (1610), where he argues that any human creature possesses all the qualities of mankind at large:

> Man is a lump where all beasts kneaded be,
> Wisdom makes him an ark where all agree,

so that it is sensible to arrange and regulate one's vices and weaknesses, much as a prudent forester might clear a wilderness to cultivate the soil and control his game:

> How happy's he which hath due place assigned
> To his beasts, and disaforested his mind.

Disafforestation is a mental act that unites the ancient sage, the Renaissance humanist and the modern novelist and psycho-analyst, and it amounts to an act of sympathy shared by history and fiction alike. A sense of what might or must have been is not distinct from an act of historical imagination, so that fiction, like history, is not simply free. It is bounded by probabilities; and a novelist – not least a realistic novelist – can get it wrong, and be told so. To write a novel, as a practitioner has recently remarked, as one rightly concerned with the sheer accuracy that even romantic fiction requires, is rather like trying to remember something that has not happened yet. But of course it could happen. In fact the reader demands to be convinced that it could happen, and happen like that.

There is a classic instance in Montaigne – so commonplace and self-evident, in fact, that it may strike the modern mind as merely tedious, its utter familiarity deflecting from the rich significance of the point. When Cato committed suicide, Montaigne argues, he must have felt pain – however much of a Stoic he may have been – simply because it is in the nature of man to suffer when wounded by a knife:

> When I see him dying and plucking out his bowels, I cannot be satisfied with believing that his mind was free of distress and horror; I cannot believe he merely maintained an attitude prescribed by the rules of the Stoic sect – calm, impassive, without emotion.   (II.xi)

That 'cannot' represents the must-have-been of history, the due licence of the interpreter; and it is an act of interpretation where poet and historian are one.

That train of reflection, if abandoned there, might risk appearing to argue as if fiction and history were indivisible.

In terms of interpretative procedures, at least, they often are. The novelist does not stand outside a tradition of historiography, even when his fiction is non-historical. As an interpreter of the human condition he is altogether a pretending historian. 'It is impossible to imagine what a novelist takes himself to be,' Henry James remarked in his essay on Trollope (1883), chiding Trollope for his over-fondness for fictive devices, 'unless he regard himself as an historian, and his narrative as history.' That downright view is not subject to exemption. 'To insert into his attempt a backbone of logic, he must relate events that are assumed to be real.' Logic means credibility. To weep for Hecuba is to accept and respond to it: even a queen, however remote in time and place, must have grieved at the loss of kin and state. It is idle to protest, as the anti-humanist often does, that tears cannot be shed for a truth so utterly familiar: 'it needs no ghost come from the grave to tell us this.' It is only because it is known that it can be accepted at all. On the principle of Plato's *Meno*, one could only be told, in such matters, what one already knows. Telling is an act of reminding, and novels are only superficially about novelties. They cloak old truths in new garb: they tell what we already know and cannot always clearly see.

What difference would it make, then, to discover a story once thought true to be a fiction?

The question is not merely hypothetical. *The Memoirs of an English Officer, by Captain George Carleton* (1728) was accepted as genuine in its own century but attributed to Defoe, as a fiction, in the next. The circle is now complete, and it is again supposed a genuine autobiography, though perhaps in part rewritten by Defoe. In an age of unshaped fiction like the 1720s, when many novels lacked conclusive endings, that confusion between truth and fiction might the more easily be made, and it is instructive in its implications. For if a real Captain Carleton is recounting details of his wars against the Dutch and French, then they are happenstance, like much of real life: there because they happened and for little else. But if the work is a novel by Defoe, then the significance of its details is willed and purposive: there because Defoe thought they should be there.

That, it may be objected, is to draw the boundary line between fiction and history much too clear. The temptation is naturally strong: it is always tempting to suppose seemingly distinct literary forms to be bordered from each other as France is bordered from Germany. Henry James exaggerated the same linear clarity in his preface to *The Spoils of Poynton*, where he speaks of life as 'all inclusion and confusion' and art as 'all discrimination and selection'; but he must have known that 'all' is hyperbole here. The biographer or autobiographer – he too – discriminates and selects: the novelist can feel bound to include a detail because, untidy as it is, it has to be there. He may even include pointless details, as Dickens often did, to make a point of the pointless, so that his fiction may appear faithfully to imitate the sheer happenstance of life. (Even pointlessness, after all, can have a point.) History and fiction are parts of one intimate family, then, as the case of Captain Carleton suggests; and as with Wittgenstein's family resemblances, they are not distinct and contiguous, as forms, but subject to overlaps and criss-crossings. Novels can even inform uniquely about what may in fact have occurred. When D. H. Lawrence, in his highly autobiographical novel *Sons and Lovers* (1913), shows the hero and his sister poisoning their mother as a mercy-killing – she is dying slowly of an incurable disease – the reader wonders, and is perhaps meant to wonder, whether Mrs Lawrence died in that way.

Fiction, then, and especially realistic fiction, is unbordered and not a discrete category, though it has emphases characteristic of itself. To return to *The Spoils of Poynton*, where the heroine is a virtuous and sensitive young woman called Fleda Vetch: if James's narrative were indeed a history, like Captain Carleton's, and not just a pretended history, there would be little enough to say about that name, beyond the passing reflection that life has its little ironies. Given that it is a novel, however, an ugly name can only be purposive – the more so because James is well known to have been fascinated by names, collecting long lists of them in his notebooks. *Poynton* is the most extensively self-documented of all his novels, as it happens, in his surviving notes,[5] and his mind can be watched at work as he conceived and shaped his theme. The book began in history, or at least in a real event: at a dinner-table in December 1893 he heard how a young Scot on marrying found his widowed mother had jealously removed the treasures of his ancestral home out of resentment against her daughter-in-law, even resorting to the desperate and useless device of claiming her son was not the son of his dead father. That last detail, at once true and tremendous in its dramatic potentialities, is one James chose to omit as too bold and big for the delicacies of his own technique. The gestation of his idea was slow. By May 1895 the young woman had emerged as Muriel Veetch, which is bad enough as names go, though not as bad as Fleda Vetch; and James was later to invent as 'my working hypothesis for a dénouement' the final burning of the treasures, which gave him the 'dim sense' of an ending he eventually resolved to follow for want of a better. The fire might have happened, after all, though one cannot exactly say it must have happened.

James's novel begins with a real event reported from life, but it is not a historical novel. So fictions other than historical fictions can be about real events. That is a conclusion to give thought. Many fictions, after all, are about real events – at least as real as Hecuba to the understanding of Shakespeare's audience – though in James, at least, one is not meant to know or guess what the event was, and he was an expert at covering his tracks. Fictions are built out of facts and out of a sense of the sheer inadequacy of facts. We have an imagination, as a great poet once said, 'because we do not have enough without it'.[6] Beryl Bainbridge has told how she reads old newspapers until she finds the seed of a plot, and then 'you wrap your own life around it'. Fact or fiction? There are few clear boundaries here: the possible cases stretch all the way from painstaking historicity to far fantasy and back again.

Where, it will be asked, does that leave the fictionality of fiction? In no very certain place . . . Hamlet's phrase about 'a dream of passion' reminds us that dreams, too, are about something real, even if they muddle what is real; and the helpful notion that they warn and instruct is far older than Freud. But if fiction is above all things pointful and purposive – what Aristotle called more philosophical than history – then it demands that its point and purpose should be taken. It is tempting, with a name like Fleda Vetch, to conclude that anything can happen with names and leave it at that. But surely it cannot be left at that. James must be making a point: the point, perhaps, that names (like words) are arbitrary and do not always suit those who bear them. But if *Poynton*, like *Captain Carleton*, were discovered to be a history, that thought would not arise. We should know that Fleda Vetch was called that because that was her name.

It is here, perhaps, in the criss-crossings and overlaps of history and fiction, that each begins to achieve a mild and tentative distinction of its own. Fiction is more purposive than history, it is tempting to say, in the sense of being purposive down to its last details. Unlike real events, it has no happenstance, though it may have the appearance of it. That is to press the Vetch point as far as it will go, and perhaps further; and it is not in doubt that, distinguish as one may, the overlaps between what the novelist and the historian do remain enormous. So enormous, that in the end there are no lines to be drawn, only blurs to be discerned. In some novelists, like Smollett or Christopher

Isherwood, the interface between fiction and autobiography is so complex and unclear that the novels represent successive attempts to write a life. Stephen Spender when young wrote a novel he prudently suppressed, quarrying parts of it years later for an autobiography called *World within World* (1951) and finally, in a more permissive age, issuing the original, or something like it, as a novel called *The Temple* (1988): a fiction, once more, but explicitly a fiction about himself. Truman Capote's *In Cold Blood* (1965) is a novel, so it says, based on a real murder and researched from newspapers and interviews, and it is subtitled 'a true account', which perhaps it is. At least it may be as true as many a history, and the names are real.

What is to be said, in the face of such borderline instances, to Hamlet's question? Hamlet thought the player's tears all imagination, and wondered that he should weep. But he did not behave as if he thought so. In fact the experience gave him the idea of writing a play of his own, which suggests how quickly he saw the point. He had ceased to wonder at the power of Hecuba. Imagination may not be about reality, but it is emphatically about the real; and fictions move not in spite of any doubt that they occurred, but because they did, or might, or must.

Notes

1. G. T. Shepherd, 'The emancipation of story in the twelfth century', in *Medieval Narrative: a symposium*, ed. Hans Bekker-Nielsen (Odense, 1979).
2. C. S. Lewis, 'The anthropological approach', in *English and Medieval Studies Presented to J. R. R. Tolkien* (London, 1962), p. 223. See also his *Of This and Other Worlds* (London, 1982), which collects his papers on narrative theory; Colin Radford, 'How can we be moved by the fate of Anna Karenina?', *Proceedings of the Aristotelian Society*, supplementary volume 49 (1975); and Eugène Vinaver, *The Rise of Romance* (Oxford, 1971), pp. 53f.
3. See M. I. Finley, introduction to Thucydides, *History of the Peloponnesian War* (Harmondsworth, 1972), pp. 25f.
4. I am indebted here to an unpublished lecture by the Rt Hon Enoch Powell on St Luke delivered to the Oxford University Literary Society in January 1983.
5. Henry James, *Notebooks* (New York, 1955), pp. 136–8, 198–200, etc.
6. Wallace Stevens, 'Imagination as value' (1949), in his *The Necessary Angel* (London, 1960), p. 150.

PART II

9

SHAKESPEARE THE CRITIC

An anonymous sixteenth-century painting in the Palazzo Barberini in Rome knowingly exposes the critical dilemma of Renaissance humanism.

A sculptor is shown completing a heroic nude in marble, his instruments at his feet; and he is listening in pardonable bewilderment to the advice of bystanders, who are urging him to finish it. One points to the world of men, where the figure of perfect man is deduced by laborious inferences from multitudes of real but imperfect cases. Another brandishes a manuscript full of critical advice about how to carve; another looks upward for divine inspiration; another points vaingloriously to himself.

There is no one and certain place, then, for the artist to look, and it is a marvel he ever finishes, or even begins, anything: not man, or men, or books, or God himself. Doubly a marvel that the humanistic case for representing nature in works of art could ever be believed, or sustained, or lived. No wonder the artist looks puzzled.

In European terms, Shakespeare was a late humanist; and the descriptive task of the humanist-artist, from the start, was seen to be at once demanding and critically puzzling. Art is about life both as it is and as it might be: a puzzling demand, since it means there is always more than one direction for poet, painter or sculptor to look – the world, books, God, oneself – and it is unclear how to choose between them, or even whether one must choose at all. Mimesis – the representation of the real – was never a simple doctrine, whether in Aristotle or his successors: it forced the poet to meditate a choice of possibilities, and he was not required or allowed by the rules to choose only one.

Shakespeare's drama points unequivocally into the world of

men, like the Tuscan bystander, and his plays are never far from a knowledge of how real beings live. Ben Jonson's attack on the *Henry IV* plays in the prologue to *Every Man in his Humour* (1598), where he calls his characters monsters rather than men, is no more than a jealous jibe by a rival that can have carried no conviction even when it was made. But Shakespeare is far from ignorant of learned opinion about the complexity of critical issues, which he quotes as well as exemplifies; or of what others have created, as his borrowings from story-books and his mocking allusions to contemporaries like Montaigne and Marlowe show; or of the Christian-Platonic doctrine of divine inspiration, which could dismiss the poet as a madman or elevate him as a god. '. . . In a fine frenzy rolling': Theseus' speech in *A Midsummer Night's Dream* (V.i) speaks of the poet's eye glancing 'from heaven to earth, from earth to heaven', giving shape to 'things unknown' and conferring on 'aery nothings', or mere events of mind, a specificity they need to make them urgent as well as true, 'a local habitation and a name'. I am not aware that Shakespeare has any eminent reputation as a literary critic or theorist; but Theseus' speech, supported by similar instances, might justly earn him one. Its grasp of the non-alternatives of great art, so to speak – of its not-needing-to-choose between the particular and the universal – has seldom been outdone in concision in the entire history of critical interpretation. Shakespeare can see that a work is all the more universal for being particular, all the truer for being fictional: 'the truest poetry is the most feigning', as Touchstone puts it in *As You Like It*. Ezra Pound was to make the same point three centuries later, and without improving it: when he reviewed T. S. Eliot's *Prufock* for *Poetry* (1917), he acutely remarked that art 'does not avoid universals: it strikes at them all the harder in that it strikes through particulars'. Pound had grasped the point of the non-alternative too – universal because particular, particular because universal – as accurately as Shakespeare, if less memorably; and his remark shows that the humanistic paradox was alive and lively in twentieth-century Modernism, at once felt and known. But a paradox, if a soluble paradox, it remains. The Tuscan sculptor is after all right to look bewildered. *Why* is fiction, or 'feigning', truer than history, as Aristotle taught? Why does the poet, though at times frenzied like a lunatic or a lover, see further and see more in the human condition than other men? Or, as

Hamlet asked wonderingly of an actor, 'What's Hecuba to him?'

Theseus' speech, and Touchstone's, illustrate at once the strength of Shakespeare's critical gifts – often, as here, a gift for brisk critical summary – and the ignorance of the historian who confronts them. On the one hand, his claim that the poet, mad as he looks, gives specificity to perfect forms unknown on earth is so accurate an account of the ancient debate about poets in Plato and Aristotle that you could use it in a schoolroom. On the other hand, the question of sources is ultimately insoluble. Shakespeare could have found such doctrines in intermediate texts like Sir Philip Sidney's *Apology for Poetry*, which appeared posthumously in two editions in 1595; and given that the *Dream* was probably written at just that time, in 1595–6, nothing is likelier than that he did find it there. It is now possible, in fact, to assert what should never have been in doubt: that Shakespeare's reading may have been vast, his acquaintance with ideas mediated through conversation probably even vaster.[1] Shakespeare is a learned author, and disparagements of his learning by Ben Jonson and later by Milton cannot, in the end, be swallowed.

But a busy dramatist in his early thirties is likely to be in a hurry, and a mind as impressionable as this might have taken fire from a mere glance at a page of Sidney's *Apology* or a remark about it from a friend. Again, the public theatre demands a large element of shared knowledge between playwright and audience, or at least some part of an audience: it thrives on known truths, not on the singular and the new. Humanism, in any case, hardly admits of the concept of ideas at once new and true; it held belief all the better for having been widely believed, originality an affectation and a vice, consensus a virtue, and ancient authority the starting-point of all thoughtful and rational life. If Shakespeare was an original critical mind, he was so only by accident; and it is likely enough that he would have denied that he was, and denied that one could be so. The only originality that counts lies in what you make of what others already know, where 'every bosom returns an echo', as Samuel Johnson once put it: to be original, in point of dogma and principle, is to be mistaken, to 'affect a singularity'. No wonder Hector drops the name of Aristotle in *Troilus and Cressida* (II.ii) to make a moral point drawn, with knowing anachronism, from the *Nicomachean Ethics*. Chronology does not matter much, and Shakespeare must have known that

Aristotle lived and wrote centuries after the Trojan wars. But authority matters. Aristotle himself, after all, had held that a view was to be seriously regarded if it was *endoxon*: the opinion of all or most men, or more particularly of the wise and informed, or what his most recent English translator has rendered as 'reputable'.[2] That is a rooted assumption of European humanism. Consensus-thinking can so easily be made to sound easy and discredited in our own times that it is salutary to reconsider the arguments of thoughtful minds like Aristotle and his sixteenth-century followers: that a consensus, or at least a learned consensus, is necessarily the best place to start any argument, even if it is not always and necessarily the best place to finish it. It is where you begin.

A glance at Sidney's argument will make Shakespeare's look plainer. All the arts are mimetic, or descriptive of the world: 'there is no art delivered to mankind that hath not the works of nature for its principal object', as Sidney puts it – all the arts being 'actors and players, as it were, of what nature will have set forth' (pp. 99–100). The arts describe. As an astronomer observes stars, or grammarians speech, so do poets describe the universal nature of man in his moral relations. But there is a difference, which Sidney arguably overdraws. The task of the poet, though descriptive, is never purely so: 'Disdaining to be tied by any such subjection', he creates 'a second nature' finer and more exquisite than the world itself – a world of gold, as Sidney boldly puts it, instead of the world of brass around us. Here, at the heart of Sidney's paradox, lies the puzzle of the Tuscan sculptor and of the humanist-artist in general. The poet creates a better world than any he has observed. Mimesis, or poetic representation, describes the visibly real through the more-than-real: it improves as it describes.

How can one describe and improve at the same time? That paradox, which lies at the heart of humanistic criticism, is taxing but in no way insuperable. Nor is it confined to the world of the arts. In many practical matters we take for granted that a description may be clearer, 'more golden', than what it describes – an astronomer's diagram of a planet, for example, a manufacturer's of a domestic gadget ('Directions for Use'), or a grammarian's rule. In fact a grammarian, like a poet, may easily find it clearer to invent an instance of his rule than to report one he has overheard. It is odd that mimesis should so readily be taken for granted in day-to-day matters like the directions on a packet, and yet found so problematical in the arts. 'The skill of the artificer', as Sidney puts it,

> standeth in that idea or foreconceit of the work, and not in the work itself. (p. 101)

There are explanatory as well as artistic advantages, then, in invention:

> ...forms such as never were in nature, as the heroes, demigods, cyclops, chimeras, furies

of epic and romance: what Shakespeare called 'the forms of things unknown' to which the poet gives place and name. That is why Sidney's poet, in an engaging hyperbole of the humanistic case, is no mere servant of nature but her equal:

> ...he goeth hand in hand with nature, not enclosed within the narrow warrant of her gifts, but freely ranging only within the zodiac of his own wit, (p. 100)

as in Sidney's own *Arcadia*, or Spenser's *Faerie Queene*, or Shakespeare's *Tempest*. Such lofty descriptions of moral nature, existing beyond any visible world, exist much as rules of language or laws of physics exist. Man is divinely derived and physically circumscribed: 'participating in the intellect of God,' as Ficino had put it, 'but operating in a body of his own'. That is how he knows more than his senses tell, and sees patterns in the visible world that are God-given:

> ...tongues in trees, books in the running brooks,
> Sermons in stones, and good in every thing.

Humanistic mimesis, then, is a theory about the certainties that literature offers; and it remains forever hard to disparage and harder still to rebut: far more than a museum-piece of critical history, and easily more sophisticated and reflected than a good deal that has passed for critical theory since. It is certainly proof against the facile complaint of escapism. It is no serious charge against *Arcadia*, *The Faerie Queene* or *The Tempest* to say that they are not like life as lived by mortals, then or ever, since Sidney, Spenser or Shakespeare might reply that they are not meant to be. A non-realistic description may still describe – a salutary reproof to the sort of critic who imagines that a realistic novel is necessarily more mimetic, at least in its claims, than highly formal fictions like allegory or romance. 'Nature never set forth the earth in so rich tapestry as divers poets have done', says Sidney, skilfully anticipating that objection; and the notion that realism is more mimetic than formalism is one he would have been expert in refuting. Of course the world shows no friend as constant as Pylades was to Orestes, as he argues, or any hero as virtuous as Aeneas: such ancient models of constancy and virtue are imaginary. But then if the world around us were as lucid as literature, the poet would have slight reason to exist, or none, and even slighter reason to be valued. The humanistic case for literature as certain truth about the human world is carefully and knowingly protected from objections of the simpler sort. What map of a country, after all, fails to simplify and to omit, to invent lines and colours that are diagrammatically vivid rather than severely imitative? The ocean is not in truth and in every light blue, as every sailor knows; and nobody but a simpleton was ever deceived by an atlas into thinking it was.

Shakespeare grasps and summarises literary humanism in masterly style, and he can see where it goes. It is in that last respect, above all, that he surpasses his contemporaries, who often impress with an awareness of the knowledge that literature can give but seldom show much clear sense where the doctrine leads. Ben Jonson's accounts are limited in just that way: they do not usually go anywhere. Consider, for example, his reference to mimesis in his commonplace-book *Timber*, where he links it to the ancient doctrine of the sister arts:

> Poetry and picture are arts of a like nature, and both are busy about imitation. It was excellently said of Plutarch, poetry was a speaking picture, and picture a mute poesy. For they both invent, feign and devise many things, and accommodate all they invent to the use and service of nature. (cix)

Accurate enough, as a restatement: but also strikingly uninteresting and unproblematical. As some would say, Shakespeare's remark that 'the truest poetry is the most feigning' problematises mimesis, and brilliantly: Jonson merely rehashes it. In a similar way, Marlowe rehashes the ancient doctrine of a 'grace beyond the reach of art' in Tamburlaine's famous soliloquy on Zenocrate:

> . . . Yet should there hover in their restless heads
> One thought, one grace, one wonder, at the least,
> Which into words no virtue can digest.   (Part I, V.ii)

Accurate again: but no one has ever shown what it is doing in the mouth of an exterminating conqueror. Dramatically speaking, Tamburlaine's soliloquy goes nowhere. If a mass-murderer can fall in love, which may be, it is a paradox that at least deserves to be explored: doubly so if he can invoke a doctrine of critical theory to justify his love. Marlowe does neither: Shakespeare would surely have done both. When he puts a critical view in the mouth of a character, it is commonly there because that character has some active and serious business with it.

Touchstone, after all, is a highly intelligent and inventive clown. Theseus compares lovers to poets because, at that moment, he is himself a lover on his wedding-night; and *A Midsummer Night's Dream* as a whole shows that love is itself a creatively imaginative act – its lovers enamoured of an idea or ideal rather than of real beings. In a play where Titania can fall in love with an ass, the dramatic context of the doctrine is potent: we love our conceits of others, and those conceits may be as remote from what we see and touch as the ravings of lunatics or the imaginations of poets. Hamlet, in a similar way, is a strikingly fitting spokesman for mimetic doctrine – 'to hold, as 'twere, the mirror up to nature' (III.ii), as he tells the players – since he is about to do just that to the recent murder of his own father by producing *The Mousetrap* before the guilty king. In fact the relation between *The Mousetrap* and the entire play called *Hamlet* is an exact diagram of Aristotelian doctrine: the play-within-the-play simplifying and clarifying – eschewing ambiguities, nuances and smudges (Bad Kinsman kills Good Kinsman, no frills) with a simplicity that the abundant life of the whole play fails in its fertile and deliberate complication to match. To understand a critical doctrine, for Shakespeare, is to understand what it does and what difference it makes. That is quite different from Marlowe cheerfully recalling his Cambridge rhetorical education as he composes Tamburlaine's soliloquy – magnificent, in a detached sense, as the soliloquy is. An idea in Shakespeare has the urgent power to prompt action, solve problems, do damage.

Fifteenth-century Florentine humanism, then, and the long shadow it casts across the ensuing century in the writings of Sidney and Shakespeare, is the first sustained and articulate theory of fiction in modern times: the first modern version of the view that fiction offers knowledge, even certain knowledge, and a knowledge clearer and more certain than life itself; and because more certain, necessary to all living beyond mere unthinking life, since it clarifies the endless confusions of life itself. That is the earliest modern version of literary certainty. The second was the European Enlightenment, where it largely frees itself of established Christianity, though still theistic; the English, now far from latecomers, sharing the palm with the French. The third version, or fictional realism, grew up in the shadow of the Enlightenment with Fielding, Richardson and Smollett, though it has somehow acquired the critical reputation of being a nineteenth-century idea. Shakespeare's humanism, then, which in European terms is late, is at once the most Christian and the least English of the three great phases of the doctrine of literary humanism. The religious aspect – Christian, Deist or agnostic – counts only marginally here. The national counts for rather more; and my contention here is that though Shakespeare came late to European humanism, in the 1590s, he contributed massively, though almost invisibly, to that tradition. True, his contribution to literary theory was not, at least as far as the surviving documents allow us to judge, noticed at the time. More surprisingly, it has hardly been noticed since. But it can still be demonstrated, from within the matrix of the plays themselves; and it is a contribution to theory that is still worth pondering.

Among his many minds, Shakespeare had the mind of a critic. That he never wrote a critical essay, so far as we know – or even a preface to a play, as Ben Jonson did – is not of itself remarkable. It is also inessential, since the evidence, though scattered, is abundant in the plays and poems themselves. First, by implication: it can hardly be accidental, for example, that his career begins and ends, to speak approximately, with plays that largely observe the unities of time and place – *A Comedy of Errors* and *The Tempest* – so that his defiance of those unities, for which Sidney and his Italian sources had strenuously argued, looks first and last like a matter of conscious decision. That he could observe them when he chose is a ground for thinking that when he defied them, as he usually did, he did so in full critical consciousness of what he was about.

Secondly, he could be openly explanatory about it. When Time enters as Chorus at the beginning of the fourth act of *The Winter's*

Tale, he announces that the play will knowingly defy the unities:

> Impute it not a crime
> To me, or my swift passage, that I slide
> O'er sixteen years, and leave the growth untried
> Of that wide gap, since it is in my power
> To o'erthrow law, and in one self-born hour
> To plant and o'erwhelm custom.

If law and custom here refer to the so-called 'Aristotelian' unities of sixteenth-century critics, then the speech makes nonsense of Voltaire's famous remark that Shakespeare was a gifted barbarian who wrote without the least knowledge of the rules. He plainly knew them; he chose, for the most part, to break them. He also knew the theory of the literary *genres*, as Polonius' speech shows: '. . . tragedy, comedy, history, pastoral, pastoral-comical, historical-pastoral, tragical-historical, tragical-comical-historical-pastoral – scene undividable or poem unlimited' (*Hamlet*, II.ii). That all should come from the lips of an old fool presumably represents some disdain, on Shakespeare's part, for the neo-classical system of literary kinds; but it does not suggest ignorance.

His knowledge of Aristotle's *Poetics*, too, or at least of the principal arguments contained in it, is more than probable. Hamlet's remark about 'the dram of evil' looks much like a reference to Aristotle's argument about *hamartia* – the tragic flaw in every virtuous man – and the only reasonable dispute here can be whether Shakespeare's knowledge was or was not at first hand:

> So, oft it chances in particular men
> That for some vicious mole of nature in them . . .
> Being Nature's livery or Fortune's star,
> His virtues else, be they as pure as grace,
> As infinite as man may undergo,
> Shall in the general censure take corruption
> From that particular fault.   (I.iv)

Since *Troilus* and *Cressida* refers openly to the *Nicomachean Ethics*, it does not look like a large presumption to suppose that Shakespeare was acquainted with some Aristotelian texts, whether in the original Greek or in some version or commentary. When Hamlet, again, speaks to the players of 'some necessary question of the play' (III.ii), urging them against clowning, we are very close to an outspoken critical intelligence, since it is precisely in that sense of plot-necessity – if this, then that – that Shakespeare excels his contemporaries. And in *Coriolanus* there is a brief couplet which, with supreme concision, puts a theory of dramatic conflict at its most intense:

> One fire drives out one fire, one nail one nail.
> Rights by rights falter, strengths by strengths do fail.   (IV.vii)

Coriolanus is the last of Shakespeare's tragedies as well as the last of his Roman plays, so that there is something extraordinarily fitting about that two-line summary by the greatest of all tragic poets of a doctrine usually associated with modern critics: that drama is only trivially a conflict of good with bad, only seriously a conflict of good with good. Aufidius' couplet makes one wonder whether Shakespeare ever read the *Antigone* of Sophocles, and in some ways it fits Attic tragedy better than his own. But then one remembers that it is in *Coriolanus*, and that it fits that.

To speak like Hamlet, or Aufidius, or even Polonius – and certainly to speak of poetry as Touchstone does – is to demonstrate a power of critical mind. Modern Shakespearians have had to grow accustomed to easy derision on the subject, and it is still commonly imagined that critical perception is something one brings to Shakespeare's plays rather than something to find in them:

> . . . Which Shakespeare answered rather badly
> Because he hadn't read his Bradley,

as the old jingle about the Civil Service examination goes. But it is surely more plausible to suppose that Shakespeare might have answered a Shakespeare paper extremely well. It is the last presumption of Shakespearian critics to suppose that their own intuitions exceed anything Shakespeare would have been capable of having for himself. The reverse is easier to credit, and harder to rebut. We follow, as critics, in his footsteps, and follow at a humble distance. This was a thoughtful and a learned genius. Not, it may readily be conceded, a scholarly one; and not necessarily, like Ben Jonson's, a bookish; but learned in the sense of well read and well advised in the great documents of Renaissance humanism and their classical sources. Remarkable, still more, as a genius that faces both ways, as the Tuscan sculptor was bidden to do: at once into literature and into life.

Notes

1. See Sir Philip Sidney, *An Apology for Poetry*, ed. Geoffrey Shepherd (London, 1965), pp. 99–100. Future references are to this edition. I am also indebted to Emrys Jones, *The Origins of Shakespeare* (Oxford, 1977), who sees him as a well-read and informed humanist as well as a genius.
2. Jonathan Barnes, in *The Complete Works of Aristotle: the revised Oxford translation* (Princeton, 1984), based on his discussion in *Revue Internationale de Philosophie* (1980).

10

THE CLASSIC MARX

Karl Marx loved the classics. 'Those old ones, at least,' he wrote warmly in a private letter of 21 December 1857, on rereading his Thucydides in exile, 'always stay new.'

Marx may have been even more of a classic and humanist than he ever understood, and decidedly more than his admirers have supposed – not least in his doctrine of class war. And the ground for proposing all that is ultimately simple. It is that ancient history is full of wars between rich and poor, as if prefiguring Marx's predictions about industrial society; and modern history – even the modern history that Marx could have known or guessed at – is not. The case is cautionary. It is not in doubt that a faith in literary parallels can mislead as well as instruct, and this chapter is a study of a humanist misled: a certainty – for Marx was classically certain – misplaced.

Marx's interest in the Ancients was lifelong. At school in Trier, where he was felt to be no more than an average pupil, he learned Greek as well as Latin, and from a noted teacher who had edited classical texts. As a boy he was thought better at literature than history, though his school-leaving exercise, composed in Latin in 1835 at the age of seventeen, was a historical essay on the reign of Augustus Caesar[1]; and as a student in Bonn, where the great Niebuhr had recently taught, he continued with Latin and Greek, as well as French and German, and attended classes on Roman law and classical mythology, his reports commending him as no more than industrious and attentive.

His writings, both public and private, maintain an intermittent flow of classical allusion throughout his life. The Berlin thesis he wrote between 1839 and 1841, on the difference between

Democritus' philosophy of nature and Epicurus', deals in human-istic style with correspondences between ancient and nineteenth-century thought, and a recent critic has aptly called it 'a kind of literary superimposition technique that brings old and new intimately together'.[2] That, after all, is the essence of humanism. The classic notion of superimposing the old on the new, familiar as it was in Renaissance and Enlightenment uses of the classics, may have influenced Marx even more than he was aware, inclining him as an early Victorian to see recent and future events exclusively through a veil of ancient commentary and interpretation. He was a prophet who, more than he knew, looked back, and Heidegger's remark that 'the humanism of Marx required no return to the antique' suggests a very modest acquaintance with his writings.[3] Such superimpositions can be conscious and overt even in his most political writings. In the first volume of *Das Kapital* (1867), for example, he cites Thucydides and Xenophon on the division of labour in ancient times; and his late notes on race, family and kinship in prehistory and among primitive nations, recently published from manuscript as *Ethnological Notebooks* (1972), are thick with references to the historical writings of the Ancients as well as to modern anthropology.

On the other hand, for one so steeped in ancient history, he has some odd omissions. His published writings rarely mention Livy or Polybius, for instance, though they both figure in his late notes on race; but there is reason to be sure that Marx and Engels knew these authors early in life. Engels had been commended for his knowledge of Livy in the certificate he was given on leaving school; he refers to Polybius' account of military organisation in his contributions to the *New American Cyclopaedia*, and quotes Livy in *The Origin of the Family*. It is a reasonable conclusion that both men were familiar with the works of the chief historians of antiquity throughout their long working lives as intellectual partners and as friends.

Marx was born three years after Waterloo, and it is natural that his view of human conflict throughout history should be an outgrowth of the fervent European debate about the French Revolution, its institutions and its wars: not least its use and misuse of ancient history to explain the present and future of mankind. Roman history in the highly conservative age of the restored monarchies after 1815 could be seen as inflammatory: not altogether surprisingly, since it had animated the *philosophes* whom many held intellectually responsible for the convulsions of 1789 and after. The usurping Napoleonic system, what is more, had boasted the trappings of ancient Roman authority, both republican and imperial. When Napoleon seized power in 1799 he adopted the title of Consul, and five years later that of Emperor: a title not known in France for nearly a thousand years. The new France laid claim to dignities Cicero had known, much as the young republic of the United States had recently done; and the republican paintings of Jacques-Louis David, who as a member of the French National Assembly voted for the execution of Louis XVI – his 'Brutus and his Dead Sons' that hangs in the Louvre, for example – still show how austere Roman virtue, above all the heroism of violent self-sacrifice, could be used by a revolutionary artist to make the artistic fashions of the age of Louis XV and XVI look like rococo fribbles. And after 1804, aptly enough, David was to move from republican austerity to the military pomp of imperial grandeur, as in his vast canvas of Napoleon distributing the eagles to his troops.

By 1818, when Marx was born, these same Roman virtues could look subversive. That is a sense now lost. Niebuhr's *Römische Geschichte* (1811–32) does not strike one now as an inflammatory work; and in his published conversations he appears essentially a liberal nationalist of the Prussian sort, an admirer of English moderation and a fervent hater of the French occupation of his homeland. 'The evil times of Prussia's humiliation', he told a friend,

> have some share in the production of my history. We could do little more than ardently hope for better days, and prepare for them. . . . I went back to a nation, great but long passed by, to strengthen my mind and that of my hearers. We felt like Tacitus.[4]

So Niebuhr's history of Rome, in his own estimation, was a radical-minded contribution to the Prussian war of liberation against Napoleon. Though dedicated to the King of Prussia it supported plebeians against patricians in the struggle of the orders in republican Rome; and if its style hardly burns with Tacitean indignation against tyranny, or anything else, it can be read as a warning against the megalomania that accompanies arbitrary power. That was sometimes the view of hostile contemporaries quick in a nervous time to scent radicalism at home and abroad. Early in 1829 an anonymous article in the Tory *Quarterly Review* accused Niebuhr of having influenced a recent bout of student militancy in German universities – the 'very hives of sedition and turbulence' – and the reviewer rejoiced that in a later edition of his book he had 'rejected and disowned these political principles'. Niebuhr died in 1831, a few years before the young Marx arrived in Bonn as a freshman; but it is likely enough that his reputation there was still felt to be dangerous, at least in nervously conservative quarters, and that the study of ancient history was as politically suspect as sociology in the 1960s.

Marx's debt to the intellectual sources of revolution – the French Enlightenment and its disciples – though already studied by historians as an accumulation of detail, still needs to be seen in a more sharply argumentative light. It is curious that Marx, who can be abundantly, even tediously generous in acknowledging his sources, should still be accorded a reputation for so much originality in matters concerning what is now called the sociology of thought: the theoretical study of how mankind thinks, believes and acts as it does. That is emphatically not because he claimed any such far-reaching originality for himself. Indeed, like many Victorians, he was all too inclined to amass details of past authorities, even to the point where it could become difficult or impossible to complete a masterpiece he had elaborately planned and replanned. He was a born footnoter, and some of his writings never managed to emerge from their notes. He amassed facts and opinions as a squirrel collects nuts. There is more than a little of Lord Acton about him, in that respect, especially in his last years; and like Acton he was never to complete his great work, in the event, so that only the first volume of *Das Kapital* ever appeared in his lifetime.

Marx repeatedly gives his sources and scrupulously acknowledges his debts. In a letter of 5 March 1852, for example, he justly denied having discovered either the concept of class or of class war: his contribution, he insisted, being rather to show how classes are linked to phases in productive development, and how class war must inevitably lead to a dictatorship of the proletariat. All that relates Marx convincingly to his intellectual predecessors in the eighteenth century and earlier. And the debt can be made to look still more convincing by showing that his doctrine of class arose out of an Enlightenment concern with individual man as partly or largely conditioned by the social forces that shaped him. That concern, too, can be glibly attributed to the inventive mind of Marx, though not by Marx himself. Montesquieu in the 1740s had encouraged men to see *mœurs* as influenced by climate and geography; Voltaire soon after by cultural history; and a reading of Montesquieu was to teach the young Gibbon, and eventually Macaulay, to see history as a complex of social forces rather than a treasury of exemplary or cautionary lives. It is an illusion to suppose that either social history or social theory was a creation of the early Victorians, or that early Victorians thought that it was.

Much of this has by now faded from view, even the view of specialists, and it would probably be a matter for astonishment to latter-day Marxists – and not only to them – to learn that William Godwin, whose reputation today is of an almost fatuous utopianism, wrote a chapter for his *Enquiry concerning Political Justice* (1793) headed 'The characters of men originate in their external circumstances' (I.iv), arguing that 'the actions and dispositions of mankind are the offspring of circumstances and events, and not of any original determination that they bring into the world'; that there are no innate ideas; and that it is education and environment that make opinion, not what a man is endowed with at birth. 'The pride of philosophy', remarks the narrator in Godwin's novel *Caleb Williams* (1794), 'has taught us to treat man as an individual. He is no such thing. He holds necessarily, indispensably to his species' (III.xiv). That heritage from Locke, damagingly simplistic as it can easily look, was a commonplace of European intellectual debate decades before Marx's birth.

It is not that Godwin, for all that, or Marx after him, believed man to be always and necessarily the impotent victim of his environment. The problem of nature and nurture goes wider and deeper than that, as both men knew. But Marx's thought is highly derivative of eighteenth-century sociology, and he was always candid in acknowledging that debt. His classicism was well attested by himself, which raises the question whether Marxists have read much Marx, and indeed whether anyone beyond a few experts has. Passages where Marx and Engels propose racial extermination, for example, still seem not to be widely known, though Stalin commended one of them in *The Foundations of*

Leninism (1924).[5] We need to pay closer attention to texts and less to commentators. Marx's awesome intellectual reputation stands as high as it does today, it may be suspected, less through the loyalty of his never-say-die disciples than through the praise heaped on him by non-Marxist historians and sociologists persuaded that his thought contains much that is originally and indispensably important to methods of social and historical analysis. Ask them what that something is, and such non-Marxists will reply in terms to do with the economic base, or social conditioning, or the theory of class: with Enlightenment propositions familar to French and English political theory, in fact, decades before Marx was born. It is hard to understand why that should be so, unless on the hypothesis of radical chic. Many a middle-aged professor still imagines that to drop Marx's name with a wink or a nod will render him immune from the charge of looking fuddy-duddy. That Marx was old-fashioned in his political and social theories, even by the standards of the early nineteenth century, and seen to be so, is a notion that still looks new.

Voltaire opened the introduction to his *Essai sur les mœurs* (1756) with a remark to imply that every new philosophy, including the enlightened, feels itself bound to reinterpret the history of the Ancients. 'You would like the *philosophes* to have written ancient history because you would like to read it as a *philosophe*.' For Marx, too, that reinterpretative view of the ancient world was inescapable. His education was classical. His doctrine was itself a theory of history – past, present and to come. And the events of ancient history had been the substance of humanistic polemics for generations before his birth. Machiavelli in the *Discorsi* had turned early Roman history into a battery of instances of how power in any age is lost, kept and won. The Enlightenment had confirmed that highly contemporary view of the Ancients and added the theoretical dimension of a sociology of thought; the American and French revolutions had decorated their institutions with Roman nomenclatures like Senate and Consul. The quest was not for originality but for precedents. Futures are governed less by novelties than by interpreting the past.

More than that, ancient history was more than ever, in the early nineteenth century, the common currency of educated men and above all of radicals. Some recent historians of humanism have found it difficult to understand how radical classical studies could once look: one recent study speaks of them in routine style as 'supportive . . . of the Establishment' and designed to train a conservative social élite.[6] That is not how Marx understood the matter, or Matthew Arnold after him. Ancient parallels can subvert. No doubt Marx's fondness for classical allusion dates his writings in a faintly damaging sense, to modern tastes. But it represents something common enough in the century between Waterloo and the First World War, and especially in the radical thought of that age. In his last years, it is true, he was to widen his interests far beyond Europe, as the notes on race show: in time, back into prehistory; and in place, outwards into Asia, Africa and the Americas: all that went with a dedicated reading of anthropologists like Sir Henry Maine and Lewis Morgan. But not much of that extra-European reference enters into the confidently revolutionary years of the classic Marx in the 1840s and 1850s, when newly industrial states in western Europe ripe (as he supposed) for civil conflict consumed his hopes and energies. The stage for class war, as he believed, was set: a vast, necessary and redemptive act of violence, to begin within weeks or months. The road to *stasis*, or a war between the classes, was excitingly open.

Marx's sense of what such a war must mean, so far as it was based on ancient sources, is more likely to have been derived from primary texts like Aristotle's *Politics* than from Niebuhr or Mommsen; though his abuse of Mommsen's *Römische Geschichte* (1854–6) in *Das Kapital* shows he had read that book too. Like other writers of antiquity, Aristotle saw *stasis* or revolution as a struggle between rich and poor. Such struggles, in his view, are exceptionally bitter, an oligarchy by its rapacity exciting the sudden violence of a *jacquerie*:

> For the few, or many, to have power is an accidental feature of oligarchies and democracies, since the rich are few everywhere, and the poor numerous . . . The real point of difference is poverty and wealth; and it follows that wherever the rulers owe their power to wealth, whether as a minority or as a majority, this is oligarchy; and where the poor rule, it is democracy. (1276b)

That blunt view of the economic base of all civil strife was bound to have appealed powerfully to Marx, and it did. Early in *Das Kapital* he calls Aristotle 'the great investigator who was the first to analyse value', remarking that Aristotle's analysis of the question had been blocked, as he himself had recognised, by the lack of a conceptual tool to clarify the issue, namely a labour theory of value (I.i.ch.3). By superimposing Ricardo's labour theory of value upon Aristotelian *stasis*, Marx believed he could at once solve the problems, and predict the future, of nineteenth-century industrial society. He fully accepted the certainty of literature. The poor, who are necessarily more numerous than the rich, would soon claim by violence the total value of what they had produced by their own labour – provided, that is, that they could achieve an adequate consciousness of their historic role. In the early 1840s the prospect of consciousness, though ultimately promising, still sadly left much to be desired. 'A German Aristotle who wished to construct his *Politics* on the basis of our society', he wrote bitterly of his native Germany in a letter of May 1843, six years before his English exile began, 'would begin by writing: "Man is a social but wholly unpolitical animal".' The remark, if not exactly funny, is of course a joke, since Marx was pedantically aware that Aristotle's *zoon politikon* does not mean 'political animal' but refers to the *polis* or city-state; indeed he proffers the correct translation in a painstaking footnote to *Das Kapital* (I.iv.ch.13). Not for nothing, one often feels as one reads him, the careful philological training of a Trier *Gymnasium* and the universities of Bonn and Berlin.

Marx's solution to class conflict, it is true, was radically different from Aristotle's, who had envisaged an authority representing neither rich nor poor holding a balance between them. Marx, by contrast, wanted *stasis* or revolution, and for a reason altogether his own. But considered as diagnosis, the views of the two are compellingly similar, and there is no need to doubt the one is deeply indebted to the other. 'The greatest thinker of antiquity', Marx calls Aristotle in *Das Kapital* (I.iv.ch.15), approvingly quoting from the *Politics* a passage where the need for labour to operate machinery is discussed. Earlier in the book, in a long footnote on Aristotle's theory of barter and trade, he had praised a section in the first book of the *Politics* concerning the difference between economics and 'chrematistics', or the deplorable practice of making money limitlessly and for its own sake rather than for use: a tendency he saw as one of the most contemptible elements in modern finance. Such passages in Aristotle make one see how utterly natural it was for the classic Marx to admire him.

To read the Greek and Roman historians, what is more, is to realise how plentiful are the ancient instances of wars between rich and poor. Thucydides, whom Marx enjoyed rereading so much, tells of a violent revolt in Corfu 'caused by greed and ambition in pursuit of office' (III.82). The notion of an economic base to revolution, which seems to some modern minds a striking and even original feature of Marxist dogma, would have looked comfortably familiar to the Ancients and to the humanists who revived their study; nor is it likely to look notably original to any historian of Greece and Rome today, whatever his political views. Such historians, like Niebuhr and Mommsen, interpret a lost world in which violent struggles between rich and poor were a matter of ordinary occurrence. Similarities, to be sure, are not identities: Marx, for example, did not believe that a difference of class was ever as simple as a difference of wealth. But he believed that the imminent and inevitable triumph of the proletariat would be won by achieving a consciousness within itself of its own increasing impoverishment under bourgeois rule: the spectacle of that impoverishment, first of all in the rich industrial states of the West, leading to the imminent combustion of workers' revolution. To that extent, the future of mankind would vividly resemble its classical past, and Aristotle would be vindicated.

It is useful to recall here that class war is not a metaphor in Marx, and it could mislead to translate *Klassenkampf* as class struggle. Until his last years, at least, Marx was always emphatic that the revolutions he promised the industrial world would be violent and bloody. That is because, as with Aristotelian *stasis*, the coming proletarian revolution must be a contest for the same objects. The transition from feudalism to capitalism had sometimes been peaceful, in Marx's view, because the one had been based on land and the other on manufacture. But in the coming contest between bourgeoisie and proletariat, the prize was all one: the mines and the factories, the very means of industrial production itself. To hope or suppose that such a contest could be other than violent was to convict oneself of bourgeois delicacy, in his view, or utopian illusion. Class war is emphatically a kind of war, and not a metaphor. But then ancient history, too, is not notable for its peaceful transitions.

There is no grave difficulty, then, in appropriating Marx's own jocular phrase to himself, and in seeing him in aspiration at least as the German Aristotle. The social diagnosis is similar, the sources avowed, and the title from his own pen. Disciples could enthusiastically echo the call. H. M. Hyndman, who knew Marx and idolised him, hailed him in his autobiography as 'the Aristotle of the nineteenth century';[7] and that perhaps is the intellectual tribute Marx would have valued most. His tradition was humanistic. He had imposed a classic theoretical order on the multifarious facts of the new industrial age, and proved himself as mighty a systematiser of modern knowledge as Aristotle of the ancient. He was ardently certain, and it was a certainty based on documents and on literature. The industrial age by the 1840s had found its Aristotle.

Such is the tribute of the English acolyte. But by hindsight one might venture a different and more searching interpretation of that phrase about the Victorian Aristotle. The sober truth is that Marx's theory of class war works better as a view of ancient history than of modern. Where in human events has it even once been validated since Marx published it to the world in the 1840s? What war between his time and today can be seen in its essence as a *Klassenkampf*, as he conceived it, or for that matter any kind of war between rich and poor? The overwhelmingly significant fact about industrial class war is that, like the Second Coming, it has not happened; and the very instances that looked so promising to the expectant faithful, like the Spanish Civil War of 1936–9, have failed dismally to satisfy social prophecy or even to show that such prophecies can be self-validating. There is no confirming evidence, and the great conflicts of the modern age have been and have remained wars between regions and nations. No lack of instances of war over the past century or more: the sample is large. But it does not contain a single clear and substantial instance of what revolutionary socialists so ardently predicted as inevitable in the early and middle years of Victoria's reign.

And that, in all likelihood, is because what Victorian socialists once thought a prophetic gaze into the future was an unwitting obsession with a remote and richly documented past. Literature can delude as well as instruct: indeed it could not instruct unless it could also delude. It is tempting to conclude that Marx was a historian deceived enough by ancient literature to believe that history foretells the future as it recounts the past. Generals, it is said, would prefer to fight the last war but one – after all, they were trained for it – and it is a natural peril of the bookish mind to suppose that the future will look like past history with only a modest list of superadded and highly specific adjustments. One can be too certain of literature, if too literal. Marx was not given to observation. Though he lived after 1849 in the world's first industrial state, as an exile, he never once troubled to visit a British factory. He was a German and a theorist. He was also an early nineteenth-century classic in love with the Ancients, and above all Greek philosophy; not least with what, in his sixth notebook on the Epicureans, he called the 'frank philosophical consistency' of Greek thought. He loved things to fit together and to answer to a single formula, and he saw human reality as one: a unitary, given complex of data. The undetermined and the indeterminate did not interest him. The Greeks, he wrote in his notes in 1839, an ardent student of twenty-one,

> will forever remain our teachers, by virtue of their magnificent, objective naïveté, which makes everything shine, as it were, in the pure light of its nature, however dim that light may be.

Naïveté can be magnificent. That is something like Schiller's view before him, and it remains illuminating – of the ancient Greeks and of the modern Germans. Whether modern industrial societies are to be accurately accounted for in such a spirit is another matter.

Notes

1. Carl Grünberg, 'Marx als Abiturient', *Archiv für die Geschichte des Sozialismus und der Arbeiterbewegung* (1925–6). For a collection of studies on 'Marxism and the Classics', mainly by academic disciples, see *Arethusa* (Buffalo, N.Y.), 8 (1975); and E. M. and Neal Wood, *Class Ideology and Ancient Political Theory* (Oxford, 1978), which defends Marx's theory of class as an account of ancient history against M. I. Finley, *The Ancient Economy* (London, 1973).
2. S. S. Prawer, *Karl Marx and World Literature* (Oxford, 1976), p. 25.
3. Martin Heidegger, *Über den Humanismus* (Berne, 1947), p. 11.
4. Francis Lieber, *Reminiscences of an Intercourse with Niebuhr* (London, 1835), pp. 90–1.
5. See 'Race and the Socialists' in my *Politics and Literature in Modern Britain* (London, 1977); and 'Hitler's Marxism' in my *The Idea of Liberalism* (London, 1985).
6. Anthony Grafton and Lisa Jardine, *From Humanism to the Humanities* (London, 1986), p. xvi.
7. H. M. Hyndman, *The Record of an Adventurous Life* (London, 1911), p. 271.

11

THE IDEA OF PROGRESS

The Victorians are widely reputed for their faith in progress: a faith which, since their day, has done their reputation little good.

That is something of a paradox in itself, since no era in human history, it seems likely, can equal the first industrial age in terms of material advancement. It is far from obvious, in fact, that the Victorian theory of progress was wrong – a thought that leaves a good deal of scepticism among historians looking odd and un-explained. Some of that scepticism, it may be, is based on consid-erations that lie outside historical evidence altogether: on the sheer intellectual prestige of pessimism, perhaps, in circles where looking-on-the-dark-side can easily be represented as more sophisticated than looking-on-the-bright. (Dark always means deep, for some.) For whatever reason, it is unusual to find recent historians altogether even-handed in the matter, in the sense of being ready to take the idea of progress seriously and coolly on its proven merits. One of them, indeed – J. H. Plumb in *The Death of the Past* (1969) – has presumed to call Macaulay's mind 'coarse and obvious', which is a bold claim. No one, I imagine, would dare level that charge at John Stuart Mill; but it is still unusual to hear it suggested that the progressive idea might be justified on evidence, or that progress in living standards in the last century and in this has shown Macaulay and Mill, writing in the 1830s and 1840s, to have been strikingly and substantially right in analysis and in prophecy.

I believe they were both. 'If we were to prophesy that in the year 1930 a population of fifty millions, better fed, clad and lodged than the English of our time, will cover these islands . . .', wrote Macaulay in 1830, viewing the future hopefully through his cen-tennial telescope in a famous attack on Southey's *Colloquies* in the

Edinburgh Review; and sure enough, the population of the British Isles by 1930 was little short of fifty millions; and few historians, if any, doubt it was better fed, clad and lodged than a hundred years before. Not all Macaulay's predictions, it is true, were so happy. Right as he was to foresee that 'machines constructed on principles yet undiscovered will be in every house', he was mistaken to suppose that by the 1930s 'there will be no highways but railroads', since one of the machines based on still-undiscovered principles proved to be the automobile. Still, his theoretical confidence has not proved folly, by and large; nor Mill's cooler, more analytical prediction in the *Principles* of 1848 of some future 'stationary state', or high plateau of prosperity (I.xi.3). These men have proved perceptive, though not infallible, prophets. They were also boldly original. Little or nothing in the sources of Macaulay or Mill, after all, encouraged optimism. They *discovered* progress, so to speak: discovered general material progress to have happened, not just the enrichment of a few; and discovered it to be likely to go on happening. The progress of whole societies is a concept practically unknown, after all, to ancient, medieval and early modern man; and since it is less than commonplace in our own century, one may call it a classically Victorian view. In that case it may be worth something more than a passing tribute, and easily more than a smile. It is exceptional, surely, in so large a matter, for social theorists to have proved at once original, certain and right, or for literature to be vindicated by events themselves.

Consider first the sources, or lack of them. There was little enough in the eighteenth-century Enlightenment, whether French or British, to encourage the view that mankind was ever likely to advance in popular affluence. Macaulay read the *philosophes*, but they failed to move him. In his early thirties he projected but never wrote an essay on Voltaire, Prince of Buffoons (as he later called him), that would have presented him as 'a strange mixture of greatness and littleness', as he put it in a letter (13 February 1834); and though he distantly recognised Rousseau's genius, 'he does not attract me' (19 November 1844). The reasons are easily guessed. By 1830 the Whigs were again the natural party of government in Britain, in their own confident estimation; and Macaulay the Whig was too little of a sceptic, too much the lover of political establishments, to take much pleasure in the finicky, mocking dissidence of the Enlightenment mind. Voltaire had helped topple ancient dynasties – an ambiguous recommendation; but, as he once wrote to his father in doggerel verse, time had erased his achievements and left nothing but a grin.

Mill's view of the Enlightenment was not much different. Though an unbeliever both by upbringing and lasting conviction, the mocking voice of the *philosophes* seems to have left him equally cold. In tone and substance alike, such minds were simply alien to the Victorians. To be secular, like John Stuart Mill or his father James, was to be solemnly that; and to be more or less conforming, like Macaulay, still left the Religion of Humanity looking little more than a pale anachronism from the age of Gibbon or Robespierre. The very term 'Enlightenment' was to be coined, or reapplied, as late as the 1860s, or after Macaulay's death, by an obscure British philosopher as an ironic dismissal of a subversive idea that had spent its force in the French Revolution and its horrific aftermath of Terror. Its intellectual confidence had been shown to be self-delusion; it cast no more than a fitful light on the parliamentary world the Victorians knew.

The British classical economists, too, were ambiguous as a ground for hope. Mill and Macaulay speak of them with respect: in fact in his *Autobiography* (1873) Mill unexpectedly remarks that the main argument of Malthus's *Essay on Population* (1798), which had been 'against the indefinite improvability of human affairs', had seemed in the 1820s to the young Mill and his friends a doctrine of hope, providing only that 'a voluntary restriction' of population-growth could be secured. That is an optimistic reinterpretation of Malthus's case, only partly warranted by revisions he made to his essay in 1803 and after. But Mill was not alone in making it. In a letter of 12 February 1831, Macaulay reported happily that he had just heard the great Malthus, by then in his sixties, had been pleased with an article he had written in his defence. So the pessimism of one age, duly reinterpreted, could look like optimism to the next. Adam Smith, Ricardo and Malthus in their day had accepted the possibility, even the fact, of local and individual ameliorations; but they held that entire nations cannot improve their standard of living, in the long run, if only because wealth promotes population, and population negates wealth. 'The liberal reward of labour', wrote Adam Smith in *The Wealth of Nations* (1776),

as it is the effect of increasing wealth, so it is the cause of increasing
population. To complain of it is to lament over the necessary effect
and cause of the greatest public prosperity.   (I.viii)

In a word, you cannot win, since economic growth always tends
towards self-cancellation. That sober or dire prediction about
industrialism, more often known nowadays by Malthus's name
than by Adam Smith's, was based on two false premisses: that
birth-control could never become commonplace, as it did; and
that a variety of cheap energy-sources – coal, oil, natural gas and
eventually nuclear power – would not transform, as it has, the
productivity of the industrial world. The classical economists
monumentally failed to see that the industrial revolution might
some day enable mankind to solve the problem of poverty. Theirs
was 'the dismal science', as Carlyle mockingly called it in *Fraser's
Magazine* in 1849, piling up epithets to ironic effect: 'a dreary,
desolate and indeed quite abject and distressing one'. Karl Marx,
who settled in London that year, shared his implied view that
such pessimism was intolerable: both unaware that it had
recently ceased to be a required view among political analysts.

The theoretical optimism of Macaulay and Mill, then, by the
1840s is a startling phenomenon, and there is little or nothing in
their available sources to justify it. The classical economists had
offered only limited grounds for hope; romantic Tory revivalists
like the ageing Southey or the young Disraeli saw only regress
and stagnation since the Middle Ages; and revolutionary socialists like Engels or Marx pronounced the imminent doom of the
system. And they were wrong, where Mill and Macaulay were
right. By the 1850s, if not earlier, real wages were rising within
the existing order of things and, though subject to checks, were to
continue to rise. By the 1860s even economists were ceasing to
sound pessimistic or look dismal. Progress was plainly happening – and within a system that had once been supposed to render
it impossible. By the 1860s the cant of doom and revolution, Tory
or socialist, had given place to cant of a reverse order, and of a
kind still highly familiar. By now the system was *too* successful. It
encouraged materialism, it was said, and the moral disorders that
materialism allegedly brings. The same men who had claimed
industrialism could not solve poverty complained as loudly when
it did. But the cant was answered, and in the last months of his
life Charles Dickens himself ordered an end to it. If the object of

industry was to reduce and eventually abolish poverty, he told a Birmingham audience in September 1869, then it makes no sense to grumble when it does. 'I confess', he said,

> that I do not understand this much-used and much-abused phrase – 'the material age'. I cannot comprehend – if anybody can, I very much doubt – its logical signification. . . . Do I make a more material journey to the bed-side of my dying parent or my dying child when I travel there at the rate of sixty miles an hour than when I travel thither at the rate of six? . . . When did this so-called material age begin? with the use of clothing? with the discovery of the compass? with the invention of the art of printing?[1]

and pointing dramatically to the wall of his lecture-hall, where gas burned, he asked his audience to consider which was the more material object: 'the farthing tallow candle that will not give me light, or that flame of gas which will'.

In the generation and more since the death of Malthus in 1834, public opinion had passed from a qualified despair about material progress to Dickens's paean of confident if still qualified hope. The turning-point of certainty may be proposed as 1848–9: not because it was a year of revolution – in England, as it proved, it was nothing of the kind – but because it saw the appearance of two books. In 1848 the first edition of Mill's *Principles of Political Economy* appeared, arguing drily in favour of rising living standards through private competition until the achieved felicity was reached of a stationary state where wealth, if justly distributed, would suffice for all; and in 1849 Macaulay issued the first volumes of his *History of England*, celebrating the Whig revolution of 1689 as the true and visible foundation of British success in trade and arms both at home and abroad. By 1850 progress had won, as idea and as fact. Mill had provided a theoretical framework, Macaulay a background of political and constitutional history. Tory reaction and Marxian revolution were equally discredited, for all but a few; apocalyptic thinkers like Marx and Carlyle could retire to their studies to live out the harmless, shadowy lives of men-of-letters and hope – not without cause – that future generations might some day read them and heed them. By 1892, nine years after Marx's death, Engels himself felt compelled in a new foreword to his *Condition of the Working Class in England* (1845) to admit that there had, after all, been a real advance in the living conditions of labourers over the past half century. The rapid immiseration of the worker by the factory

system had simply not happened: quite the contrary. No wonder
the revolutionary sage looked an incredible figure to the mid- and
late Victorian mind. Disraeli, a working politician intent on the
premiership, would allow his prophecies of doom from the
hungry Forties to be gently forgotten, and must have found
Coningsby (1844) and *Sybil* (1845) an embarrassment in later life.
Progressives had not thought much of them at the time. 'As for
Disraeli and his *Sybil*,' Mill wrote dismissively in a letter in the
spring of 1849, 'I cannot imagine its being received as testimony,
or supposed to be anything but a commonplace story.' There were
sudden grounds for hope, even for complacency; and a taste for
glimpses from the English past of the causes from which a peaceful and prosperous nation had come.

What were those grounds? And how was it that after 1830 it
became possible for thoughtful beings to reverse the warnings of
earlier times and foretell a prosperous time? The step was sudden: in fact the idea of national progress seems to spring fully
armed from the minds of Macaulay and Mill in the years that surround Victoria's accession to the throne in 1837. The two seem to
have arrived at their progressive views, what is more, independ-
ently of each other, at least in large measure. Though acquainted,
they were neither friends nor allies. Six years older than Mill,
Macaulay had as a young man in London attended the Debating
Society founded by Mill at the tender age of twenty. But he is not
known to have spoken a word at it; his silence may have been less
than approving, since he was never a Utilitarian like Mill or his
father James; and in 1829 he attacked the ideas of Bentham and
James Mill in an *Edinburgh Review* article of such eviscerating
scorn that J. S. Mill was still smarting from it years later when he
came to write his *Autobiography*. Cold syllogisms like the
Greatest-Happiness Principle cut no ice with Macaulay, even in
his youth; and he dismissed the Benthamites in devastating terms
as 'smatterers whose attainments just suffice to elevate them
from the insignificance of dunces to the dignity of bores'. In the
Autobiography Mill was to call the attack erroneous, but he bitterly
admitted it had forced him to conclude the premises of his
father's argument had been 'too narrow'. No easy sympathy
here, at all events, no meeting of minds; a deep gulf in style and
temperament divided the two great progressives from first to

last. Macaulay plainly thought Mill a prig. Mill, for his part, thought Macaulay over-rhetorical and blandly indifferent to facts and statistics: excessively English, he wrote to his wife years later, in the sense that he was culpably ignorant of continental thought, and

> what all cockneys are, an intellectual dwarf – rounded off and stunted, full grown broad and short, without a germ of principle of further growth in his whole being. (19 February 1855)

Plainly the party of progress was divided, if it had ever been one. In the very letter where he had dismissed *Sybil*, Mill had already spoken out against Macaulay as well as Disraeli. 'Anything that Macaulay says is not a matter of observation', he wrote warningly, since Macaulay hardly bothers about evidence at all outside literary works, building his case airily on 'inference and argument' and spinning streams of exciting and excited rhetoric in the comfort of a gentleman's library without recourse to statistics or experience. And as to the great question itself, the condition of labourers and their families,

> I incline to think them worse off as to quantity, tho' not quality, of food than three centuries ago, and better off as to clothing and lodging – but there is a sad dearth of facts that can be relied on.

Macaulay, by contrast – or so Mill implies – was seldom put off by a dearth of facts.

The remark is fittingly cautious, for by 1849 Mill secretively knew something about the difficulty of collecting facts about poverty, and something about the still greater difficulty of doing anything about it. Long before, at the age of seventeen (or so it was whispered against him for the rest of his life), he had idealistically scattered pamphlets on contraception around London – some of them over area railings where they might be picked up by housemaids, a class of woman notoriously prone to unwanted pregnancy – and had been imprisoned for several days at the pleasure of the Lord Mayor of London, though released without a trial. As always, his motives were unimpeachably high-minded. He had seen the remains of murdered infants hanging from trees in London parks in 1823, as he walked to work in the India Office, and had later passed the hanging bodies of executed felons; and the double spectacle made him certain that over-population was a prime cause of crime and misery. He had been 'imprudently benevolent' over contraception, as a friend defensively put it years later, having been 'young during an over-population panic'.[2] Mill himself never referred to the incident, whether in the *Autobiography* or elsewhere, and may have felt it more absurd than shameful. But Macaulay knew the story – indeed all London seems to have known it – and his comment was characteristically acid. When Mill visited France after the July revolution of 1830, Macaulay derisively wrote to a friend that he must have gone there 'to preach up the republic and the physical check' (August 1830). The physical check is contraception. Old Whig and new Liberal divide here; and the fact that Macaulay should suppose Mill a republican as well as a sexual radical suggests how obstinately alien their two minds were.

Only months before, in January 1830, Macaulay had written his anti-Tory article against Southey for the *Edinburgh*. Its optimism, though bounded, was enormous, and it was not confined to his native land. Not only the English have grown more prosperous: all reasonably well governed nations, Macaulay held – provided only they enjoy prolonged peace – habitually grow more prosperous. It would be surprising if it were otherwise. Far from being pie-in-the-sky, progress is simply natural to peaceful societies and a law of history:

> We know of no country which, at the end of fifty years of peace and tolerably good government, has been less prosperous than at the beginning of that period. . . . History is full of the signs of this natural progress of society. . . . 'The industry of individuals, struggling upwards against wars, taxes, famines, conflagrations, mischievous prohibitions, and more mischievous protections, creates faster than governments can squander,

so that 'we see the wealth of nations increasing', as he puts it in a passing allusion to Adam Smith's title, in spite of the corruptions and over-spending of those who govern. Progress, in a word, is not only possible but natural to man. It is unremarkable, then, to remark on it; unboastful to boast that it is there.

Material progress is based on what individuals do, never on what governments try to do. Like socialists in this century, Conservatives in the last were habitual advocates of big government; and Macaulay's especial scorn for the Tory Southey is reserved above all for his superstitious worship of state power. 'The omniscient and omnipotent state' is ever Southey's idol, he complains, as his party is forever the party of Church establishments and centralised power. But it is not from state 'intermeddling', as Macaulay calls it, that British prosperity has grown, and may continue to grow, but uniquely from 'the prudence and energy of the people'.

As wealth increases, so does knowledge; and progress is cognitive as well as economic. Five years later, in an essay on Sir James Mackintosh, Macaulay was to propose the intellectual equivalent of his argument about rising living standards. As wealth increases, so does moral and political knowledge. You learn how to govern by governing, much as you learn to live by living – educating oneself through one's mistakes.

> The science of government is an experimental science, and ... generally in a state of progression.

So political science advances like medicine and engineering, 'depositing impurity after impurity'. The sciences themselves advance through error, after all, so that scientific error is not a ground for denying that they advance. Just as natural scientists were once misled by astrology and alchemy, so did rulers once commit such follies as persecuting heretics, founding monasteries and starting crusades. Now we know better: 'Time advances: facts accumulate, doubts arise.' And it is to intellectuals, Macaulay insisted, that we owe the first glimmerings of truth which statesmen eventually follow – an emphasis of Macaulay's highly unusual in earlier eras of Whiggery. 'The highest intellects, like the tops of mountains, are the first to catch and reflect the dawn', as he grandly puts it. Politics are no longer seen as the self-interested compromises of a hereditary aristocracy. They are ideas-in-action, they are a product of literature.

> First come hints, then fragments of systems, then defective systems, then complete and harmonious systems. The sound opinion held for a time by one bold speculator becomes the opinion of a small minority, of a strong minority, of a majority of mankind. Thus the great progress goes on, till schoolboys laugh at the jargon which imposed on Bacon, till country rectors condemn the illiberality and intolerance of Sir Thomas More.

That confident summary of the power of theory makes Macaulay sound a little like a Whig version of Lenin, for whom politics, too, was literature in action. Genius first conceives, in libraries and lonely rooms; disciples heed; then men of action act. It is an apprehension more natural to the nineteenth century than to the eighteenth, and more natural to our own age than to either. Politics, in that view, is not mere happenstance. It is certain knowledge, based on the book. It is word made flesh.

Macaulay's most striking contribution to the doctrine of politics as ideas-in-action lies in his realisation that the actors in the drama need not be great men, and may be all the more effective because they are not. The obscure, like the makers of the revolution of 1689, may succeed where a dazzling talent like Napoleon failed. Years later George Eliot was to end her greatest novel, *Middlemarch* (1872), with a reminder that lasting achievements spring from the unsung deeds of obscure people – 'unhistoric acts', as she calls them – the good of the world being half owing to those who 'lived faithfully a hidden life, and rest in unvisited tombs'. That resounding utterance, in substance, is wholly Macaulayesque. Macaulay had already rejected, in his attack on Hallam's *Constitutional History* of September 1828, the over-heroic notion that great events are of necessity made by great men. The English Revolution of 1689, on which the political greatness of the nation was founded, was indeed a great event; but it was not made by great men. It was little men, he insists, who had brought William of Orange from Holland and put him on the throne of England. 'It was assuredly a happy revolution, and a useful revolution; but it was not what it has often been called, a glorious revolution.' In fact the event was almost wholly 'discreditable to England':

> That a tyrant who had violated the fundamental laws of the country
> . . . could not be pulled down without the aid of a foreign army is a
> circumstance not very grateful to our national pride. Yet this is the
> least degrading part of the story . . .

and Macaulay goes on remorselessly to detail the personal discredits of 1689: the fawning insincerity of the English nobility; the perfidy of James II's advisers; the lies shamelessly spread by a Protestant establishment against the indubitable legitimacy of the new-born Catholic heir. . . . And the Tory opposition had been no better than the Whigs, he argues, 'ashamed to name what they were not ashamed to do': the only sacrifices made, as Macaulay witheringly put it, being Marlborough's sacrifice of his honour, which was no great matter, and Anne's of her filial affection for an exiled father, which was little more. Great events *can* be made by little men, and are. That, so to speak, is Macaulay's Law.

Hypocrisy and self-interest can establish good and lasting constitutions, as the revolution of 1689 did, where virtue and dedication like Robespierre's can altogether founder and fail. It was 'fortunate' for England and the world, as Macaulay put it, that the Reformation was made by men who cared little for religion, and the Revolution a century and a half later by men who cared little about political principles or family virtue.

It is unusual, I suspect, to hear Macaulay spoken of as a theorist; still more unusual to hear his theories spoken of as profound and just. But surely both claims are to be reasonably made. Macaulay was indeed a theorist, and far more concisely one than Mill; and the assumption that he was only interested in 'event-history' is simply false. The Whig historian selects and theorises – selects, as he knew, in order to theorise. The theories are above all in events themselves, as chosen and presented: to be briefly pointed, to be curtly and memorably judged. Macaulay knew that no modern historian can pretend to offer all the facts. 'No history can present us with the whole truth', he wrote in an early article 'History' (May 1828), any more than a painted portrait could do. All history is necessarily omissive; and the difference, as he argues, between Clarendon's history of the Civil War and Goldsmith's 'vanishes when compared with the immense mass of facts respecting which both are equally silent'. The panorama of English social life in the 1680s, what is more, that Macaulay offered in the famous third chapter of his *History of England* should have disposed forever of the myth that he was a master only of narrative – powerful as his sense of narrative undoubtedly is. The pattern of that chapter is not narrative at all but synchronic; it is a study of the total life of an age, viewed systematically from top to bottom of the social scale. Macaulay is a trenchant theorist and analyst both of history and of human affairs.

Can theories of history, in the end, be worth having? In 1945 Karl Popper proclaimed they cannot: the 'host of trivial universal laws' that historians take for granted having no serious interest, as he argued, and no total ordering function equivalent to those of science. To instance a law of history that contrives to be true only at the cost of being trivial, Popper parodistically suggests that where two armies are equally well led, big ones tend to defeat small ones.[3] Macaulay's laws of history suggest that

Popper was mistaken. No one would call them trite or trivial: in fact the Whig interpretation of history has been so often derided, in that century and in this, as to leave no doubt whatever that it is seen even by its enemies as a fallacy of vital and dangerous potency.

How fallacious, on the other hand, is it? Its first tenet, which Macaulay could have found eloquently in Burke and abundantly in the talk of his Whig friends at Holland House, was that constitutional liberties slowly acquired and in cherished memory of ancient rights, such as the English, are more likely to survive than those which, like those attempted by the French in 1789, are based on an arrogant denial of a national past. Liberty is not to be achieved by a single leap. History has not dealt badly with that law of history since Macaulay died in 1859: indeed the recent story of many a Third World state – the relative stability of India, for example, contrasted with its neighbours – leaves Burke's point, and Macaulay's, fresh and new. His second law, of which the English Revolution of 1689 is a favoured instance, is that great events do not need great men to make them – may indeed be the better without them – and that decisive turning-points can be the work of tainted ambitions and mediocre minds. And the third is that, given peace and a minimum of economic interference by the state in the life of a trading nation, material progress for all is something more than possible: it is a natural expectation, it would be surprising if it were otherwise. The point must have sounded new in the 1830s. It was certainly contested, by conservative and socialist alike. Neither Macaulay nor Mill profited much, if at all, from inherited thought, whether Whig or other. They discovered progress; and they left it to ensuing generations to discover, and to their surprise, that they were right.

Notes

1. Charles Dickens, *Speeches Literary and Social* (London, 1870), p. 252.
2. Letter by John Robertson, *Amberley Papers*, ed. Bertrand and Patricia Russell (London, 1937), II. 247–9. I am indebted to E. A. Wrigley for his advice and his recent edition of Malthus's works, 8 volumes (London, 1986) and to editions of the letters of Macaulay by Thomas Pinney, 6 volumes (Cambridge, 1974) and of J. S. Mill by F. E. Mineka 6 volumes (Toronto, 1963–73), and dates in my text refer to these editions.

3. Karl Popper, *The Open Society and its Enemies*, (London, 1945), II.251. See chapter 4, above. Popper's point has been rebutted by J. O. Wisdom, 'General explanation in history', *History and Theory*, 15 (1976), who concludes that history is a 'generality-impregnated narrative' – a phrase that aptly characterises Macaulay – and that its theoretical aspects are not required, as Popper claims, to be trivial or false.

12

THE LOST PROPHETS OF
REALISM

Henry James's critical essays, collected complete for the first time,[1] show the march of his analytical mind from the 1860s down to the First World War, and that mind can at last be conveniently viewed as a single whole. He was publishing criticism before he ever published fiction and well before he settled in England in 1876 – his abiding home, as it turned out, for forty years; and the crown of his task, as one can now see, lay in the prefaces he wrote for the New York edition of 1907–9, by which time he was over sixty, having composed all his principal fictions. So the scope is wide, in terms of years – even wider than the novels. It is also deep: so deep as to give pause. Has the theory of fiction advanced in the years since James died? and do we nowadays read novels better than our grandparents – or, for that matter, as well?

James was a realist in fiction, and it is by now commonplace in critical circles to hear realism spoken of as a thoughtless and un-theoretical creed, or one that novelists perform with little reflection for readers who do not reflect at all. It is widely imagined to be cosy. It is also spoken of, sometimes by academic critics who should know better, as if it monopolised nineteenth-century fiction, and even as if it were invented in that century. All these propositions are implausible, and it is hard to see how they could survive a reading of the essays and prefaces of Henry James. He was an unremitting theorist of realism as well as its practitioner; and nothing like its first, as he perfectly knew. In fact his year in Paris, in 1875–6, had revived in him a vivid sense of that busy world of fictional theory in a land where he had always felt almost as much at home as in London. He was well aware that realism had failed to triumph in England, in any case, as his strictures against certain unrealistic tricks by Dickens and Trollope suggest; and his attitude to his immediate English predecessors can be disdainful even when he strives against the odds to be appreciative. That is partly because he began as a young man with his way to make in the world, and ended as an old one who sometimes felt he had been undervalued by it. But it was also a matter of just observation: realism did not, in fact, possess Victorian fiction. That was the sense in which, in his view, it was unserious – even frivolous; and it was a frivolity he set out sternly to correct.

James knew, too, that the theory of fiction was nothing like new even in England. As early as the 1740s Henry Fielding had fitted out his two greatest novels with an elaborate apparatus of prefaces designed to accommodate a new realistic fiction into the ancient system of literary kinds – the 'comic epic in prose', as he venturesomely called it – and since the 1850s George Eliot had been publishing formidable critical essays in the *Westminster Review* and elsewhere, defending the philosophical claims of the realistic novel against recent theorists and sociologists. Her essays were to be collected soon after her death by her husband, in 1884, and they represent a capacious body of evidence that, for the greatest of all Victorian realists native to England, realism was not cosy or unreflected at all. It was a school which, like the Dutch painters she loved to compare it with, was consciously radical, even subversive in its purpose, and armed with powerful conceptual weapons of defence and attack. Her argument, in a nutshell, had been that a novelist who listens, observes and reports the life of a community he intimately knows is revealing more than those who, like theory-bound sociologists, believe that the end of social enquiry is the devising of general laws pertaining to whole societies; so I enlist her here, along with Fielding and James, as one of the lost prophets of realism, since all three enjoy far too little reputation as critics or theorists in the present age. And for a fourth and living prophet, Iris Murdoch – another critic-novelist – might be adduced, though her literary essays of the 1950s and 1960s unfortunately remain uncollected. Her point, as a professional philosopher, is closely akin to George Eliot's and Henry James's: that recent theorists have commonly underrated the power of realism to defend itself philosophically in critical argument, and gravely underrated too its power to inform the world or to change it, mistaking it for some tame, cosy cat-by-the-fire. In fact it is more like a tiger. Realism in fiction can damage easy assumptions about life as it is lived, or ought to be lived. It is nothing like reassuring; it is not even meant to be.

The point runs wider than modern prose fiction. England has known fictional theory at least since the sixteenth century, and theorising about the arts is a very old game in the West. That does not forbid any given theory to be called new; but if it is seriously to be called that, in fiction or elsewhere, then it would first need to be conscientiously compared with other theories available to the European mind for the past two thousand years. Unfortunately the enforced 'newness' of critical theory is a pretence that has been laboriously maintained in recent years, especially among anti-realists. In February 1986, for example, members of the Yale School of English, where theoretical interest flourished, were interviewed by a New York newspaper; and when asked whether it was true that they denied language could refer to reality, one professor painstakingly replied that he had come rather to believe, after a careful study of recent theorists, that language is 'only problematically referential'. The implication that he had once supposed the relation between literature and life to be without problems is arresting: either he had not read Plato, Aristotle and Sidney, or else he had not noticed that this was the very problem they were about. In a similar way, a British Deconstructionist has recently remarked that modern theory has finally debunked empiricism, or what he calls 'the empiricist assumption that the only way to get at the world is by dropping all the problems and simply telling things like they are'.[2] He did not mention what empiricist philosopher he had been reading, but it can hardly have been Locke, or Bishop Berkeley, or David Hume. Locke was so far from believing human understanding to be unproblematical that in 1690 he published an essay hundreds of pages long grappling at length with the issue. And it was not things as they are that he supposed to be the source of all knowledge, but ideas: 'whatever is the object of the understanding', as he exploringly put it, 'when a man thinks', be they phantasms, notions or species. Such ideas, as Locke insisted three hundred years ago, need not be based on things at all: as when one imagines monsters that never existed, or reads a romance or novel about events that never occurred. The notion that British empiricists were practical, no-nonsense types only interested in the solid objects around them could not survive even a cursory glance at their texts.

A recognition that the status of fiction is problematical is nothing like a discovery of this century, then, and it is not a view that would have remotely surprised the four prophets of realism I have just mentioned – Fielding, George Eliot, Henry James and Iris Murdoch – or, for that matter, ancient or Renaissance man. Fielding's theories adapt Aristotle's theory of story to eighteenth-century narratives in prose; and he shows no sign, in his prefaces to *Joseph Andrews* and *Tom Jones*, of imagining the task to be in any way unproblematical. Some would say he over-elaborates the problem. Several of George Eliot's most trenchant essays defend modern realism against easy and ignorant theorising: they speak out boldly for experience and sympathy, that is, against the crippling obsession of sociologists, then and now, with stated criteria, laws of behaviour and verbal definitions. Henry James's immersion in Paris literary life, as a young novelist, had taught him to respect its supreme consciousness of deliberate form, though not its morality. And Iris Murdoch has recently written an entire treatise on a two-thousand-year-old critical theory, Plato's view of art, in *The Fire and the Sun* (1977), having interested herself in such questions as a professional philosopher in Oxford since the 1940s. The suggestion that we needed 1960s Deconstruction to tell us that language and fiction are problematical will look strange to future historians, as it would doubtless have looked to Plato or to Locke.

So would the recent slogan of an 'undetermined text'; and the view, confidently supposed to follow from it, that one can no longer certainly know what novels mean. 'That the reading of a novel is a highly individualized performance by the reader, its virtue depending upon his competence, is surely common know-ledge,' Frank Kermode has justly remarked.[3] Reading texts differently, whether they be novels or the constitution of the United States – or, for that matter, interpreting events in real life differently – is indeed common enough; but it does not alter the fact that such texts and events are what they are or that some interpretations are wrong. A real event, like a quarrel between friends, might in life be subject to numerous and conflicting inter-pretations, both by the friends themselves and by onlookers to the dispute; and the parties might to the end never manage to agree on an interpretation of what happened between them, or who was mainly to blame. If 'undetermined' means something like that, then it is easy to accept that in that limited sense both life and literature are undetermined. It does not follow that no interpretation is ever false or that the truth is never to be certainly known. Critics who dogmatise about indeterminacy, what is more, are notorious for failing to live or to read as if they believed in their own dogmas. In life, as in fiction, we necessarily accept the duty of making judgements, and necessarily retain the right to think others, or ourselves, to be sometimes mistaken. Even the claim to know what constitutes a proof of indeterminacy is after all a judgement, and a contested one.

Such contradictions between theory and life have already been noticed and dissected. In *The Sovereignty of Good* (1970) Iris Murdoch, then in mid-career as a novelist, usefully revived the concept of 'attention-giving' in moral life, or what she called 'the idea of a just and loving gaze directed upon an individual reality' – instancing, in a passage of analytical philosophy that reads uncommonly like one of her own novels, a virtuous mother-in-law striving to reconsider an unsympathetic attitude towards her son's wife, whom she secretly finds silly and vulgar.[4] That attitude is undetermined, no doubt, if only in the sense that the introspective mother-in-law, who is inclined to reproach herself for a culpable snobbery, can never confidently arrive at the end of all the considerations bearing on her problem – the young woman's voice and dress, her son's evident happiness in his marriage, her own over-correct upbringing, perhaps, and its damaging effect on herself and her sense of tolerance. Such moral dilemmas, which at once require us to give attention to relations with others and yet forbid any certainty of having reached the end of everything that needs to be known or taken into account, are utterly familiar in life, and equally familiar in realistic fiction. If, in calling the meaning of a novel undetermined, it is meant that one can never certainly reach an end to the reasonable interpretations to be laid upon it, then nothing has been done by that assertion to weaken its claim to describe life, since life too is endless in the interpretative tasks it imposes. The sheer fidelity and accuracy of fiction may be all the more for that.

Endless interpretation is a proposition that the theorists of realism for two hundred years and more would have warmly endorsed. Life is more complicated than you think or, as James once put it in his notes, 'the whole of anything is never told'. Fielding's hero Tom Jones makes one wonder if the lapses that young men commit under female temptaton are rightly to be seen as lapses at all, since courage is a virtue and the young must learn through mistakes to learn at all. When George Eliot's heroine in *Middlemarch* high-mindedly married an old man out of admiration rather than love, a similar balance is finely struck; or when James, in *The Wings of the Dove*, shows a young heiress who knows herself to be dying enter into an act of willing collaboration with a conspiracy to defraud her of her inheritance through marriage, a balance is struck again. What is one to say about such cases – or do about them? Nothing simple, certainly like Do or Don't; and if it is the point of calling great fictions undetermined to say that they are not simple, then the point is uncontroversial. But it is highly confirmatory of the claims of realism to describe the real world. Life is like that. The similarity between fiction and the real is a point highly familiar, both in practice and in theory, to novelists of the last two hundred years.

Recent theorists, unfortunately, have tended to retreat in needless bafflement from indeterminacy rather than advance beyond it; and that retreat has led to a revival of the hasty notion that morality too is in its very nature irrational. The step from calling a text undetermined to asserting that no one can certainly know what it means is not a long step; nor the step from calling all morality unknowable, on the one hand, to behaving ruthlessly on the other. Perhaps, indeed, those who insist that all morality is merely personal do so because they are already resolved to behave ruthlessly, or at least to hold themselves more or less free to do so. Indeterminacy is an easy licence to do what you please.

James himself never made the mistake of doubting the moral intelligence of art. His sense of the ethically problematical is unimpeachable, and he always leaves a problem looking more complex than he found it. But complex in a radiant and inviting way. 'The house of fiction', as he put it in the preface to *The Portrait of a Lady*, has 'not one window but a million', noting the diversity of readers and their interpretations; and at each of its windows

stands a figure with a pair of eyes, or at least with a field-glass, which forms, again and again, for observation, a unique instrument, insuring to the person making use of it an impression distinct from every other.

So the notion of the undetermined text is full-blown dogma in the theoretical writings of the great Victorian realists. James's fiction is never simple-mindedly about things as they are. The millions who read are all 'watching the same show', as James puts it,

> one seeing more where the other sees less, one seeing black where the other sees white, one seeing big where the other sees small, one seeing coarse where the other sees fine,

so that, as he concludes, they are as nothing without the guiding moral intelligence of the novelist – 'the posted presence of the watcher' – whom James uncompromisingly dubs 'the artist', since he endlessly shapes the formless into form.

The artist is a technically trained being, for James: trained, that is, by reading the great masters of form. The problems of fictional form do not solve themselves artlessly or by nature, as he knew, and they are not solved by instinct: the novelist needs to have learned his trade as surely as a surgeon, or his work is a botch. For one thing, he must learn how to contrive beginnings and endings where none naturally exists. 'Relations stop nowhere,' as he put it in the preface to *Roderick Hudson*, 'and the exquisite problem of the artist is eternally but to draw, by a geometry of his own, the circle within which they shall happily *appear* to do so.' 'Appear' is italicised by James himself, and it is plain he sees realism as an artifice as refined as the silversmith's or the miniaturist's. That is why he describes so minutely the creative process of fiction: the 'germ' of an idea – heard or overheard (perhaps) at a dinner-table; its reshaping, by which the artist rejects 'the fatal futility of fact', as he gaily calls it, where real events look eager to threaten all symmetry and point; and the resolute pull of popularity, to be hearkened to and yet resisted, like the unending demands of publishers for more and more dialogue. Realism is high artifice here, beyond a doubt; and no easy assumption that realism as conscious artifice was a discovery of the last half century could survive a reading of what James wrote.

The realist's first duty is moral attention-giving. 'Consider life directly and closely', James told a class of students in 1889; and do not be 'put off with mean and puerile falsities, and be conscientious about it'. A novelist looks at life, and goes on looking – hard.

That emphasis is powerfully cognitive. Virtuous conduct demands not so much will-power as a more profound attention to details already known or glimpsed, so that the moral life in James often looks rather like typing or playing a piano where, as everyone knows, you are more prone to make mistakes when careless or exhausted. James is above all the prophet of moral alertness. It is less that we do not want to behave well, as he believes, or do not know how to, than that we are betrayed by inattention. And the problem is far more insistent than with typing or piano-playing, since moral choices are uniquely omnipresent. You cannot stop playing, so to speak, in morality, as a pianist might, just because you happen to feel tired.

James's claims for morality as a form of knowledge will strike some as his most subversive claim. But it is something ordinary people, it may be, understand better than some philosophers, as the popular phrase about 'knowing the difference between right and wrong' aptly suggests. In *The Sovereignty of Good* Iris Murdoch has chastised her own academic profession for refusing to accept something the common man usually sees to be squarely obvious:

> The ordinary person does not, unless corrupted by philosophy, believe that he creates values by his choices. He thinks that some things really are better than others, and that he is capable of getting it wrong. (p. 97)

James would not have put it quite like that, but he would not have dissented. In his magnificent Philadelphia lecture of 1905, 'The lesson of Balzac', he claimed as Balzac's distinguishing strength an ability to convince his readers that he has 'really bought' his information, as James puts it: '. . . his spirit has somehow paid for its knowledge'. It is James's uncompromising use of terms like 'information' and 'knowledge', in the context of the moral life, that by now looks strikingly subversive. Unlike Zola, he argues, Balzac has lived and not merely observed; his knowledge of moral choices was not just overheard from acquaintances, that is, or quarried out of books. In a similar way, one of George Eliot's essays is called 'How we come to give ourselves false testimonials, and believe in them'. So there is a longstanding and advanced tradition of realistic theory in England before the dawn of the twentieth century in the essays of the great novelists themselves. It is a tradition hostile to bookish abstraction and its easy self-justifications, and as openly sceptical of simple moral rules as of sociological laws.

'There is really too much to say', James engagingly remarks at the end of one of his New York prefaces, shying delicately away from such serious questions. If you want to learn morality, so he often implies, look closely, and ever more closely, at individual cases: don't ask the novelist, or anyone else, to venture dogmatically beyond the proffered instances into general propositions. James loves to speak of seeking and pursuing rather than finding; and his fastidious disinclination to pronounce on anything he has actually found may strike, at first glance, as teasing. But knowledge is none the less that for being continuously open to question and to doubt; and it is surely not unrealistic to suggest, as the great realists often do, that moral laws are endlessly subject to qualification and to exception – ill served, in the end, by the brisk formulations either of ancient moralists or of modern sages. Life apart, they tell us, it can only be fiction, in the end, that enlarges a sense of rule and exception at the same time – assuring us eternally that, in matters as fugitive and as complex as these, a tentative and enquiring certainty, in the nature of things, is all there is to be had.

Notes

1. Henry James, *Essays on Literature* and *French Writers, Prefaces [etc.]* (New York, 1985) (Library of America).
2. Christopher Norris, *London Review of Books*, 7 (1985), no. 1.
3. Frank Kermode, *Essays on Fiction 1971–82* (London, 1983), p. 73.
4. Iris Murdoch, *The Sovereignty of Good* (London, 1970), pp. 17f.

13

THE PHANTOM GHOST OF MODERNISM

A ghost called Modernism stalks our literary world.

Hardly the real thing, since few in Anglo-America are seriously trying to write poems like *The Waste Land* or novels like *Ulysses*; and the *nouveau roman* has not lasted in Paris. It is critics, by and large, not creators, who since the 1960s have reverted to the doubts, agonies, and scepticisms about language fashionable between the two world wars among the followers of T. S. Eliot and James Joyce. In academe, above all, Modernism is back.

Hamlet records that a returning spirit is supposed to have a story to tell. I want to ask what the Modernist ghost has to tell us, sixty years on and more, and whether we should heed it.

Modernism has returned with a difference. The doubts, agonies, and scepticisms of the 'Men of 1914', as Wyndham Lewis called them – meaning, above all, T. S. Eliot, Ezra Pound and himself – were about justifying claims to knowledge rather than with the far more radical scepticisms that were to dog the 1960s. Man can and does know, in the 1914 view: he merely finds it difficult or impossible to explain how he does. Scepticism was seldom total, merely provisional. With late Modernism, in the 1930s and after, that near-impossibility could convert into the very matter of poems and novels, as in Eliot's *Four Quarters* or Joyce's *Finnegans Wake*, and by then epistemological doubt had ceased to be an agony and become something like a boast. But an argument that ended as a boast began as a difficulty; a hesitant and unradical scepticism.

One salient doctrine of literary Modernism, from the start, was that no great poem could ever without fatal loss be translated, paraphrased, or explained. 'Poetry is what gets lost in translation', Robert Frost is alleged to have said. That remark, whether he made it or not, is perhaps the best summary of the school there is, and its general content may be presumed a part of T. E. Hulme's conversational legacy to Ezra Pound in the 1910s. It is certainly there in Hulme's posthumously published *Speculations* (1924): 'Images in verse are not mere decoration, but the very essence of an intuitive language'; and since that view smacks of late nineteenth-century French Symbolism, it is reasonable to guess Hulme had picked it up in Paris. That it was a late romantic doctrine of poetic language seems not to have discouraged the passionate advocate of a new classicism: Hulme took his perceptions where he found them. And Pound did not reject the view. Though a master of poetic translation, he saw it as a rigorous exercise in pastiche rather than the faithful reflection of an original – an act calculated only to widen the gap between original and translation and underline the uniqueness of both.

By the 1920s and after, Eliot's formulations of the principle of untranslatability make it clear that it was to be understood, in his view, in some absolute and unnegotiable sense. 'It is a commonplace', he remarked in a late lecture of 1942, 'The music of poetry', 'to observe that the meaning of a poem may wholly escape paraphrase.' With that 'wholly' Eliot apparently spurned any tentative prospect of compromise – the hopeful notion, for example, that a paraphrase might be helpful but not sufficient. This was defiant stuff and strong meat. And if it was a commonplace by 1942, it had been contentiously proclaimed many years earlier. In his unpublished Cambridge lectures of 1926 on the Metaphysical poets, for example, Eliot had distinguished three ways by which thought can turn into poetry: by elegant truisms like 'Gather ye rosebuds . . .'; by extended exposition, as in Pope's *Essay on Man*; and by an act of original intellection, Hulme-style, as in Dante or Donne, where a great image stands indispensably as thought itself, newly minted, irreplaceable and unique. That last is of course the supreme poetic act: 'poetic thought', as Eliot called it years later, as opposed to mere prose conviction, which he called 'the thought of a poet'. In the supreme grandeur of poetic thought, form and content are inseparable. Little use, then, ever to ask what the meaning of a poem is.

All that, however interpreted, plainly leaves great poetry

honoured in the possession of meaning. Modernism even enhanced that claim to meaning, since it proposed uniqueness in place of translatability. There is no substitute for leather, it is said; and in Modernism there was no substitute for literature. All that is light years away from the radical scepticisms of the 1960s: contrast, for example, Roland Barthes's sweeping claim in *Le degré zéro de l'écriture* (1965) that modern poetry 'destroys the spontaneously functional nature of language, and leaves only its lexical basis', words being emptied of their content and grammar shown as bereft of all purpose outside itself. Eliot and Valéry did not remotely believe anything like that, or behave as if they did; and it by modern poetry Barthes means such poets as these, then he gravely misreports them. The early Modernist held that it was teasingly difficulty, indeed, to believe in language as instrumental of meaning; and more than difficult – even frankly impossible – to explain its relation to thought and reality. But he still believed that those relations were indispensably there.

If the French New Criticism of the 1960s was the child of inter-war Modernism, then, it was a child that mocked and belied its own parentage. And that is no way to behave to a ghost. *La nouvelle critique* was a sort of juvenile-delinquent offspring of Anglo-American New Criticism, and its mocking denials went nowhere further than in its reckless rejection of meaning. For the true Eliotian, poetic meaning had been a touchstone. 'Poetry *is* meaning', that lifelong and inveterate Eliotian F. W. Bateson was fond of saying with memorable emphasis, quoting Coleridge's remark about the best words in the best order. That the meaning of a great poem is ultimately unsayable except in its own terms in no way weakens that conviction. On the contrary: a poem is all the more precious if it cannot without loss be offered in other terms. Modernism dignified literature and the meaning of literature.

It also made it endlessly difficult of approach, which may help to explain why its critical successors in the 1960s reacted to it in so impatient and inaccurate a way. If we cannot say what the relation between language and reality is, the *nouveau critique* concluded, then we do not know what it is; and if we do not know, then it is not there. Not exactly a persuasive case, that, as stripped down to its bare bones and exposed to view; but then inter-war Modernism could easily make for impatience. By the 1950s, if not earlier, it had come to look something of a charmed circle, its acolytes proudly armed with talismans like Eliot's *Sacred Wood* and uttering invulnerable slogans like 'A poem should not mean but be'; and such spectacles do naturally stir to impulsive reactions. Put up or shut up, its sceptics may naturally have come to feel. It was always, after all, a sort of chastity-belt notion of literature – a doctrine of literary language smugly concerned with its own inviolability and eternally protected against any attempt to accost, to question or to board.

It could also lead to a characteristic incuriosity. Happy in the pursuit of the butterflies of ambiguity, the Modernist critic never wanted to be told in blunt terms what anything meant: that would have spoiled the chase. Nor was one ever encouraged to investigate the merely human origins of the faith. When an entirely respectful play about the tragedy of Eliot's first marriage was first shown in a London theatre in 1984 – Michael Hastings's *Tom and Viv* – a host of disciples in the columns of the *London Review of Books* (March–April 1984) declared their outrage at the sacrilege and their virtuous determination never to read it or see it. That the life and reputation of a dead poet might be in the public domain had plainly never occurred to them; that Eliot, being a man, might be fallible, was a possibility which, however remote, they did not wish to entertain. The critical crisis over *Tom and Viv* showed that, late in the day as it is, Modernism is still a faith and a cause: an impressively well-armoured and self-protected doctrine that repels any offer, however friendly, to probe or to question.

That armour derives above all from the Modernist dogma that great poetic utterance, like Dante's or Donne's, is untranslatable into other terms. There is, in that view, a sort of 'ghost in the machine' of great poetry; which is why Modernism may be seen as ghostly in more senses than one, and insubstantial even for a ghost. Unlike Hamlet's father, this returning spirit refuses to speak clearly or tell us what to say or do. And it is no use questioning it, in the very nature of the case, as Hamlet once questioned his returning parent. For if a poem can only be expressed in its own terms, then to ask what it is about is to ask a question always to be disallowed; nor does the usual distinction between prose and verse operate here, since much of what Pound and Eliot proclaimed as critical truth they proclaimed in verse. If meaning can 'wholly' escape paraphrase, as Eliot said,

then there can be little point in asking for a paraphrase or in
venturing one's own. Modernism cannot be interrogated, then; it
can only be swallowed whole, much as Moonies swallow the
claims of their church. That is not because its literature is about
nothing, as the 1960s formalists seem to have imagined, but
because it is about something so important that any bid to paraphrase could only falsify what is there.

If all that smacks of self-importance, as it must, it may also help
to explain the elaborate stratagems of modesty that Eliot often
employed, in verse and prose alike, to ward off that entirely
natural suspicion. Eliot is our great poetic master of modesty –
none greater:

> That was a way of putting it – not very satisfactory,

he abruptly slips into *East Coker* (1940), after a moment of poetic
inflation:

> A periphrastic study in a worn-out poetical fashion,
> Leaving one still with the intolerable wrestle
> With words and meanings. The poetry does not matter.

Backtracking like that, highly Eliotian as it is – 'By this I do not
mean to say that . . .' – surely deserves, even at this distance,
something more sympathetic than a smile. Eliot was a good man
as well as a great one, and a nice man as well as good; and he lived
out his life, by choice, in a nation where self-recommendation, to
be forgiven at all, needs to be artfully disguised.

The problem, after all, was real. A great man is always likely to
have noticed that he is that; and a great poet who sets out to
reclaim poetry from triviality cannot, in the end, fudge the fact
that he is claiming to offer mighty truths. What to do? Insert
modest disclaimers, he may have resolved, which no perceptive
reader is meant in the end to take literally. And, in the end, we do
not take Eliot's claim to have found the wrestle with words and
meanings intolerable. He chose to practise it, after all, for over
half a century; and he must occasionally have noticed that he
practised it well.

But if great poems are untranslatable, and if you offer your own
as nothing less than great, then you must forever deny any sort of
attempt to explain. Explanation is always open to the charge of
reduction. Hence the vatic style of late Eliot, punctured by
moments of self-effacing disavowal. If there are ever occasions

when mock-modesty is a good idea, Modernism was surely one of them. No wonder it was fond of denying explanation and writing poems about how nearly impossible it is to write a poem, or novels about how nearly impossible to write a novel. Near-impossibility was at once its dogma and its defence. 'It is not to be read,' said Samuel Beckett in *Our Exagmination* (1929), of Joyce, 'or rather it is only to be read . . . to be looked at and listened to', since *Work in Progress* is 'not about something, it is that something itself'; and Wallace Stevens remarks in a late letter (18 April 1944) that there had once been a time – presumably when he was a young poet in the 1920s – 'when I felt strongly that poems were things in themselves'. Stevens, to be sure, got over it. But clearly Modernism in his heyday was a credo defiantly self-enclosed and impervious to external complaint or abuse. 'You cannot imagine how marvellous it felt', I remember an ageing acolyte recalling, 'reading T. S. Eliot when everyone else was reading John Masefield.'

But can we, in the end, believe the Modernist ghost?

I approach that fundamental question head-on, though shyly conscious that no head-on battle can be easily won or lost in such a matter. No use asking what the ghost means, since his utterances (as he often remarks) are immune. And if that sounds desperately like an impasse, it may be that one should not take that road at all – or at least that one should try one or two other roads as well. Better, perhaps, to outflank and surround, in the hope of wearing down an outer defence or two. Modernism is not an enemy, after all: merely an old friend who may in age have grown over-complacent and too big for his boots.

I simply do not believe, as a teacher, that great literature is unparaphrasable or untranslatable, except in a sense so absolute as to be patently overdrawn. We translate the Bible, after all; indeed most know Scripture in no other way. As for modern literature, I have paraphrased and translated too many poems, and watched others paraphrase and translate too many, to believe that poetry is 'what gets lost' when you do. If it is objected that those who spend their lives in that way could hardly be expected to think otherwise, I accept the jibe at its face value, and only wish it were true. Some teachers of literature are themselves Modernists, after all; and the contradiction is one they should be invited to confront. It can help, in life, to believe that you are achieving something – as opposed to merely claiming or pretend-ing to do so. Teachers and translators deserve to be assured they need feel no shame. If the whole Modernist claim were true, it would after all have shattering implications for any system of literary education that there is; and it is a certain mark of serious-ness in argument to be ready to follow a conviction where it leads, and to accept its consequences, however unpalatable, when one gets there.

The Modernist bluff might be called down in practical terms. There is a telling parody of a Modernist instructor in Mary McCarthy's early campus-novel *The Groves of Academe* (1953); she is a nice, naïve young woman called Domna, and she regularly preaches the inseparability of form and content to her classes. In the end, for the good of the college, a friendly colleague has to call Domna off her high horse. 'Content *can* be paraphrased', he remarks in affectionate exasperation; and the effect of denying it has been to starve students of intellectual substance and to turn them into 'sophisticated hollow men without general ideas'. Eliot once wrote a poem against hollow men, and that cannot have been exactly what he wanted. But it is what he got: it is what we all got. There were those in the 1940s and 1950s who (in under-graduate phrase) had been fatally bitten by the tsetse fly; and one remembers them still as the burnt-out cases of literary culture.

On a longer view, classic Modernism was a late, even decadent version of literary humanism. That meaning is the principal justi-fication of literature, that moral guidance is the principal object of meaning, was the fundamental insistence of Sidney's *Apology* and of the Italians from whom he borrowed; and it was the view – though not the unwavering view – of Dryden, Samuel Johnson, Wordsworth and Matthew Arnold.

Modernism departed from classic humanism in its insistence on unique formulations and its open disdain for translatability. That was its innovation, though it was not without its precursors. Shelley, a critical source Eliot would not happily have acknow-ledged, had spoken in *A Defence of Poetry* of 'the vanity of translation', comparing it with casting a violet into a crucible. But one can better judge how substantively innovative Modernism was here by comparing it to Samuel Johnson. Johnson, a classic

humanist in the old style, held that it could be a serious objection
to a poem to show that it could *not* be translated. 'The lines are in
themselves not perfect', he commented severely on *Cooper's Hill*
in his 'Life of Denham' (1779):

> for most of the words thus artfully opposed are to be understood
> simply [i.e. literally] on one side of the comparison, and metaphoric-
> ally on the other; and if there be any language which does not
> express intellectual operations by material images, into that lan-
> guage they cannot be translated.

That passage refers to Denham's famous couplet on the Thames:
'Though deep, yet clear; though gentle, yet not dull; / Strong
without rage, without o'erflowing full'. In a brisk defence of translatability, Johnson carries the humanistic credo of an indivisible
moral world to its extreme, even outrageous, conclusion; and to
minds educated on nostrums like Eliot's or Frost's – 'Poetry is
what gets lost in translation' – the suggestion is so alien that one
gropes eagerly for an escape-hatch. The whole notion is sheerly
unnerving. Can Johnson be teasing?

Not at all. 'Custom can never conquer nature,' said Cicero, 'for
nature is unconquerable.' If the common understanding of mankind outstrips, in its lasting interest, any merely historical,
regional, or individual difference or local custom, then translatability *is* after all a necessary condition of great literature. It is a
hard doctrine; hard because its very premiss, for modern man, is
so hard. And so are its consequences. It would utterly forbid
punning or equivocation, for one thing, like the coruscating
language-play that Beckett praised in Joyce's late prose; just as it
explains Johnson's celebrated contempt for Shakespearian puns
in his preface of 1765. The doctrine looks all the harder in that
Johnson refers here not only to literary languages commonly
known to learned opinion but also to any language there is or
could ever be, real or imaginary. In French, as it happens, *profond*
and *clair* do have metaphorical senses much like those of *deep* and
clear in English, when applied to what Johnson calls 'intellectual
operations'. But that appeal would not have satisfied him. It would
have to work for Hottentot too; and it would have to work for any
language you cared to invent, and not only Esperanto. In other
words (since humanism encourages the use of other words), the
literary property Modernism prized most dearly – whatever it is
that mysteriously inheres in a given language at a given time –

was something the classic humanist rejected outright as contingent, transitory, and trivialising.

It is a contrast to give thought. Why has our own century chosen to lay so approving an emphasis on the unique and distinctive capacities of a given language at a given moment to speak wisdom to its time? A great language can surely speak folly. Eliot sometimes sniffs around that issue, both in verse and prose, as one understandably troubled by what he might find there. But his voice is muffled. In *East Coker* he calls his efforts in the 1920s and 1930s 'largely wasted' – speaking of his grasp of English, which most would think enviable, as 'shabby equipment always deteriorating'; and it is characteristically hard here to sort out the modesty from the conviction. Yet he nowhere appears to imply that there could ever be any instrumentality fitter than poetic language to proclaim urgent and profound truths to a troubled time. For Eliot, language teaches, being the best there is. A troubled humanist, then; but a humanist still.

A few years later André Gide joined in the chorus for the inviolable truth of a native tongue. French syntax was not a fetter, he announced in a radio talk; years of writing French had taught him that. On the contrary it was a 'marvellous school of logic, and the submission of thought to rules – to superior, universal laws' – laws so logical, indeed, that they triumphantly resisted 'the assaults of barbarism' if duly obeyed.[1] Gide only barely stopped short of implying that in good French one can only talk good sense. Two years later, in a similarly speculative spirit, George Orwell in an appendix on Newspeak to *Nineteen Eighty-four* (1949) suggested that a future totalitarian state might enforce a language in which no one could ever tell the truth. That is the other side of Gide's strange medal: nothing but truth, nothing but lies. Orwell wriggles so earnestly over his mind-stretching hypothesis that one senses, and hopes, that he cannot quite have believed in it himself; and I do not suppose, for that matter, that Gide would have gone to the stake for his generously grateful claims on behalf of the French language. In Newspeak, Orwell says, it might be 'well-nigh impossible' ever to express an unorthodox opinion; and he meets the most obvious objections to all this – that all languages use negatives – by an argument that borders engagingly on the desperate. One could still call a dictator evil, admittedly – 'Big Brother is ungood':

But this statement, which to an orthodox ear merely conveyed a self-evident absurdity, could not have been sustained by reasoned argument, because the necessary words were not available.

But in the end that does not persuade. However loaded a language may be, it surely remains possible to unload it, laborious as the process might be: by inventing and adapting new terms, for example, by reviving old ones, by inserting or deleting negatives ('Freedom is not slavery'), and by using a host of qualifiers like paradox and irony. If there exist 'systematically misleading expressions' – to quote the title of a famous old article by Gilbert Ryle – it is none the less possible, as Ryle equally showed, to expose them. *Possible* here means linguistically possible. The state might choose to forbid such behaviour; but it remains bluntly implausible to suggest, with Gide, that a language could make one talk nothing but sense or, with Orwell, that it could make one talk nothing but lies. It is not even possible, I suggest, to *conceive* of a language like that. I should be happy to offer a cash prize to anyone who can invent one or find one.

Modernism was usually less extreme than that. It was not Eliot's case, or Pound's, that a given language might be all truth or all lies. Nor did they claim, like post-structuralists such as Barthes, that in its very nature it cannot perform any instrumental or realistic function. The Modernist case, at once humanistic and yet critical of classic humanism, lay somewhere in the middle. That is its interest; that is its abiding appeal; that, perhaps, is why in academe it is back, or why it never quite went away. Its interest and appeal lie in that precarious balance it once struck between literary realism and scepticism. Modernist language describes – but only just; mankind can know – but only laboriously, fragmentarily, and after painful assessment of the difficulties; and there are no certainties, least of all immediate certainties. 'We have no direct (immediate) knowledge of anything', the young Eliot concluded his Harvard thesis of 1914, when he was a philosophical pupil of Bertrand Russell: 'The "immediately given" is the bag of gold at the end of the rainbow. Knowledge is invariably a matter of degree: you cannot put your finger upon even the simplest datum and say "this we know."' Those words ended an academic thesis on F. H. Bradley published late in Eliot's life as *Knowledge and Experience* (1964), and the chosen topic guarantees a philosophical source in nineteenth-century German idealism and its recent interpreters like Bradley and Russell. As a conviction, it was to change rather little during Eliot's lifetime. He was still a self-critical Idealist a quarter of a century later, writing about the problems of language in *East Coker*: a poem that restates in verse the solemn contention of his 1914 thesis that 'the mental resolves into a curious and intricate mechanism, and the physical reveals itself as a mental construct'. That precarious view, forever certain about uncertainty, was a constant in his thought over years and decades; and it helps to explain the prevailing intellectual tone of *The Waste Land* and of *Four Quartets* alike: a solipsism earnestly contested and only narrowly evaded, as of a claustrophobe fearful of entering a dark tunnel. Or so it may have seemed to Eliot, to whom total scepticism was always fearful. To the reader, by now, it all looks more elegant than alarming, like the high-wire act of a supreme circus acrobat, and latter-day Modernism is more likely to startle an agoraphobe than a claustrophobe. In Borges, Beckett, and Calvino, still more – that BBC of postwar Modernism – it is amusing rather than taxing, a way of showing oneself off in an accomplished mood of metaphysical whimsy. When a real professional does it, vertigo can be fun. And when the danger stops, in acrobatics, so does the interest. In Modernism, as in circuses, the danger *is* the interest.

It is in that danger, perhaps, that the return of Modernism to critical favour may ultimately be explained. Its lasting appeal, at least, was plainly never political or religious. Among the early advocates of Eliot, few shared his dogmatic interests, which from the late 1920s were Christian-conservative; still fewer Pound's enthusiasms for Mussolini or fiscal reform. The great Eliotians were spectacularly secular and radical minds, on the whole: I. A. Richards, William Empson, F. R. Leavis, F. W. Bateson, and their long host of successors. The paradox was known and felt at the time: hero-worship of Eliot persisting awkwardly down the years in an embarrassed consciousness of a vast dogmatic divide.

That leaves the task of discovering the causes of a revived Modernism somewhere outside politics and religion altogether. Recent Modernist critics like Frank Kermode or Christopher Ricks have tended to be a bit unspecific about all this – apart from a continuing insistence, which no one contests, that Eliot wrote good poems. As friendly onlookers, we have to struggle to compensate for that vagueness with our own precision; and I suggest that such precision is to be found, though not easily found, in untranslatability.

Untranslatability, it must be said, leaves the Modernist ghost as insubstantial as ever. But then its insubstantiality is essential to it, as it always is to ghosts. The hero of Noël Coward's *Blithe Spirit* (1941) discovers he cannot touch his first wife, Elvira, when she inconsiderately returns from the dead, but finds her none the less attractive for that. Non-substance lies at the heart of the Modernist mystery. And it is no disrespect to living disciples of the faith to say that they have taken a tactical argumentative shelter behind untranslatability, as if content to gesture toward Eliot's doctrines about truth and language and leave them much as they found them. 'We have our inheritance.' As faithful disciples, in the end, they had no choice but that.

For their refusal to argue about essentials is in the end essential to the creed, their incuriosity a hallmark of their school. No wonder they stayed away from *Tom and Viv*; no wonder they should be so anxious in their public protests that the world should know they had stayed away. That refusal to discuss is inescapably at the heart of their doctrine. If great poets cannot be paraphrased, they can only be worshipped; if great poems cannot be translated, they can only be praised.

Nor is this to be dismissed, in all the instances, as a canny evasion of critical responsibility. There is too much passionate sincerity at the heart of radical Modernism in our times, crucified as it is on the manifest contradiction of acknowledging a religious conservative as its poetic leader, to admit much place for guile; though it is undeniable that the movement has been kept alive, at least in part, by that continuing academic passion for what the Germans call a *Problematik* – a complex of problems endlessly inviting admiring debate and never ending in a conclusion. A good deal of such critical theorising reminds one of some vast dam-building project in southern Asia, where the unspoken fear lies in the thought that the work might some day run out and the World Bank turn its attentions elsewhere. Criticism has its over-manning problems nowadays, like other industries in western economies since the 1970s; and some of the agonies of late Modernism are not only sincere but real.

To the outsider, however, happy as he may be to call Eliot a great poet and Joyce a great novelist without endorsing a dogma or sharing a cult, the phenomenon of a revived Modernism has its provoking aspects. Eliot's achievement after *Ash-Wednesday* (1930) in plays and poems looks more than ever like a matter of scattered aphorisms rather than a coherent wisdom; his later critical achievement likewise; and fragments do not cohere merely by parading their fragmentariness and propounding a faith beyond themselves. Eliot's claim in *Ash-Wednesday*, that radiant poem that appears to track his own religious conversion, seems to be that devotion would somehow put it all together for us, if only we let it, and that the Church of England can be called in to finish a job that Hegel and F. H. Bradley between them could not quite manage. I do not believe that will wash. You cannot really get from critical idealism to Anglicanism, as an argument, and even the eloquence of Eliot fails to show that you can.

Dogmatically speaking, Modernism has latterly come to enjoy some of the convenient advantages of a way-station or perch. As hairs grey and arteries harden, so do radical critics by stages turn conservative. They turn earlier, often, than they are ready to admit they have turned – even to themselves. And there can be a tactical advantage in sitting on the Modernist perch as one wonders where in the world next to lodge. In recent years Modernism has proved a godsend to the politically disillusioned. It is an apt place for the ironist; and irony can be the best defence there is against the charge of apostasy, being a habit of mind that forbids serious questioning. It may be no coincidence that the last-but-one bout of critical formalism, which was the American New Criticism in the years after 1945, occurred during another era of fading radical enthusiasm: a turning away from admiration of the USSR, in the era of Arthur Koestler and George Orwell, facetiously known to some at the time as the Retreat from Moscow. Formalism puts little dogmatic strain on its acolytes. Detachment is its substance; irony is its style. Its instability is its charm. Nobody could feel under any obligation to canvass wet streets for a conviction as nebulous as this.

For how *can* one explain or test a doctrine that no one is ever allowed to paraphrase? If we may not say, 'By this Eliot meant that . . .', then the critic is forever bound to an uncomfortable or admiring silence, or to a display of language seldom better than self-regarding.

That, at least, is how a loyal and consistent disciple would behave, were his loyalty and consistency altogether unwavering. It is in his occasional failure or refusal to do so – in the disparity between what he says and what he does – that the first chink in that armoured doctrine may appear.

Notes

1. André Gide, 'The French language', in *From the Third Programme*, ed. John Morris (London, 1956), p. 201, from a BBC broadcast of July 1947.

14

THE WHIG INTERPRETATION
OF HISTORY

In 1931 Herbert Butterfield's *Whig Interpretation of History* appeared; and by now its exposure of the distortions of the vantage-point represents something like a professional orthodoxy in the English-speaking world. The book 'brought to an end', one historian has remarked with evident approval, 'an epoch of historical writing';[1] and when Butterfield died in 1979, an obituary by a Cambridge pupil exultantly declared that the book had 'finished off for good the cosy notion that English history was a pretty smooth and undoubtedly designed and masterly progression from tyranny to liberty, and from poverty to wealth'.[2] The anti-Whig today speaks with the certainty of one who brooks no debate. He believes he has finally discredited not just a long liberal tradition of political interpretation but the wider humanistic view that the past could ever teach mankind how to govern or to live – the ancient and Renaissance notion that history is a moral enquiry and that instructive patterns and recurrences are to be ascribed to the past. Among professional historians in Anglo-America, at least, the humanistic sense of history as an edifying fable, with rare exceptions, has by now become a matter for detached debate or easy derision.

That is to turn the tables. 'Our ancient history is the possession of the Liberal', Freeman wrote triumphantly in 1872,[3] with equal certainty. No era is now that. In fact two recent books on the nineteenth-century English mind – J. W. Burrow's *A Liberal Descent* (1981) and *That Noble Science of Politics* (1983) by Collini, Winch and Burrow – seek only to confirm Butterfield's sceptical claims, though not without the echo of a sigh for enviable moral certitudes now vanished, as they suppose, beyond recall. *That Noble Science* calls itself anti-Whig in its very prologue, and specifically in Butterfield's non-party use of the term, since the Whig interpretation was never the property of a single party – scorning the notion that history could ever help us to draw 'nourishment, or some other form of comfort, from the past' and taking for granted, as usual, that the Whig interpretation was optimistic, even cosy. And the victorious anti-Whig stands ever-viligant to repel any attempt at revival. A new study of the parliamentary crisis of the 1750s, J. C. D. Clark's *Dynamics of Change* (1982), darkly complains that Whiggism may have secretly survived the frontal assaults of Butterfield and Lewis Namier under guiltily assumed names, 'to provide foundations for new misrepresentations', so that it may need to be rooted out of its underground hide-outs and exterminated anew.

All this historical *machismo* is surely very quaint. Historians are commonly amiable, harmless beings in their private lives, which tend to be quietly herbivorous in tempo, complacent in the enjoyment of civil rights like immunity from confiscation and arbitrary arrest, and almost tediously respectable whether in suburban villa or country cottage. Perhaps that helps to explain why in public they are so eager, by over-compensation, to look hard-faced, cynical and morally detached. At all events, it is notable that only the boldest among them in Anglo-America today would openly dare to speak for moralised history, and he would know that he risked the lively derision of his colleagues if he did. Teaching history is not supposed to concern itself with what history has to teach: all that belongs to our ancestors, it is thought, somewhere between the habit of painting themselves in woad and the happy invention of scientific methodology. In some continental traditions, it is true, like the *Annales* school in France, didactic theories fitfully survive; but with exceptions mainly on the extreme Right and Left, the Butterfield view of 1931 is largely triumphant throughout academic history in English – an established certainty – and conservatives can be as anti-Whig and as anti-moralising as anyone. Past events, Michael Oakeshott wrote some years ago, 'have no overall pattern or purpose, lead nowhere, point to no favoured condition of the world, and support no practical conclusion'.[4] Like literary theorists, historical theorists in recent times can be marvellously proud of doing nothing, achieving nothing, asserting nothing. There are no lessons in history, in the anti-Whig view, except that there are none – an interesting self-exception. Burke, Macaulay and Acton were wrong.

I want to ask whether such widespread acceptance of anti-humanism among historians, and more especially of anti-Whiggery, can be justified as argument or principle. And for that purpose two related issues need in turn to be confronted: whether there are patterns or recurrences in history at all; and if so, whether they are Whig.

Patterns and recurrences

If recurrences did not happen in history, it is hard to see how one could use words. The milder term 'recurrence' may perhaps be preferred here, since patterns are usually thought of as repeating at exact intervals. A recurrence, then, is a loose pattern. The larger movements of heavenly bodies are precisely recurrent; political and social events are not often as certain and exact as that unless, like presidential elections in the United States, they are created by human fiat in fixed terms. But then even those who propose bold laws of human flux, like Nietzsche in the last century or Oswald Spengler and Arnold Toynbee in this, do not usually suggest that events return at stated and precisely predictable periods.

It could only be strenuously paradoxical, surely, or heavily over-defined, to deny altogether the humanistic claim that classes of events recur. Humanism goes further. It is based on a recognition that recurrences and likenesses are not only more significant than differences but represent an indispensable means of understanding ourselves and others. In a preface to Plutarch (1683), for example, Dryden remarks in conventional vein that history is not only entertaining but instructive, helping 'to judge of what will happen by showing us the like revolutions of former times' – mankind being 'the same in all ages, agitated by the same passions, and moved to action by the same interests'. That classic view of history is one Plutarch himself, or Erasmus or Samuel Johnson, would have echoed. It has regrettably few defenders nowadays among professional historians, who have trained themselves studiously to discern uniqueness rather than like-ness; but then that training can sometimes secrete a stubborn mis-understanding of what humanism means and of what it can do.

Writing only five years before the English Revolution, Dryden did not seek to deny that any given revolution is unique: only that what revolutions have in common could plausibly signify less than their differences. He held that likenesses come first. And rightly: for if we did not believe that revolutions were alike, we should not use the same word to describe what happened in Eng-land in 1688–9, in France a hundred years later, in Russia in 1917 and in Iran in 1979; and if, similarly, we did not believe the Eng-lish, American and Spanish civil wars were alike, we should not use the same term to describe all three. That is as clear in dis-agreements among historians as in agreements. 'Simon de Mont-fort was not Asquith in armour', an anti-Whig historian once remarked, denying that his assembly in 1265 was in any sense popular or parliamentary. But to judge whether his assembly is rightly called a parliament involves seeking likenesses, as well as differences, between the thirteenth century and the twentieth, so that the argument necessarily concerns what is like and unlike at the same time. Or again, there are historians, mainly from the Old South, who prefer to call the American Civil War a War between the States, on the scrupulous or partial ground that an attempted secession like the Confederacy of 1861 fails to satisfy one necessary condition of all civil wars: that they should be fought, as Cromwell and Franco once fought, for power over a whole nation. That too is a dispute about likeness. Revolutions, again, are sometimes held of necessity to be popular and left-wing – though, as Kerensky often insisted, the October revolu-tion in Russia was not popular, and though the Iranian revolution in 1979 was far from left-wing. To settle such disagreements, which might after all be of substantial interest – or even to try to settle them – would be to debate the respects in which these events were at once like and unlike other instances of wars and revolutions.

Butterfield rightly called an emphasis on likenesses the hall-mark of the Whig interpreter such as Macaulay and Acton, as it is of the humanist in general. The Whig is 'viligant for likenesses between past and present,' he protested in 1931, 'instead of being viligant for unlikenesses' (pp. 11–12). But that is one of the oddest

of disjunctions to be made here. We observe likenesses and unlikenesses in a single and continuous process, as contested cases
like the American Civil War or the Iranian revolution suggest,
and could not do one without the other. Likeness is not identity,
and it would be a perverse objection to humanism to insist that
every human event is in the end unique. Nor is likeness necessarily dependent on a single property or group of properties being
held in common, as Wittgenstein's famous analogy of family
resemblances shows: 'Don't say "There *must* be something in
common, or they would not be called games"', he argued. 'Don't
think, but look.'[5] That is as true of parliaments, civil wars and
revolutions as of games. In fact Wittgenstein's talk of overlapping
and criss-crossing is much to the point here: we do not need a
common set of properties, for example, in order to call a given
event a revolution or a civil war. The American Civil War might
after all have been unique among civil wars in that it was not
fought for power over a whole nation, and still, one might conclude, represent an instance of civil war. The overlapping and
criss-crossing in that case is simple in a plain and exemplary way:
most such recognitions in daily life – 'Is that a bed or a sofa?' –
would, under analysis, prove far more complex to unravel. It is
none the less extraordinarily difficult to persuade the anti-Whig
historian that he is necessarily engaged in a study of likenesses
when he uses familiar terms. Those whose avowed interest is in
the uniqueness of events, and only in that, need to be told that
they cannot judge an event to be unique without first comparing
it with other and similar cases; and for that purpose they would
first have to perceive similarities. In fact it is only because cases
are alike, on the whole, that it is worth commenting on their
unlikeness. People seldom ask 'Is that a bed or a lamp-post?'

It is sometimes thought, for all that, that terms like civil war,
revolution and parliament are uninteresting instances of pattern
and recurrence, and that the great pattern-mongers of history are
usually hunting bigger game than triflingly lexical issues like
these. With Nietzsche, Spengler and Toynbee that was certainly
true; equally with Marx and the Marxians. Even superstitiously
progressive theories of history, after all, denying return or regress
as they dogmatically must, accept recurrence in another sense –
as Marxists have traditionally believed that proletarian revolution
in one land must inevitably recur in others. Such views, it is now

clear, are sadly vulnerable to events themselves. Whiggery is not vulnerable in that sense, as it happens, since it embraces no dogma of inevitability: it studies the conditions by which human liberty can thrive and has thrived, but makes no claim that it must.

There are two large weaknesses in the anti-Whig case here. One is to suppose that procedures as allegedly obvious as the naming of revolutions, parliaments and civil wars are not procedures at all, since they come so naturally to mind. But how naturally, in fact, do they come? When the historian employs such terms, he can easily forget how much of the business of comparison and connection-seeing is built into the very words he imagines uncontroversial and uncommittal. A dissentient voice like the American Old South, or Kerensky on Lenin, or the questioner who asks whether socialism is left-wing, at least serves to show how committal and potentially controversial such terms can be. And they do not cease to be that merely because it is easily forgotten by common usage that they are. When the work is well done, it is perilously easy to forget that it ever needed to be done at all; when ill done, it can be hard to undo. Not that the Butterfieldian openly denies how committal such terms are in identifying likenesses. It might be better to say he simply has not noticed it, veiled as it is by sheer familiarity. It may be sorely tempting, for just that reason, for him to undervalue the humanistic case in general and the Whig in particular.

The second anti-Whig claim, often made with a touch of glee, is to gesture towards an absurd theory or generalisation with the implication that any belief in historical recurrence would require acceptance of any theory of recurrence there is. Popper's ironic instance of big armies defeating smaller ones is an example.[6] But all that is too easy. To cite a reverse case: suppose it were suggested that a belief in uniqueness and unlikeness required the historian to accept any factual claim ever made – that Augustus Caesar or Napoleon, for example, never existed, or that Bacon wrote Shakespeare. Anyone can see what is the matter with that. It is easy enough to accept that some grand theories of history are merely fatuous. So, for that matter, are some factual claims. But exposing the laws of Toynbee's *Study of History* as truistic or false does no serious damage to humanism in general or to historical theorising in particular – just as studies in the Bacon-wrote-Shakespeare tradition do no serious damage, of a general sort, to factual enquiry. There can be bad instances where not all instances are bad.

The case for humanism in history, then, stands, and not uncertainly. If there were no recurrences in the past, there could be no language. And if no language, no historians.

Whigs and anti-Whigs

So much, in summary, for the wider issue. The case for the Whig interpretation needs to be more specific.

In 1819 Lord John Russell, a future Prime Minister, ended a life of his martyred ancestor Lord William Russell, executed with others by Charles II for treason in 1683, in these ringing terms:

> It is to their spirit, and to the spirit of men like them, rather than to any unalterable law, that we owe the permanency and the excellence of our ancient constitution.

Russell was to alter that ancient constitution himself a dozen years later, in 1832, with the first Reform Act; and the remark may be accepted as a classic statement of Whig interpretations of British political history by one determined to make more of it. That at least disposes of the easy charge of complacency. It was not an unalterable law of history that made British liberty but the readiness of men to die for it; and it is a mindless slander on the Whigs to suppose that they thought of human progress as inevitable or easy. Though Macaulay was an optimist, in many ways, Acton could be monumentally pessimistic, and the entire tradition of Whig historiography is neither clearly bright nor clearly grey. It is, however, clearly striving. The Italian Risorgimento, G. M. Trevelyan once wrote, 'was not inevitable, but was the result of wisdom, of valour, and of chance'.[7] Of *chance*: the Butterfieldian view may not be reliably deterministic, but the Whig view is always reliably anti-deterministic. That is what makes the phrase initially quoted so strikingly unjust: 'to draw nourishment or some other form of comfort from the past'. The Whig does not draw only comfort from the past, and not even mainly that. He praises the valour of heroic men whether they succeeded or failed, and his lessons can be bitter. 'Laws exist in vain for those who have not the courage and the means to defend them', wrote Macaulay starkly in 1832 in his essay on Burleigh, during the Reform Bill crisis. More like a cold shower than comfort. The Whig past is not cosy but strenuous, and you sometimes have to die for it.

By 1849, when Macaulay's *History of England* began to appear, there were cautious hopes of a peaceful solution to a prolonged constitutional crisis. The anti-Whig has latterly chosen to look blandly unimpressed by that surprising outcome in the first industrial nation on earth. His own cosiness is notable. Butterfield emphatically denied there were any general conclusions to be drawn, here or elsewhere. The 'value of history', he maintained, 'lies in the richness of its recovery of the concrete life of the past' (p. 68), its meaning not to be conveyed by 'dry lines' or by any 'species of geometry'. But diagrams can have the useful truth that belongs to diagrams, and it can, on occasion, be just the sort of truth that is needed. There is a well-known diagram of the London Underground by which travellers find their way; its value would not be enhanced, and might easily be impaired, by a greater richness of detail. Dry lines can be helpful, similarly, in great issues of state. Many in the 1830s and after believed that parliamentary reform was necessary to preserve ordered liberty, and that Tennyson's diagram of broadening precedent, or one thing at a time, was the safest way forward:

> Where Freedom slowly broadens down
> From precedent to precedent

– a better way, as their reading of the seventeenth century suggested, than a more violent path taken by Pym and Cromwell after 1642. A double shift towards industrialism and political democracy was achieved in Britain without bloodshed. That was the Whig victory. No other nation could do it; no other nation did. And if the geometry of the Whig interpretation did not contribute massively to that achievement, then it needs to be said why actors and observers alike believed at the time, and on visible evidence, that it did.

The anti-Whig is fond of attacking his adversaries for oversimplistic judgements, as if Whiggery and priggery were much alike. Butterfield opened his essay in 1931 with a claim that Whig assertions were in their nature over-simple, and one remembers with a shock of recognition that the essay appeared only a year after a little comic masterpiece called *1066 and All That* (1930):

One may be forgiven for not being too happy about any division of mankind into good and evil, progressive and reactionary, black and white. . . . (p. 1)

And he later complained of 'simple and absolute judgements' (p. 75) and the Whig 'abridgement of history' – only possible because in that tradition 'all the facts' are never told 'in all their fullness' (p. 24). Knowingly or unknowingly, Butterfield here echoes an ampler plea for many-sidedness that Stubbs had made over sixty years before, in an Oxford inaugural of 1867, where he placed these principles high among the lessons of history:

> That there are few questions on which as much may not be said on one side as on the other; that there are none at all on which all the good are on one side, all the bad on the other; or all the wise on one, and all the fools on the other.[8]

Telling all the facts in all their fullness. . . . But is it even *possible* to write history in that way? Butterfield pursues his point by comparing the historian to a witness rather than to a judge or jury (p. 131), and he does not seem to understand how fatal to his own case that court-room analogy is. For if a witness were allowed or required to tell all the facts that he knew or thought he knew, he would never finish; and if he never finished, the trial would not.

Butterfield might reply that when he speaks of facts here – 'all the facts . . . in all their fullness' – he means all the facts relative to the question to hand. But the decision whether a fact relates to a question is one for a judge, not for a witness. The historian does not cease to resemble a judge, then, when he resolves to tell all he knows. He judges as he tells, if only in what he admits and omits. Abridgement is unavoidable, then, however history is written; so is selection. Sir Karl Popper used to ask his class in Vienna to write down everything they could observe, prompting an understandable bafflement; and he tells the story to illustrate the ultimate poverty of induction:

> Observation is always selective. It needs a chosen object, a definite task, an interest, a point of view, a problem.[9]

The real question is not whether judgements are made. They are always being made, one way or another. The question is whether they are well made. In writing history, as in living lives, there is no escaping the task of judgement.

Anti-Whigs often assume that judgements of value are merely personal or subjective. Butterfield opened his essay in 1931 with a brief disparagement of 'partial judgements and purely personal appreciations' (p. 2), as opposed to reliably expert pronouncements on matters of fact; and towards the end of the essay, where he opens his main attack on Acton, his deeper assumptions about the necessary subjectivism of value-judgements become disarmingly clear:

> Such judgements are those of the historian himself; their value is the measure of his acuteness; their bias is the clue to the inclinations of his mind. They are not the judgements of history, they are the opinions of the historian. (pp. 104–5)

And again:

> The problem of their sinfulness is not really an historical problem at all. . . . Moral . . . responsibility lies altogether outside the particular world where the historian does historical thinking. (p. 118)

And his reasons are twofold: that it is difficult or impossible to win agreement on points of morality, as he imagines, and equally so to 'find the incidence of these upon any particular case'.

But why should moral truth, or any other kind, be thought in any way to depend on agreement? Much that is true is unagreed, and none the less true for that. Flat-earthers dispute the shape of the globe; historians contest among themselves such factual questions as the origins of the First World War; and in law the accused are liable to punishment whether they believe murder or forgery to be wrong or not, and courts do not even seek their agreement on such matters. We do not *need* to have agreement about the truth in order to have it, and it is not reasonable to expect it or even to want it. Silly people continue to believe silly things.

The difference between the factual and the moral, in any case, is not at all like the difference between what is agreed and what is not. Historians frequently disagree about points of fact as well as about morality, and factual disagreements such as those over the origins of the 1914 war are fertile of debate. Conflicts of views often are. In his Cambridge inaugural of 1895, Acton invited his audience to remember Charles Darwin

> taking note only of those passages that raised difficulties in his way; the French philosopher complaining that his work stood still because he found no more contradicting facts,[10]

since it is by considering objections and counter-opinions that scholars contrive to advance at all. To conclude that moral judgements are personal to the historian rather than agreed does nothing, then, to put them outside what Butterfield called 'historical thinking'. It might rather put them inside. Thinking needs disagreement to move on; it thrives on reasoned dissent.

If it were sufficient to show that no agreement is to be had to call an issue subjective, then many highly factual issues in history would have to be deemed subjective. And if the reverse were true, then many moral issues like the modern condemnation of slavery would have to be deemed objective, and on that ground alone. But of course the difference between objective and subjective judgements is nothing like the difference between what is agreed and what is not.

Nor is it clear that value-judgements are regularly distinguishable from factual statements. 'He is good at chess' means much the same as 'He usually wins at chess', but most would call the first remark evaluative and the second factual. That illustrates, in a simple and diagrammatic way, the extreme artificiality of fact/value distinctions. If the historian is to be called a witness, then witnesses too often have views on the guilt of the accused; and such views are factual and evaluative at the same time. It is a factual matter whether the accused is a forger or a murderer, or which government bears the heaviest responsibility for a war; and a value-judgement too, since it is better to be innocent than guilty. (Not just better for the accused or his reputation, that is, but better absolutely.) When Acton, in a note on the detested Inquisition, wrote bluntly 'They sent forth murderers', his assertion is factual and evaluative too. The historian does not abandon the evaluative function in history, then, when he confines himself to facts. Knowing and judging are one.

Butterfield's anti-Whiggery was proclaimed, it may be recalled, in 1931, or some years before the theoretical writings of Karl Popper or R. G. Collingwood on the nature of intellectual enquiry were widely available to historians. Philosophically speaking, his view was not entirely old-fashioned at the time; but it is astonishing that historians have questioned it so little since. It is still common to hear them talk as if preconceptions were an unfortunate personal intrusion into historical research, rather like catching mumps – to be regretted or dismissed as bias, prejudice, or (in the most severely reductive sense of the word) ideology. But historians need preconceptions to work at all, and they are under no obligation to apologise for what they cannot dispense with. Any expedition, even the most scientific, starts from home. Any intellectual enquiry starts from somewhere. That is not a matter for regret. In a chapter called 'Question and answer', Colling-wood in his *Autobiography* (1939) argued how absurd it would be to read an author or excavate an ancient site without starting from a testable hypothesis as to what the author or builder meant when he wrote or planned. It is no serious objection to Whig historians, then, if they interpreted British political history to determine how one nation established a continuous rule of law that lasted for decades and even centuries. Their answers may be right or wrong. But it is hard to believe that they were wrong to ask the question or to answer it.

Butterfield's model of piling fact upon fact in the hope of an ever richer complexity is in the end an absurdity – an absurdity, fortunately, that he preached but did not practise. *The Whig Interpretation of History* is a suavely shaped and sharply worded historical polemic in a rhetorical tradition that owes much to Macaulay; a classic instance, in fact, of an argument-against-itself. If it had tried to observe its own stockpiling precepts, it would never have been written at all.

Beneath anti-Whiggery, in our times, has lain what might be called a terror of anachronism: an echoing insistence that histori-cal events are best interpreted in terms of their own age rather than one's own.

Butterfield repeatedly inveighs against judging matters 'apart from their context' (p. 30); and in an exceptionally interesting analysis near the close of his essay he comes astoundingly close, for so virtuous a man, to condoning persecution and political murder:

> Faced with the poisonings of which Alexander VI is accused, it is for the historian to be merely interested, merely curious to know how such things came to happen. . . . (pp. 119–20)

He invites his ideal historian to set moral judgements to one side 'for the time being', striving rather to 'explain how Mary Tudor came to be what she was'. That approaches an extreme of dogmatic relativism, at least for the time being, and in a manner highly ambiguous. It is uncontroversial, no doubt, to suggest that no one should condemn the Smithfield burnings of heretics before the pertinent facts are clear; and helpful to urge the historian not to write like a prude or a ranter. But the advice plainly goes further than that. It seeks to expel morality. Acton, similarly, has been intemperately attacked by a more recent historian for his 'heavily moral attitudes' and a naïve 'astonishment at the commonplace'.[11] And the same old anti-Whig ambiguity remains: does that mean morality is to be excluded from history altogether, or that it should be admitted only in some lighter vein? (Strange to accuse Acton, of all people, of doubting that religious persecution has been commonplace in human history.) There are undeniable differences in pace and tone between Victorian historiography and our own, and something should be conceded here to a shift of style. But such differences are not always to the advantage of the moderns; and anyone who disparages the style of Macaulay and Acton should pause to ask himself, in all modesty, whether he can write as well.

The demand to see everything in context, and only there, remains an odd one: all the odder because Butterfield himself can occasionally see how odd it is. Whether as historians or as readers, we are what we are. 'History must always be written from the point of view of the present', he incautiously concedes (p. 92), the historian's task being to translate the past into terms that are understood today. But it is a question whether translation is enough, and the implication that to understand is to withhold condemnation does not, on reflection, convince. Suttee, for example, or the enforced suicide of widows, is a notorious limiting case here, and there have been others. Butterfield wrote before the advent of Hitler, and his entire argument has a cosily academic air about it, as if at once pre-Bolshevik (which it was not) and pre-Nazi. Reality is held at bay. On the first day of the Second World War he stopped a Cambridge colleague in the street, it is said, and remarked: 'Wouldn't it be wonderful if neither side won?' That was not his last word, to be sure, and *The Englishman and his History* (1944) shows that a complacent relativism did not survive the war. In that generous retraction he regretted a 'misguided austerity of youth' that had possessed him a dozen years earlier, and he warned that a room swept clean 'cannot long remain empty' (pp. 3–4). Knowing the past is not a luxury for professionals, as he came to see. Mankind needs history, and the interpretations of historians, in order to live in civilisation and at peace at all.

The retraction was not credited at its value, and the dogmatic demand for context-and-nothing-but has not ceased since Butterfield first wrote; in some quarters, in fact it has even grown more ardent and extreme. There is talk of the 'misuse of the vantage-point' and the 'mythology of prolepsis' or anticipation. Events can only mean what their agents meant by them, it is said: absurd, then, to see Petrarch's ascent of Mount Ventoux in 1336 as the dawn of the Renaissance, or to suppose that Locke anticipated liberal theories of the state.

> No agent can eventually be said to have meant or done something which he could never be brought to accept as a correct description of what he had meant or done,[12]

though psychoanalysis is instantly admitted as offering some awkward exceptions. So Marsilius of Padua cannot have contributed to the Enlightenment debate on the separation of powers, since he did not intend to do so; and because Locke did not intend to anticipate Berkeley's metaphysics, it is meaningless to say that he did.

And yet people often effect what they did not mean, and begin what they had no intention of beginning; and if psychoanalysis concerns subconscious intention here, then it is nothing like inclusive enough to cover the cases. The Emperor Franz Josef of Austria is famous for having earnestly remarked, as the First Word War dragged miserably on: 'This is not what I meant'; but few historians would think that a reason to deny his share of responsibility for the war. Nor would psychoanalysing him greatly help: it is what he did that matters. Accountability can be as difficult in history as in courts of law; but it is seldom enough – though it is often something – to protest in all honesty that one meant well.

It is ultimately implausible to ask of the historian to abandon hindsight, and vantage-points are there to be used. The wisdom of hindsight is one of the richest blessings the historian has, and he may well feel he has yet to hear sufficient cause why he should give it up, even if he could. Petrarch on the mountain, like Locke writing his *Essay*, caused more than he intended, and probably more than he could ever have been brought to understand.

Winston Churchill is said to have remarked on the fall of Singapore that only then could one understand the meaning of Pearl Harbour a few months before. That is to profit from a vantage-point. The intention of an agent at the time of acting is one historical consideration among many; it may reasonably alter interpretation, much as a court might be swayed by evidence of intention in judging whether a violent death was manslaughter or murder. But whatever the verdict, the case starts with a corpse. What court, after all, has ever supposed that the probable intention of the accused was a limit to the evidence it could take into account?

It is sometimes suggested, in reply, that the historian is concerned with what happened rather than the uses it might be put to in later ages – that Macaulay's moralising emphasis, and Acton's, on what the past has to teach the present is unprofessional as well as misconceived, and ultimately 'not the business of the historian'. But that argument is itself misconceived, being based on a distinction between the past and its interpretation that is no more than a figment of the anti-Whig mind.

Butterfield himself came close to conceding just that when he candidly remarked, in evident self-embarrassment, that in the end 'history must always be written from the point of view of the present'. The concession, fatal as it is to his case, speaks boldly for his intellectual honesty. For if history must always be so written, then it is vain to demand of the historian that he should write otherwise. And yet the whole case of *The Whig Interpretation of History* is that the historian should write otherwise. In other words, Butterfield offers advice which, on his own admission, cannot be taken. Hence the noisy rumble of argumentative gears as he almost, but not quite, excuses the crimes of Renaissance Popes and modern dictators. He cannot doubt, as a good man, that in the long run the historian must come down against murder: but how long is the long run?

It is the brisk certitude of Macaulay's judgements, one suspects, and Acton's – 'They sent forth murderers' –, not their spirit, that discomforted him. Such certitude smacks of the glibness mocked at in *1066 and All That*: '...and this was a Good Thing'. The professional wants to look as if he is doing something difficult, after all, and moral judgements in that style can be made to look damagingly easy. You do not need to be a historian to see that murder is murder, or that murder is wrong. The anti-Whig historian cannot help feeling that, if historical perception is as easy as that, then as a historian he is left with no special place to stand. He aches, as an expert, to do something only an expert can do; and humanism, with its emphasis on what unites mankind, is deflating to his professional pretensions. 'Great abilities', as Johnson told Boswell, 'are not requisite for a historian' (6 July 1763), and the remark is too candid to be comfortable. With other professions, such as surgery or the law, a special competence is not in doubt: there is no room for amateurs there, and we consult professionals because we have no choice. In history, by contrast, there is all too much room for amateurs – or so the historian must occasionally feel as he anxiously scans the weekly journals and Sunday newspapers. Whig historiography can even be a best-selling activity, as Macaulay's *History of England* and Winston Churchill's *History of the English-Speaking Peoples* proved: anti-Whig historiography, by contrast, flourishes in scholarly monographs and journals, and harbours the grudging envy of the tired professional against easy commercial success.

The anti-Whig disjunction between events and interpretations is open to deeper objection. To put it at its simplest: if an event never occurred, then the historian (whether Whig or anti-Whig) has small grounds for concerning himself with it at all. In other words, the case against him lies not in interpreting it in one way rather than another, but in admitting it to debate at all. That summary would need to be enriched before it became convincing; and 'events' is a word that needs to be broadly understood here, to include mental as well as physical. Historians rightly discuss King Arthur, who may never have existed, and hypothetical questions about Hitler's invasion of England in 1940, which never occurred. That the Welsh believed in Arthur, that Hitler intended to invade, are after all events of a kind. Modern history, under anthropological influence, has been eager to concede importance to the study of mental events in regard to remote tribes and peoples – remote whether in place or in time. But out of a nagging fear of ethnocentricity, perhaps, it has been profoundly reluctant to apply the same techniques, unless destructively, to what for centuries the English-speaking peoples have admired in Magna Carta or the Revolution of 1689; and it is notable that conservatives like Michael Oakeshott have been as eager as Marxists to deflate Anglo-Saxon self-confidence here, as if a reasoned patriotism were a natural preserve of Whiggery and as foreign to the Tory mind as to the socialist. Burke's long eulogies of the English Revolution of 1689 are seldom seen by Butterfieldians as anything better than blandly self-persuasive or crassly overweening: a cosy myth designed to justify British self-conceit and an illusion of political uniqueness. But another possibility, to be entertained only secretively if at all, is that Burke may after all have been right about the English Revolution; and that, as Churchill in his *History of the English-Speaking Peoples* plainly implied, those peoples are in truth unique, and remain in the realm of political stability and liberty-with-order uniquely qualified to teach.

Whig historians were in no doubt that history is only instructive because it happened, and they nowhere defend distortion or invention. It is because Magna Carta and the English Revolution occurred, and only because they did, that their part in English constitutional evolution arises at all. The history of institutions, Stubbs wrote in the preface to *The Constitutional History of England* (1874),

> abounds in examples of that continuity of life, the realisation of which is necessary to give the reader a personal hold on the past, and a right judgement of the present. For the roots of the present lie deep in the past, and nothing in the past is dead to the man who would learn how the present comes to be what it is.

As Stubbs says, history 'abounds in examples'. No need to invent them, then. The interest of the remark lies as much in what it takes for granted as in what it asserts. It is the past itself, not an invented past, that it is the task of the Whig historian to present and to interpret.

There is, after all, an alternative, of which fiction is the grand literary instance. Parents sometimes invent comfortable stories to console small children with; and modern dictatorships employ entire ministries, Goebbels-style, to invent flattering national myths. That is not the Whig way. Faced with the task of defending Macaulay, no one would say he distorted nothing. But it would be profoundly unjust to say that he ever in principle allowed distortion to be justified; and his claim that the English Revolution was among the great events of political history would have no standing, as a claim, if it were supposed that he did not believe it happened, and happened through such causes and with such effects as he proposed.

It is precisely because 1689 occurred, in that view, that it can teach the world how constitutional liberty is to be progressively gained and preserved. That is quite different from the arrogant relativism of modern totalitarians who hold that, since the illusion of objective truth depends on social or genetic conditioning, the state is entitled to create and enforce myths of history favourable to its own claim to a heroic role. Hermann Goering used to give thanks that he was born 'without what they call a sense of objectivity'. It is easy to guess what Macaulay or Acton would have thought of that.

The humanist case for moralised history remains cogent, then – the more so because it was never meant to justify all the attempts at moralised history that there are. If there were no timeless concepts, we could not understand the past at all. T. S. Eliot, a humanist though no Whig, sonorously called history 'a pattern / Of timeless moments' in *Little Gidding* (1942). He is unlikely to have supposed it only that: a carpet is always more than its pattern. But it remains wildly implausible to suggest that patterns and recurrences are never there. If they were never there, it is hard to see how we could understand events at all, or use words to describe what we do understand.

The Whig interpretation of history, in its moral fervour, has had strikingly few friends in the present century, at least until recent years, and fewer than has sometimes been supposed in the last. Acton in his 1895 inaugural proclaimed that 'the weight of opinion is against me when I exhort you never to debase the moral currency', calling on his audience of historians to allow no one 'to escape the undying penalty which history has the power to inflict on wrong'. That, as Acton implies, was not the common view of Victorian historians, and it was not the view of the most advanced German school of the age. The Whig interpretation has always been contested; and since it believes in contest, it may be supposed that it has always sought it. The vain attempt to compose unjudging history is far older than Butterfield's essay of 1931.

And behind the continuing attempt, not least in this century, there has often festered something impressively obstinate and deep: an intellectual suspicion of morality itself – its foundations, its coherence, its precarious stability in the face of bids to legitimate or discredit it. The myth dies hard that morality needs foundations, to be certain, and agreed foundations at that. In many such attempts, as in Butterfield's, the moral effects of history are admitted, if at all, only surreptitiously and through back doors. There is muted applause in the 1931 essay for an intellectual effect he calls 'richness'; and it may be he believed that a wealth of detail about the past might encourage a salutary sense of toleration. That is guesswork. But where moral scepticism runs deep, it can easily invade any sense of moral order that there is, whether inside history or out. There is far more than a sense of history at stake when Butterfield disdainfully quotes and rejects Acton's dictum that the achievement of history is 'to develop and perfect and arm conscience' (p. 114). Acton was the implacable foe to self-exemption in moral affairs, and to any other exemption. But his fervour and assurance were simply alien to the world that followed 1918: and alien to many still, as the unbroken twentieth-century tradition of anti-Whiggery shows.

Hard, in the end, to suppress the suspicion that the glory of the Whig view of history has been lost sight of less through its failure than through the sheer longevity of its success. Certainty can breed impatience and discontent, and not least moral certainty. We take civil order and law's rule for granted, in recent times, and in a way that Burke, Macaulay, and even Acton could not. It is by now temptingly easy to call a hatred of persecution 'astonishment at the commonplace'. The historian is a restless being. Taking so much as settled, he aches to look bold.

And to that happy certitude of ordered liberty, at least in English-speaking lands, add a contempt for any argument, whether factual or moral, not bounded by verbal definitions and agreed criteria; and the unwarranted contempt into which the Whig interpretation of history has fallen may perhaps be explained.

Notes

1. Owen Chadwick, *Freedom of the Historian: an Inaugural Lecture* (Cambridge, 1969), p. 37. The lecture is largely devoted to his late colleague G. M. Trevelyan, a noted Whig interpreter who believed the book an attack on himself, though it was more largely directed at Acton. P. B. M. Blaas, however, in

Continuity and Anachronism (The Hague, 1978), pp. 9f., has shown that Butterfield's 1931 essay summarised a mood already common among British historians, attracting far less attention than Lewis Namier's early writings. On the doctrine of continuity among seventeenth-century historians see J. G. A. Pocock, *The Ancient Constitution and Feudal Law* (Cambridge, 1957).

2. George Gale, *Encounter* (November 1979), p. 88.
3. E. A. Freeman, *The Growth of English Constitution from the Earliest Times* (London, 1872), p. viii.
4. Michael Oakeshott, 'The activity of being an historian' (1955), in his *Rationalism in Politics* (London, 1962), p. 166.
5. Wittgenstein, *Philosophical Investigations* (Oxford, 1953), §66–7. See Renford Bambrough, 'Universals and family resemblances', *Proceedings of the Aristotelian Society*, new series 61 (1960–1).
6. See p. 39, above. For an attack on Arnold Toynbee's determinism see H. R. Trevor-Roper, 'Arnold Toynbee's millennium', *Encounter* (June 1957).
7. G. M. Trevelyan, *Garibaldi and the Thousand* (London, 1909), p. 5.
8. William Stubbs, *An Address Delivered by Way of Inaugural* (Oxford, 1867), pp. 26–7.
9. Karl R. Popper, *Conjectures and Refutations* (London, 1963), p. 46, from a Cambridge lecture of 1953.
10. Lord Acton, *The Study of History* (London, 1895), p. 55.
11. Geoffrey Elton, introduction to J. N. Figgis, *The Divine Right of Kings* (London, 1965); reprinted in Elton, *Studies in Tudor and Stuart Politics and Government* (Cambridge, 1974), II.195.
12. Quentin Skinner, 'Meaning and understanding in the history of ideas', *History and Theory* (1969), 8, pp. 22f.

15

ORWELL'S NAZI RENEGADE

In February 1982 an ex-Nazi died in Portland, Oregon, in his mid-nineties, a forgotten man.

His name was Hermann Rauschning. Born in Prussia in 1887, he became an early Nazi in the 1920s and president of the Danzig senate. The son of an officer and graduate of a military school, a monarchist and a Bismarckian conservative, he had welcomed Hitler's new movement as a bulwark against a Communism that had recently seized power in Russia and had only narrowly been prevented, after the national defeat of 1918, from spreading into his native Germany. Then, in 1932–4, or during the two years that surrounded Hitler's seizure of power in January 1933, he held intermittent conversations with his leader, writing them down in private memoranda. The effects were shattering. Convinced by what he had heard that Hitler was at least as revolutionary as any Marxist, and more radical than many a Bolshevik, he fled to Switzerland in 1936, published a series of anti-Nazi books like *The Revolution of Nihilism* (1938), and after a spell in wartime England settled in the United States at the end of the Second World War as a farmer in Oregon. He was the Trotsky, so to speak, of the Nazi revolution.

The rest of the story hardly matters. An old man by the 1950s, Rauschning occasionally returned to Europe, issuing occasional statements in favour of German reunification – to be accused of Communism himself, paradoxically, since the reunion of Germany would by then have meant breaking all military ties between Bonn and the West. When he died in 1982 he was so completely forgotten that no extended obituary can be found in Europe or America to mark his end. And yet he was once famous for having written a best-seller – a work praised by George Orwell during the war as the equal of Trotsky, Silone, and Koestler.

The bestseller was called *Hitler Speaks*. Based on his conversations with Hitler in 1932–4, it appeared in French and English versions late in 1939, some months after its author had been deprived by the Nazis of his German citizenship – to be published in its original German in neutral Zurich shortly after as *Gespräche mit Hitler*. The book sold well in several languages. It was never other than controversial, however, presenting Hitler as a revolutionary who openly avowed his debt to Marxism, denied the certainty of knowledge even in the sciences, and derided the Bolsheviks less for their radicalism than for their timid conservatism. It was a bombshell. More like Mao than Stalin, the Hitler whom Rauschning knew had proclaimed that one revolution could never be enough. Blood must have blood; a single socialist revolution, Lenin-style, could never suffice; and the future history of the world, even more than its past, was one of limitless and unending violence.

The trouble was that Hitler as a more-than-Marxian revolutionary simply did not fit the mood of Europe in the weeks that followed the outbreak of war in September 1939. *Hitler Speaks* was bought but not believed. Richard Crossman, an ardent young socialist too extreme for office in Attlee's government when elected to the Commons in 1945, dismissed it as a work of fantasy in a review in the *New Statesman* in December 1939: 'at the best, historical fiction'. There are verbal traditions that Neville Chamberlain, as Prime Minister, refused equally to believe in it as running counter to the Hitler he had met and known; and that another Conservative, Lord Halifax, soon to be ambassador in Washington, took a similar view on similar grounds. Since both men had treated with Hitler in the years of appeasement that had led down to the war of 1939 – and on Rauschning's own mistaken assumption, as a young Prussian monarchist, that Nazism was at least better than Bolshevism – they were shocked and incredulous to be told that Hitler was something even worse. He was anti-Marxist, it was now suggested, only in the sense that he thought Marxism-Leninism too bland and too tame.

The war once over, however, opinion took another turn. In *The Last Days of Hitler* (1947), H. R. Trevor-Roper accepted the essential authenticity of the reported conversations; and in 1972, in a painstaking German study of the book, Theodor Schieder showed that Rauschning's reports conform closely enough to later evidence – Hitler's wartime table-talk, for example, and Albert Speer's memoirs – to be accepted as substantially reliable. If they are not literally verbatim records, that is, they are at least credible summaries of what the Führer said.[1] All that should be enough to put the Trotsky of the Nazi revolution back on the map of history. But there is a further, and more potent, resemblance that has never been noticed: the resemblance between Hitler's reported remarks to Rauschning in 1932–4 and George Orwell's last novel, *Nineteen Eighty-four* (1949).

Orwell was publicly an admirer of Rauschning, though there is no record that they ever met. Shortly after Hitler invaded Russia in June 1941, he wrote an article called 'Wells, Hitler and the world state' for Cyril Connolly's *Horizon* (August 1941), drawing excited attention to a new cosmopolitan literature recently created by refugees from fascist and communist dictators, and one that made the facile predictions of H. G. Wells and Aldous Huxley look merely parochial by comparison as well as obsolete in their comparative optimism about the mechanised future of mankind. The new literature Orwell called 'renegade', being written by men who had abandoned extremism or at least dictatorial systems. Orwell lists Trotsky, Silone, and his new friend Arthur Koestler – all renegades from Communism. He also mentions Rauschning, an ex-Nazi in London at about that time.[2]

To call Rauschning the Trotsky of the Nazi revolution, then, is to borrow a hint from Orwell, and it was characteristically whimsical of him to use the damning word *renegade* as a term of praise. But then Orwell very likely saw himself as one by 1941, and with some reason: in *Homage to Catalonia* (1938) he tells how he had gone to Spain in 1936 ready to fight for the Spanish Republic under Stalinist leadership, only to be disillusioned with Communism by what he saw in Barcelona in 1937 when invalided back from the front. Towards the end of the World War, once again, he was to praise Rauschning as one of the few to recognise early how similar Fascism and Communism truly are (*Tribune*, 24 March 1944). These references have not succeeded in keeping Rauschning's name alive, and in a recent life of Orwell (1980) Bernard Crick does not mention him. But Orwell's own late fiction makes of Rauschning a more profound influence on him, in all probability, than the Communist renegades Trotsky and

Koestler ever were. Indeed Arthur Koestler once told me he
needed to teach Orwell nothing about Communism, close as
their friendship in the early 1940s had been. It was Spain that had
already taught him all that. 'George understood the whole *Gestalt*
for himself', Koestler remarked with a twinkle, amused that
nobody should have thought to ask him such an obvious question before.

Homage to Catalonia is a report on Orwell's highly personal
experience of the Spanish Civil War. It is not a history, and its
author says it is not. And it bluntly poses the larger question
whether a true and certain history can ever be written, while
making little attempt to answer it. The argument for truth is
knowingly poised here, as if on a knife-edge. In fact the motto,
which consists of two seemingly contradictory sayings from the
Book of Proverbs, suggests Orwell may have been trifling with a
faintly despairing relativism in mid-career, since both propositions look true even as they appear to contradict each other:
'Answer not a fool. . . . Answer a fool. . . .' (Proverbs 26:4–5).
Orwell had seen events in Spain for himself, and had then read
lies about them. It was no wonder, then, if he came to doubt
whether the whole truth could ever be told. That question was to
ferment in his mind for the rest of his short life, which was to end
in a London hospital in January 1950, when he was only forty-six.
He had less than a decade, then, to work it all out, in scattered
journalism and in his two great utopias, *Animal Farm* and *Nineteen
Eighty-four*; and it was renegade literature, as he called it, that
made it possible for him to work it out.

Late in 1942, and no sooner, the point began to emerge in his
mind. In the depths of World War, Orwell wrote for a little magazine an article called 'Looking back on the Spanish War', nowadays often reprinted in an expanded version as an appendix to
Homage to Catalonia, though it is no part of the book. The article is
far more advanced than *Homage* itself as an analysis of how
dictatorial power in a highly mechanised world can be won and
kept by central control of the mass media, and Orwell's final convictions about totalitarianism start here. 'I am willing to believe',
he wrote in the 1942 article,

> that history is for the most part inaccurate and biased; but what is
> peculiar to our own age is the abandonment of the idea that history
> *could* be truthfully written. In the past people deliberately lied, or

they unconsciously coloured what they wrote, or they struggled after the truth, well knowing that they must make many mistakes; but in each case they believed that 'facts' existed and were more or less discoverable.

And then, without even mentioning Rauschning, Orwell suddenly echoes the Hitler of *Hitler Speaks*:

Nazi theory indeed specifically denies that such a thing as 'the truth' exists. There is, for instance, no such thing as 'Science'. There is only 'German Science', 'Jewish Science', etc. The implied objective of this line of thought is a nightmare world in which the Leader, or some ruling clique, controls not only the future but *the past*.

The leader can simply deny that what happened ever happened, in fact – as Stalin had denied Trotsky's part in the October Revolution; facts can be pushed into oblivion down the memory-holes of the Ministry of Truth, much as Spanish Communists had denied the manifest heroism of their anarchist allies in Catalonia in 1937. Even arithmetic itself might be changed by some future leader of men. 'If he says that two and two are five,' Orwell goes on, 'well, two and two are five'; adding cheerfully, in an article penned during the London Blitz, that the prospect 'frightens me much more than bombs – and after our experiences of the last few years, that is not a frivolous statement.'

Compare that with Hitler's reported remark to Rauschning eight years earlier, in 1934: 'There is no such thing as truth, either in the moral or in the scientific sense. . . . The idea of free and unfettered science, unfettered by hypotheses, could only occur in the age of Liberalism. It is absurd. Science is a social phenomenon, and like every other social phenomenon is limited by the benefit or injury it confers on the community. The slogan of objective science has been coined by the professor[i]ate simply in order to escape from the very necessary supervision by the power of the State.' Just like Orwell's Ministry of Truth in *Nineteen Eighty-four*, one feels; or just like any Marxist militant in universities around 1968. Hitler is nowhere reported here as using the word *conditioning*, favoured as it commonly is in such arguments; but his dogma is the same. There is no knowledge, only opinion. And Himmler, so Rauschning reports, shared that view: 'Science proceeds from hypotheses that change every year or so. So there's no earthly reason why the party should not lay down a particular hypothesis as the starting-point, even if it runs

counter to current scientific opinion.' Totalitarianism is subjectivist, then, whether fascist or communist.

Subjectivism is the dogma that truth is in its nature a phantasma
– knowledge, or rather what we take for knowledge, being an
illusion genetically conditioned, as in Nazism ('Jewish science'),
or socially conditioned ('bourgeois science') as in Marxism. That
is why the party has a right, even a duty, to impose on every
citizen what, for the moment, is allowed to count for truth. Subjectivism is distinct from scepticism in that the sceptic typically
assumes that there is an objective truth: it is merely that, by and
large, we are incapable of apprehending it; whereas the subjectivist denies even that. It is a brutally convenient dogma for a
dictatorship, since it allows it to destroy its enemies by tactically
changing the party line, as Orwell's *Nineteen Eighty-four* illustrated – promptly exterminating those who hold, or recently
held, views only recently discredited. So subjectivism is a licence
not just for tyranny but for extermination – as Stalin killed the Old
Bolsheviks, or as the Nazis in 1934 destroyed Ernst Roehm and
his followers. Mao's cultural revolution of 1967–76 is another
classic instance, though one Orwell did not live to see. And here
lies the very heart and essence of his last utopia: that nightmare
world, as he calls it, which in the 1940s did not quite exist, but
which he saw as a far greater and a far more immediate threat to
mankind than the cosy or heartless hedonism of Aldous Huxley's
Brave New World.

That nightmare world, in the end, is not so much a world of lies
as one where truth and lies are not acknowledged to exist. Man
can never know: he can only believe. No perception, then, is true
or false: the party will tell you which view to embrace for the
moment, which to reject. Knowledge was a bourgeois illusion,
and the revolution has abolished it. 'Science is a social phenomenon', as Hitler told Rauschning. There can be no universities,
then, as we know them, since there can be no pursuit of truth
where there is no truth; and the state must forever dictate the
shape and content of whatever in schools and colleges may be
taught and learned.

It is curious, and unexplained, that Orwell's point about
totalitarian subjectivism has been entirely lost to view; and the

vast celebrations that inevitably accompanied his novel *Nineteen Eighty-four* in 1984 itself failed even to mention what Orwell himself would undoubtedly have seen as the vital message of his last book. It is a claim to certainty.

That critical failure arose partly, no doubt, because we no longer read Nazi or anti-Nazi propagandists of the 1930s: so little, indeed, that it is unusual by now to think of Hitler and his clique as ideologues at all. The Nazis have passed into history as a murderous gang. But to reflective spirits of the 1930s it was obvious that they were murderous because they were ideologues, and their ideology in those years was extensively studied. Rauschning's books do not stand alone. In 1938, for example, the year of Orwell's *Homage to Catalonia*, there appeared *The War against the West* by Aurel Kolnai, a Hungarian Jew converted to conservative Catholicism who viewed the new German ideology with an unmixed horror. A professional philosopher, Kolnai had left Vienna for England in 1937, a year before the Nazi annexation of Austria; he spent his last years lecturing at the University of London, dying in 1973, and his passionate and untidy book is even more thoroughly forgotten, by now, than Rauschning's. Nor does Orwell mention it anywhere in his writings. But his point is similar to Rauschning's. 'I am *subjective*', Hermann Goering proclaimed in the spring of 1933, a few months after the seizure of power, in a declaration quoted by Kolnai with an air of fastidious horror. 'I submit myself to my people', and Goering went on to praise his Maker for having created him without a 'sense of objectivity'. Kolnai calls the remark 'the essence of National Socialism' and a return to the tribal mind. Koestler too, in his *Spanish Testament* (1937), had referred in his preface to the 'subjective' and 'objective' aspects of his little memoir about his own involvement in the Spanish Civil War, as if that war had, in its turn, created a conflict of mental states. It may be too late, by now, to discover which of these sources mattered most to Orwell, and Rauschning is the only one of them he acknowledges. But he first thought of *Nineteen Eighty-four* in 1943, he wrote to his publisher Frederic Warburg in October 1948 when the book was about to appear; and it seems likely enough, from his repeated instance of 2 + 2 = 4 (or, if the Party insists, 5) that there was an unbroken connection between what Hitler said to Rauschning in 1932–4, Orwell's 'Looking back on the Spanish War' in 1942, and

Nineteen Eighty-four itself. So we have missed Orwell's vital point in his great utopia, and must now struggle to recover it. It was a point about a necessary relation between totalitarianism and a subversive theory of knowledge.

Oddly enough it is Hitler's view, and Stalin's, that has until recently looked fashionable in the higher education of the Western world, and the convenient oblivion that has overtaken Orwell's point has obscured that simple truth. It is still exceptional in universities to hear it argued that moral or aesthetic values might be objective; and even the objectivity of the natural sciences has been challenged in our times, and from within the sciences themselves.

In 1962 an American philosopher, Thomas Kuhn, issued *The Structure of Scientific Revolutions* – an immensely influential book that argued for 'the priority of paradigms' in scientific history. Kuhn made no special play with terms like *objective* and *subjective*; but the tendency, and perhaps the purpose, of his argument was to sap the pretensions of scientific knowledge. It plainly never occurred to him to doubt that value-judgements are merely personal; nor did he realise that intellectual procedures unfounded on stated and agreed criteria might still lay claim to objective standing. When scientists dispute the significance of problems, he argued, 'the question of values can be answered only in terms of criteria that lie outside of normal science altogether', so that a scientific consensus depends on 'the world of which that [scientific] community is a part'. Gropingly and profoundly well-intentioned as it was, the book was argued entirely without reference to modern dictatorship, and it has been extensively debated by philosophers of science in similar terms. Orwell is seldom mentioned in the argument, still less Rauschning; and neither Kuhn nor his followers and detractors have ever showed the faintest awareness that a totalitarian view once advanced by Berlin and Moscow was being implicitly revived. Indeed it is easy to accept that the scientific and philosophical world they inhabit would have been sincerely horrified if that resemblance had ever been suggested.

The key doctrine of *Animal Farm* and *Nineteen Eighty-four*, in short, has dropped from sight. It is now thought wildly eccentric, at best, and harshly authoritarian at worst, to suggest that moral, aesthetic, or even (in extreme circles) scientific value-judgements might be matters for objective inquiry. Tell a critical subjectivist that he is putting Adolf Hitler's view, and he will simply look puzzled; suggest that his view might be totalitarian in its implications, and he will look amazed. Subjectivism is nowadays seen as a badge of liberty, and it is supposed to guarantee the right to think and speak as you feel.

All that is very strange. Orwell is an author who is said to be widely read. He is extensively studied in schools and colleges; *Nineteen Eighty-four* has even been a television play, as far back as the 1950s, and in 1984 itself a brilliantly diagrammatic film. And there is an early moment in that novel and in that film when its hero Winston Smith, imagining himself to be out of sight of the telescreen on the wall of his apartment, scribbles his most subversive thoughts into a secret diary. It is his moment of freedom, as he hopes. And that freedom is not the freedom to think what you please, as the subjectivist imagines, but to see, and to say, that things are what they are: 'The Party told you to reject the evidence of your eyes and ears. . . . And yet he was in the right! . . . The obvious, the silly, and the true had got to be defended. Truisms are true, hold on to that! The solid world exists, its laws do not change. Stones are hard, water is wet, objects unsupported fall towards the earth's centre.' And he picks up his diary and writes: 'Freedom is the freedom to say that two plus two make four. If that is granted, all else follows.' That powerfully echoes a point Orwell had made seven years earlier in 'Looking back on the Spanish War'; it may even echo a remark made as early as 1934 by an obscure Nazi apologist called Jakob Hommes, in a passage quoted by Kolnai in 1938 under the heading 'Irrational science'. Surely, Hommes was asked, mathematics at least is free from the racial taint. But even here 'Hommes is not at a loss for an answer', Kolnai writes. 'He stuns us with the master stroke that the concept "twice two make four" is "somehow differently tinged" in the minds of a German, a Frenchman and a Negro. . . . As for sciences of a more human and historical relevancy, all pretensions to neutrality and objectivity are evil.'

Orwell may never have read Kolnai's *War against the West*; but the coincidence that it appeared in the same year as *Homage to Catalonia* – 1938 – remains suggestive of an ardent political debate about totalitarian subjectivism that needs to be revived. Freedom demands certainty, as Orwell came to see in the last years of his short life. How could one ever argue against error, unless truth is there to be known? 'If liberty means anything at all,' as he put it bluntly in a preface to *Animal Farm'*, 'it means the right to tell people what they do not want to hear.'

What subjectivism offers, by contrast, is no more than the false sense of liberty that men enjoy when they chant slogans to their leaders. If mankind can never certainly know – if human judgement is fallible by its very nature, whether on social grounds or genetic – then the case for dictatorship must in the end look overwhelmingly strong. A Ministry of Truth, Goebbels-style, would make perfect sense if mankind depended on the authority of the state even to understand that two and two make four. If there is no truth, then there is no error. So no professor can be wrong, and no student could ever reasonably think his teacher mistaken – still less tell him so. No radical discovery in science or the arts could ever be made, since discovering implies something already there to be discovered; and no radical proposal could ever be rationally made in politics either, since radicals need the Orwellian assumption of truth to make a case for change at all. 'Stones are hard, water is wet. . . .'

If we do not know even that, how could we ever pretend to know that government is corrupt, ineffective, or tyrannical? Like criticism of the arts, political debate desperately needs the concept of objective moral knowledge; the more so because, as in the arts, its debates extend deep into moral judgement. To condemn Auschwitz, after all, is to make a judgement that is moral and political all at once: and if no moral judgement is better than subjective, then that judgement is no better. Subjectivism remains eternally convenient to those who seek to keep things as they are, like the fat-living ruling class of Orwell's *Nineteen Eighty-four* or of the Soviet Union. The powerful of the world can only prosper from the conviction that there is no truth that can ever be certainly known or certainly said.

It may be, then, that Hitler's remarks to Rauschning over fifty years ago, in 1932–4, have had a long, fertile, and unnoticed literary history. The great Nazi renegade, as Orwell called him, published them in 1939 in *Hitler Speaks*; Orwell praised him with Trotsky, Silone, and Koestler in 1941; and by the end of the war his own memories of Spain, and thoughts provoked by the new renegade literature of continental Europe, had led Orwell into the profound, subversive and strangely neglected speculations of his two great utopias.

And yet it is far from clear that Orwell's last and most telling charge against totalitarianism has been understood or noticed. It is still not usually realised, that is, that totalitarianism is subjectivist, or that objectivism may be needed in order for us to disagree with one another. I do not mean in order to agree politely to differ, but to argue that another moral or political view is wrong, and why it is wrong. The crucial and neglected point of Orwell's nightmare utopias is that we forever need such certitudes, and that dictators would, if they could, destroy a sense of history itself – any certain knowledge that what happened really happened. 'To the death of Big Brother?' O'Brien challenges Winston Smith mockingly in *Nineteen Eighty-four*, as they raise glasses. 'To humanity? To the future?' But Winston Smith politely contradicts him:

'To the past,' said Winston.
'The past is more important,' agreed O'Brien gravely.

It is a sense of history that governs choices: and to lose all sense of historical knowledge is to lose all political sense as well. What liberty needs, above all, and continues to need, is better historians; to control the past, as Orwell unforgettably put it, is to control the future.

An ultimate contradiction, it is tempting to conclude, lies at the heart of any version of subjectivism, whether Nazi, Communist, or other, and it is this. If it is true that all beliefs and paradigms are conditioned, then that view, being itself a belief, must be conditioned. And if it is an objection to say of a belief that it was conditioned, as Hitler and the Marxists both supposed, then it is equally an objection to the doctrine of conditioning itself. No case has been made for exemption here. If we cannot certainly know anything, then we cannot certainly know that. Radical scepticism always contradicts itself, sooner or later, and usually sooner.

That is an argument which, so far as I know, Orwell himself never used. But I think, hope, and believe that he would have liked it.

Notes

1. I am grateful here for the revealing advice of Arthur Koestler on his wartime friendship with Orwell; and to my colleague H. R. Trevor-Roper, Lord Dacre, for information about the source of Neville Chamberlain's refusal while Prime Minister to believe in the authenticity of Rauschning's *Hitler Speaks*. The story was based on Trevor-Roper's conversation with Lord Cherwell when Cherwell was personal adviser to Churchill as First Lord of the Admiralty in 1939–40, in the last year of Chamberlain's premiership. Halifax's incredulity is equally based on hearsay – this time Rauschning's own; he reported it to Theodor Schieder, who includes it in *Rauschnings Gespräche mit Hitler als Geschichtsquelle* (Opladen, 1972), a study designed to confirm the probable authenticity of these reports of Hitler's conversations in 1932–4.

   Professor Schieder died early in 1985, before he could answer an attempt by a Swiss schoolteacher, Wolfgang Hänel (*Die Zeit*, 19 July, 1985), to prove Rauschning an imposter. Hänel fails to meet Schieder's arguments for authenticity, and his own grounds for attacking Rauschning's honesty are insubstantial: that *Hitler Speaks* was written at the instigation of a journalist, and for money; that Rauschning can seldom have been alone with Hitler – though he frequently speaks of conversations among a wider group of confidants; that Albert Speer did not mention Rauschning in his memoirs – though it remains unclear why he would do so; and that one lively incident told of Hitler resembles an episode in a Maupassant story. As every Swiss schoolteacher should know, there are few men alive or dead of whom it could not be said that they have lived episodes that resemble the stories of great literature.

2. See Golo Mann, 'Raymond Aron', *Encounter* (December 1983). There seems to be no evidence that Orwell and Rauschning ever met, though they were both in London during the Blitz.

16

THE ECLIPSE OF REASON

In his celebrated eleventh thesis on Feuerbach (1845), Karl Marx called on philosophy to change the world instead of merely interpreting it.

As a recent intellectual historian has noted,[1] the trouble is that his advice was followed to the letter. Marxism did change the modern world, and by the 1950s a third of the human race was living under Marxist governments. But it never succeeded in interpreting it. A practical success, then, at least in power terms, and an intellectual failure: not exactly what one expects of idealists, least of all lovers of high abstraction in the German mould. Communism may not have raised the living standards of any working class on earth; it may even have lowered some, as comparisons between the two Germanies or the two Koreas suggest. Nor has the logic of history, to which Marx often and confidently referred, legitimated his historical case. His certainties now look baseless. No Marxist revolution, and no class war, has ever happened in any advanced industrial state. In fact such states, to speak broadly, seem to be prone to no kind of revolution at all. They are classically stable. A Victorian certainty that industrial capitalism bore within itself, and ineluctably, the seeds of its own destruction has long since been falsified by events themselves, and it is now tacitly abandoned even by Moscow and Peking.

Marx's certainty that a new philosophy could change the world, on the other hand, has proved dazzlingly successful, provided only one is unconcerned whether change is for good or ill; and it was the severely practical success of Marxist governments in consolidating power after 1917 that proved the profoundest of all embarrassments to western literary Marxists. Nobody can reasonably call a system that lingers on for decades a total failure. Durability is the first test of politics, after all; and the Soviet system, whatever its faults, endures. Indeed some would say it looks hardly less durable with the passing years. And it is plainly implausible to argue that it bears no purposive relation to anything Marx and Engels ever sought or planned. In 1848, in the *Communist Manifesto*, they demanded nationalisation or state capitalism, and eastern Europe has it. It also had a stable system of central authority unaltered by elections, and it is hard to deny that Marx was that style of an authoritarian. In the later volumes of *Capital* that appeared after his death in 1883, he insisted that the control of production through central power would be 'even more necessary' under socialism than under capitalism; and though he believed that socialism would eventually make government superfluous – 'throwing its political hull away', as he vividly put it – he was fiercely anti-anarchistic, coined the phrase 'the dictatorship of the proletariat' in a letter of 1852, and derided any notion of human rights as a mere fig-leaf for bourgeois hegemony. Lenin was to intensify the illiberal elements in Marxist scripture, both before he seized power in 1917 and after; but they were always there. The Soviet system is not wholly unreasonable, it seems clear, when it claims the authority of Marx and Engels for what it does.

The triumphant certainties of Marxism, then, present a formidable counter-instance to any sceptic who believes that language never describes the real or that mankind never lives by the book. It is the more surprising that it is above all Marxist or post-Marxist intellectuals who have most easily adopted radical scepticism and cast elaborate doubts on what ordinarily passes for the rationality of man. Part of the explanation lies in the suspicion, entirely justified, that Marxism might itself be a mere ideology rather than an escape into reality, subject in its turn to the distortions supposed to characterise the ideologies of others. Another is the disturbing spectacle of a success wholly enacted in terms of power. The pure theorist – above all the utopian theorist – is not naturally at his ease at the spectacle of a severely practical triumph. Since the Bolshevik revolution of 1917 there have been a number of responses to that dilemma, of which recent critical theory represents one set of instances.

The first, with Georg Lukàcs, was to invent cultural Communism. 'Politics is merely the means,' he wrote , 'culture the goal.' One effect of that view was to push utopia conveniently forward into a future infinitely remote. For the most certain fact about culture as popular diffusion is that it never ideally happens. No society, taken as a whole, can easily be seen as cultivated; and once culture is the goal, not merely the abolition of poverty, perfection is infinitely postponed. All that helps to give western cultural Marxism from the start a distinctively abstract flavour. Uncertain of itself, it naturally denied certainty to others. Its world was not primarily one of party conferences or of cabals fitfully planning the violent overthrow of constituted government. Culture-Communism was different. It wore rather the rich, warm hues of the last days of the Habsburg empire, to which Lukàcs returned in 1916 from France, as a native Hungarian, after a disastrous marriage. Its tone was not one of revolutionary fervour but of the cream-cakes, coffee and endless café-talk of a dying central European order. Western Marxism, in that sense of the term, was less a programme of action than a school of conversation and of literature.

Its characteristic fear, by 1916, was intelligible. The West might soon win the war; but if it did, who would save civilisation from Anglo-American materialism, on the one hand, or from French cultural decadence on the other? Here, in the last gasp of a Teutonic *belle époque*, in the twilight of the Habsburg and Hohenzollern empires, intellectuals turned to a highly abstracted version of revolutionary Marxism, and in an atmosphere at once ostentatiously high-minded and rigorously removed from any sense of evidence. Facts are a betrayal of mind; clarity a surrender to bourgeois prejudice; certainty, self-evidently, an illusion. 'An élitist intellectual from top to toe' – a remark once aptly made of Adorno – might have described almost any member of the new school. The western Marxist combined the fierce moral fervour of the rootless intellectual with the veneration of the desk-worker for the man of action. The popular voice counted for absolutely nothing. Given the 'impotence of the workers', as Horkheimer put it, 'truth seeks refuge among small groups of admirable men'. The western Marxist was confidently self-admiring in a world where self-esteem was everything and efficacy nothing. Political reality demands compromise, but the western Marxist was not interested in compromise because he was not interested in reality. He sought a redemptive faith – a living, daring and self-justifying creed.

With the Frankfurt School in Weimar Germany, and with Sartre and Althusser in France, western cultural Marxism was soon to adopt a literary style to fit that mood: a competitive cultivation of the abstract. Though preferring East to West after 1945 as 'the better side', as Sartre famously put it, it was proudly external to party discipline. Though Marxian, it reverenced no individual scripture – rather the resonance of great names. Though passionately political, it was not exactly in politics. That would have meant entry into a system, and the western Marxist was self-assertively outside systems. He cultivated 'a sort of orthodoxy in heresy', as Dr Merquior puts it. He was above all academic in inclination, and to an extravagant degree: indeed Professor Doktor Theodor Wiesengrund Adorno of Frankfurt, a chubby, bald little man, is famous for standing on tiptoe for emphasis in his lectures, exclaiming intensely: 'Ladies and gentlemen, this is very dialectical!' The very tone was new. Marx and Engels, in sublime self-certainty, had oscillated between hard-hitting journalism and the statistic-packed treatise: the western Marxist after 1917, by contrast, was at home in neither. His mind was above all literary, fictional, fantasising. He loved plays and films and novels rather than real events, and earnestly canvassed views about novels he had read and plays and films he had seen.

Great fiction helps its devotees to feel less ill at ease in an alien universe, and it teaches as it consoles. With western Marxism a hard-nosed revolutionary tradition devised by early Victorian activists as a formula for instant revolution in industrial states turned mannered, inactive, literary. Lukàcs, under Dostoevsky's spell, dubbed novelists the 'negative mystics' of a godless age – an interesting remark improbable in the men of 1848 or in the sober proceedings of the First and Second International. Like Walter Benjamin of Berlin, Lukàcs is a considerable literary essayist; and as his adage about novelists suggests, the engaging world of cafés and carpet-slippers is never far from what such sages wrote. Knowledge, still more certainty, they largely disdained. Benjamin, on paper the most romantic of all pre-war western Marxists, was to die by suicide on the Spanish borders of France in flight from the Gestapo, having bemoaned a life imprisoned 'in the power of facts', as he once put it, until that power in its most brutal form caught up with him. Facts, he held can never of themselves compel belief: they have 'scarcely ever become the basis of conviction'. All this is a long, long way from the Scientific Socialism of the Victorians. It is not facts that count, by now, but patterns of mind, and the western Marxist was a spirit free to wander through the enticing labyrinths of his own thoughts. Even Antonio Gramsci, though a party man, writing his notebooks in a prison-cell in the early 1930s in Mussolini's Italy, was unconstrained as a spirit, though constrained in all else, and devised a philosophy of praxis that denied materialism in favour of an ideally integrated civilisation yet to be born. It was far more than the discipline of the rational he rejected in his prison cell: it was the discipline of evidence itself.

A Cambridge economist, Joan Robinson, once remarked that Marxism was the opium of the Marxists. The remark commemorates the cosy feel of an intellectual club founded by Lukàcs and Gramsci between the world wars that was to number countless French and British intellectuals, by the 1960s, among its members. Western Marxism was a good club, in its day. Clubmen are stereotypically an idle lot, like opium-takers; and being a Western Marxist never, of itself, demanded anything like hard work, though some of its members chose to work hard. Few of them troubled to study more than a few pages of the writings of Marx and Engels, authors admittedly tedious to pursue through the length of their collected editions; so that it was always easy to surprise them with quotations from those sources, such as those embarrassing passages in which Marx and Engels publicly demanded racial extermination. Fewer still thought the difference between good argument and bad mattered much, since they were radically sceptical of argument. Irrationalism, they discovered, can be fun.

It can also be backward-looking. 'Put the brakes on history', said Walter Benjamin when he heard the terrible news of the Nazi-Soviet Pact in August 1939. It is from the past, not the present, that solace is to be sought. Cultural Communism was talking about Jerusalem: a Jerusalem once believed in and now largely unbelievable, so that its task was to recapture a mood of hope when the very grounds for hope were known and felt to be dead. No wonder western Marxism turned irrationalist. There is no rational way, plainly, out of that contradiction. None, equally, in the supreme élitists of the higher education of the western world propounding the virtues of social equality. Their contradictions were inescapable. But there can still be a companionship of intellectual despair, and western Marxism leaves behind it an amiable memory of a like-mindedness that stretched eventually from Berlin to California. This was a club whose membership by 1968 straddled the world.

Some of the motives of western Marxism ran deeper than the need for companions. By the 1960s the industrial world was entering a period of academic boom, with new universities and expanding old universities; and an exploding academia means more and more people looking for more and more things to say. Mind, like matter, abhors a vacuum, and in an age when thousands were suddenly eager to appear profound, a non-party movement with its roots deep in nineteenth-century central Europe offered a convenient terminology to look profound in. And not just look profound, but feel it. This was heady stuff, equipped with its own captivating jargon about reification and the dialectic of class conflict. It was the first profundity that many adolescents of the age had ever heard; and much as there is no love like one's first love, so there is no profundity like one's first.

It was not chosen – merely there. It was not selected but found. It looked all that there was. No wonder it was eagerly and gratefully seized on. It was a solution to the riddle of history, as Marx had once called Communism itself in his Paris manuscripts of the 1840s. That riddle may in truth be insoluble, the more so because it is as hard to pose as to answer. But by the 1960s capitalism had bred within itself a contradiction Marx had never dreamed of: organs of mass popular education where a Victorian riddle and a Victorian solution could be dubbed the latest thing. East of the Iron Curtain, Marxism might look as boring as any other established faith. In the West, by sudden contrast, it looked chic.

And more than chic – virtuous. Again the defining model has more to do with fiction than fact. Virtue and vice can be lucidly opposed and duly rewarded in fiction: that, as Oscar Wilde once gaily remarked, is what fiction means. In crime-stories and in western films, above all, moral allegiances are bracingly undivided and clear. In a similar cops-and-robbers spirit, sages like Lukàcs, Benjamin and Sartre could see the dialectic of history as blindingly plain and dazzlingly imperative in its demands on the spirit: 'the better side . . .'. History was viewed as moral drama, with few dubieties. The Spanish Civil War, the Second World War after June 1941, and eventually the Vietnam War, provided ready instances. They were clear, unsmudged, urgent: a godsent change from the professorial Wherefore and Why.

Even before they came, a 'second ethic' had been born to accommodate them. A reading of Dostoevsky had profoundly impressed the young Lukàcs with the dream of virtuous terror-ism, where the assassin is possessed of a moral fervour utterly unknown to the workaday life of the professor or parliamentar-ian. The sources of that terror-worship, it seems clear, lie less in theory than in fiction, and it was out of fiction that western Marxists eagerly built their cult of violence. This was to be the adrenalin of western Marxism for groups like the Red Brigades of Italy or the Baader-Meinhof in Germany, where direct action was the favoured mode of self-excitation, the life of mind in classroom or committee representing no more than tame preparatives to heroic deeds. It was that aspect of western Marxism that was eventually to win from Habermas the title of the Fascism of the left – *Linksfaschismus* – and in the Germany of the 1960s the press was full of the doings of militants aptly known as Red Nazis. Such militancy was exclusively for the young, and it is hard to imagine Lukàcs, Benjamin or Sartre committing a terroristic act. Lukàcs read novels; Sartre chose to play no more than a passive role in the French resistance; and Benjamin's only recorded deed of blood was the act which in 1940 he tragically committed against himself. The intellectual, simply because he is that, does not act: to the end of her life, that was Simone de Beauvoir's justification for Sartre's passivity, and her own, during the Nazi occupation of Paris. The classic western Marxist is not given to violent acts. He spawns them. It is the idea of violence, not the thing, that titillates and excites.

Outsiders can be puzzled to understand how western Marxism advanced so easily and so far into academic institutions after 1960, lasted so long – at least till the American withdrawal from Vietnam in 1972 – and thrived so readily in what is imagined to be the critical and dissective atmosphere of college and campus. Such institutions are created out of a concern for knowledge, after all, even certain knowledge – emphatically not out of a glib certainty that certainty is nowhere to be had. They are in no way designed for irrational cults. Nor were Marxist theories in any way validated by social evidence or by the current of events themselves. The postwar world was not, and is not, moving towards class war: there *is* no time-bomb in capitalism, it is now clear, that inevitably leads it to self-destruct. Nor, to all appearances, has competitive enterprise lost anything in its popular appeal. A consumer society with competing brand-names is plainly what people want – not least poor people; and China and India, the two most populous states on earth, were before the 1980s choosing to move in just that direction. But it was as if these realities did not exist. Western Marxism was a dogma seraphically untouched by reality and unconcerned with mass sentiment. It was a fiction based on fiction, a romance for romantics: what Lionel Trilling once called a false seriousness – a moral earnestness that is moral luxury.[2]

Even before the end of Marx's own century, Marx had largely ceased in an age of flourishing revisionism to look like the Machiavelli of the Proletariat, as he was once proudly called, or the supreme prophet of realism for industrial states. Western Marxism always laboured, after all, under the weight of a vast initial implausibility: that of supposing that early nineteenth-century thinkers like Marx and Engels, who had arrived at all their principal convictions before 1850, could answer the problems of post-industrial societies of the mid and late twentieth century: problems which, in the very nature of things, neither Marx nor his contemporaries had known or dreamed of. But all that ignores the intellectual's recurrent passion for revivalism. Years ago, in *The End of Laissez-faire* (1926), Maynard Keynes attacked 'doctrinaire state socialism' because, as he said,

> it misses the significance of what is actually happening; because it is, in fact, little better than a dusty survival of a plan to meet the problems of fifty years ago, based on a misunderstanding of what some one said a hundred years ago.

It is understandable he should have been puzzled. But dusting down the survivals of distant ages is the natural business of the academic mind, and it is always dangerous to underrate its determination to make antique ideas sparkle and look new. Early in the twentieth century, it is said, there were only two Marxist professors in all Europe: by 1900 Marxism looked old hat, in fact – even to Marxists. By 1970 there can have been few universities in Europe, if any, that had as few Marxist professors as two. This was an amazing act of intellectual resurrection, and it makes one wonder whether any idea can ever confidently be called lost.

What looked new to the 1930s and 1960s was above all irrationalism. Even that, it may be said, is in one fashion or another old. There are manifold precedents for a sudden loss of intellectual faith in reason: in the *Bacchae* of Euripides, in some of the wilder excesses of European romanticism, in Nietzsche, in Freud, in Jung. . . . The reasoner who denies reason is an old act in Western culture. Another propellant to western Marxism was the tacit encouragement readily given it by its enemies. The West, easily bored as it is and almost as easily amused, could not resist the temptation to coddle it when it came. The economic failures of Communism are far less often mentioned in the capitalist press than the minor scandals and crises of the western economy; the failure of Soviet agriculture to feed its own people is not a matter of daily report in the mass-media of Anglo-America, though it is a matter of daily observation in the groceries and butchers' shops of eastern Europe. The intellectual prestige of Marx, meanwhile, among historians and sociologists in the universities of the West remains even now inexplicably high; and many a non-Marxist historian is content to assume that an interest in theories of social class requires him to acknowledge by name a debt to that tradition of thought. That is not a mistake Marx ever made. In fact his writings, little read *in extenso* as they are today by friend or enemy, are meticulous in detailing his intellectual debts to the eighteenth-century Enlightenment and to early nineteenth-century theorists like Saint-Simon – not to mention Ancients like Aristotle.

Marx himself never imagined he had invented an entire theory of social class; and his own original contribution to such theories, which endeavoured to link them to modes of production, has worn less well than the theories of such predecessors as Montesquieu and Adam Smith. It is as certain as anything can be in intellectual history that Europe would have had a tradition of theorising about social history, and above all about social class, if Marx and Engels had never existed; and it is an arguable proposition that such theorising would have worked closer to the evidence if they had never existed. A reading of their acknowledged sources, ancient and modern, leaves their indebtedness to a long tradition of sociology beyond all shadow of doubt.

The effects of western Marxism have been huge, as the effects of any determined pursuit of the irrational are; and any study of its rise and fall offers an irresistible challenge to sum them up.

History is often a story of unintended consequences; and it must be admitted that the effects of western Marxism, whatever its motives, have been highly conservative. That truth is occasionally glimpsed even by its adherents. 'Communism is not radical', Bertolt Brecht once remarked, in a declaration approvingly quoted by Walter Benjamin. 'It is capitalism that is radical.' Just so. The urge for private profit can play the devil with traditional institutions of tribe, religion and family – a radical urge that Communism has striven, not altogether without success, to quell. Revolutionary sentiment, what is more, being an all-or-nothing affair, can notoriously turn conservative at the drop of a hat, since a demand to do everything can offer easy excuses for doing nothing; so that the cry 'We want a revolution now' can transform itself into a sour defeatism in the quickest of quick time: 'method as impotence, art as consolation, pessimism as quiescence', to quote Perry Anderson, a disillusioned adherent of the school, writing in 1976. It is reform that conservatives find hard to defeat, after all, not revolution: reform, being studied and gradual, gives itself time to consolidate and succeed before moving onwards. A revolution of thought, by contrast, can easily and rapidly turn into navel-gazing disillusion and facile despair. The western Marxist believed for a time that he had found, or was about to find, the foundations of all certain knowledge, never doubting that theory is fundamental to certainty. The discovery that it had not after all been found and (sadder still) that it was not there to be found was worse than dispiriting. It was shattering to all hopes of progressive action and any prospect of social change.

Disappointed in his quest for the foundations of knowledge, the western Marxist could easily conclude that certainty was nowhere to be had. It was a conclusion highly and conveniently favourable to doing nothing. The growing scepticism of the 1970s may help to explain the quiescence of the 1980s. An intellectual Left had taken a wrong turn, and by 1980 it was paying a heavy price for it. Marxism 'went wrong', as Doris Lessing conceded in her 1971 preface to *The Golden Notebook* (1962), recording her own disillusionment over what had once attracted her as a 'world ethic'. Its certainty turned uncertain, its zeal ran out into the sands, its crusades looked lost. It had staked everything on a claim that could not be vindicated: an exemption from itself.

In all these ways, western Marxism can be judged a conservative influence. In its half century or so of active life, between the last days of the First World War and the 1970s, it had efficiently split the radicalism of the industrial world, helping conservative movements in an age of divided oppositions to take power and keep it. It created sympathy, at times, or at least partial sympathy, for the Soviet system of eastern Europe, 'the better side', which many a traveller from the West has rightly called the most conservative society on earth. It advanced the cause of state capitalism and central economic planning: all, in the long run, favourable to the rich, since it would be an exceptional planner who failed to plan for himself and his own. That western Marxists secretly or openly preferred a style of private opulence is a charge increasingly made against their memory; and certainly their private tastes were not commonly hostile to champagne-lunches and the life of well-appointed town houses or country estates. A utopian hope turned cynical and self-interested, and died.

Marxism as a whole was bad news for radicals: no doubt of that. Western Marxism was only fairly bad news, by contrast – its effects always limited to an intellectual élite more concerned with self-assertion and ideological purity than with reform. But élites can make an atmosphere and set a tone, and this short-lived sect created uncertainty about what is certain, made for doubt, and engendered despair. And radicals need certainty far more, in the end, than conservatives do, since the onus of proof lies and always lies with the party of change. It is that onus of proof, which may not be as intolerable a burden as the world has lately been asked to believe, that has been the theme and purpose of this book.

Notes

1. J. G. Merquior, *Western Marxism* (London, 1986), a study of cultural Communism since Lukàcs by a Brazilian critic.
2. Lionel Trilling, introduction to Henry James, *The Princess Casamassima* (New York, 1948); reprinted in his *The Liberal Imagination* (New York, 1950).

INDEX